APPLIED PEDAGOGIES

Strategies for Online Writing Instruction

Edited by
DANIEL RUEFMAN
ABIGAIL G. SCHEG

UTAH STATE UNIVERSITY PRESS
Logan

© 2016 by the University Press of Colorado

Published by Utah State University Press
An imprint of University Press of Colorado
5589 Arapahoe Avenue, Suite 206C
Boulder, Colorado 80303

 The University Press of Colorado is a proud member of
The Association of American University Presses.

The University Press of Colorado is a cooperative publishing enterprise supported,
in part, by Adams State University, Colorado State University, Fort Lewis College,
Metropolitan State University of Denver, Regis University, University of Colorado,
University of Northern Colorado, Utah State University, and Western State Colorado
University.

The paper used in this publication meets the minimum requirements of the American
National Standard for Information Sciences—Permanence of Paper for Printed Library
Materials. ANSI Z39.48-1992

ISBN: 978-1-60732-484-3 (paper)
ISBN: 978-1-60732-485-0 (e-book)

Library of Congress Cataloging-in-Publication Data

Names: Ruefman, Daniel, 1983– editor. | Scheg, Abigail G., 1986– editor.
Title: Applied pedagogies : strategies for online writing instruction / edited by Daniel
    Ruefman, Abigail Scheg.
Description: Logan : Utah State University Press, 2016. | Includes bibliographical refer-
    ences and index.
Identifiers: LCCN 2015041260 | ISBN 9781607324843 (pbk.) | ISBN 9781607324850
    (ebook)
Subjects: LCSH: English language—Rhetoric—Study and teaching—Computer-assisted
    instruction. | Creative writing—Study and teaching—Computer-assisted instruction. |
    Web-based instruction.
Classification: LCC PE1404 .A64 2016 | DDC 808/.0420785—dc23
LC record available at http://lccn.loc.gov/2015041260

Cover illustration © JOJOSTUDIO/Shutterstock

CONTENTS

INTRODUCTION

Daniel Ruefman
Abigail G. Scheg

Distance education is not an altogether novel concept that emerged spontaneously in the digital age, but one that has existed for more than two centuries. Correspondence courses emerged in the early eighteenth century when teachers, like Caleb Phillips, offered weekly shorthand lessons by mail order. These lessons continued to grow in popularity as prestigious universities began program offerings in the nineteenth and twentieth centuries, incorporating new technologies and skills as they developed. The underlying principles of early correspondence courses were essentially the same as the online courses of today. They extend access of education and vocational training to a population limited by their location or life circumstances. Much in the way email has largely replaced written letters in personal correspondence, the digital technologies available today have simply replaced the mail-order process with a more efficient delivery of course materials.

A decade ago the ability or desire to teach online was referred to in job postings as a "preferred qualification" for writing instructors at postsecondary institutions. However, as course management systems became more refined and digital literacies were more widely distributed across the socioeconomic divide, this preferred qualification evolved into a prerequisite for employment at many institutions. For example, the English and Philosophy Department at the University of Wisconsin–Stout offers summer and winter term courses exclusively in the online course format and as customized instruction (CI) programs expand at the University, roughly 50 percent of writing courses offered during any given semester are conducted online. Individual philosophies regarding online instruction have become irrelevant. As online course offerings continue to expand, it is expected that writing instructors and administrators adapt to the demands of the digital classroom or risk marginalization within the profession.

While the perpetual growth of online education demands that new and existing faculty members adapt to the demands of a digital

DOI: 10.7330/9781607324850.c000

classroom, the support that these educators are offered at institutions across the country can be best described as inconsistent. Some institutions offer workshops to help orient faculty with the content management systems, but others offer virtually no support for the faculty members who are expected to learn how to navigate the system. Even in the event that training is available, it is often insufficient, orienting faculty with the tools and functions that are available, but offering little to no assistance with online curriculum development, course design, or assessment strategies.

Lack of instructor preparation and varying standards for online teaching throughout academia, while simultaneously growing online course offerings, is a recipe for educational mediocrity that is counterproductive to the mission of higher education. This text is an attempt to address these issues by examining the pedagogical practices employed by successful writing instructors in digital classrooms at a variety of institutions. The title, *Applied Pedagogies: Strategies for Online Writing Instruction*, reflects our belief that the best pedagogical theories are rooted in practice. Furthermore, the organization of this text does not merely reflect the current climate of online writing practices, but it also includes a discussion of the future of online writing courses within the academy.

PART ONE: COURSE CONCEPTUALIZATION AND SUPPORT

Conceptualizing an online writing course is always challenging. Presenting course content in a manner that is accessible for a variety of learning styles can be as intimidating as it is frustrating. The opening chapter of this collection, "Return to Your Source: Aesthetic Experience in Online Writing Instruction" draws from experiential learning theory to provide some insight into how students are biologically wired to learn and demonstrates how writing instructors may develop supplemental materials that are more likely to connect with their respective students.

While the opening chapter discusses the importance of creating an online aesthetic, the next chapter "When the Distance Is Not Distant: Using Minimalist Design to Maximize Interaction in the Online Courses and Improve Faculty Professional Development," seeks to simplify the process of course design with a minimalistic approach. This chapter builds upon the prior discussion by providing concrete examples for how a few minimalistic adjustments to course design may ease the transition from face-to-face to online writing instruction, and maximize student engagement with course material.

Finally, Part One culminates with "Shifting into Digital without Stripping Your Gears: Driver's Ed for Teaching Writing Online." While this chapter adds to the initial conversation regarding course design, it also touches on the need for instructor training and support from their respective institutions.

PART TWO: FOSTERING STUDENT ENGAGEMENT

In Part Two of this collection, the discussion moves beyond course conceptualization and design issues to address explicitly a major concern for all online writing instructors—how to best foster student engagement. To begin, "Lost in Cyberspace: Addressing Issues of Student Engagement in the Online Classroom Community" outlines several inventive synchronous and asynchronous strategies that seek to connect students with one another as well as with the instructor.

The next several chapters ask us to consider who is enrolled in online writing classes and what their unique needs are. Building upon strategies of general student engagement discussed in the previous chapter, this collection next delves more deeply into multicultural and multi-ethnic student engagement with "A Rhetorical Mandate: A Look at Multi-Ethnic / Multi-Modal Online Pedagogy." This chapter examines how learning styles can create barriers within diverse student bodies, and how these barriers can become even more pronounced in the digital writing classroom. Awareness of who we are teaching (in terms of culture, ethnicity, and socioeconomic background) is vital to paving the way toward equitable, universal access to all students.

The concept of universal access continues on in the next chapter "Can Everybody Read What's Posted? Accessibility in the Online Classroom." This chapter explores the impact of visual, auditory, cognitive, and motor disabilities on the educational experience of students enrolled in online classes. The practical tips presented in this chapter will help writing instructors and administrators provide the support necessary to ensure that all students have equal access to course content.

When engaging students, it is important to know who they are, but it is even more important to understand how that audience is responding to the material presented to them. In an in-person classroom, non-verbal communication (like body language) offers a great deal of insight into how well our message is landing with that audience, something that is obviously missing from the online course. To address this issue, "Taking the Temperature of the (Virtual) Room: Emotion in the Online Writing Class" shows us why physical absence is often so disorienting for both students and the instructor, but also how we might better interject emotion into sterile online writing classrooms.

Collaborative writing is a key skill in the professional world today and that collaboration occurs increasingly across great distances. For that reason, many online writing classes require students to co-author texts with peers that most will never meet in person. The chapter, "Thinking Outside 'The Box': Going Outside the CMS to Create Successful Online Team Projects," attempts to address this topic by highlighting the limitations of course management systems to help students collaborate. This case study argues for the creation of functional student workspaces in the digital environment that are independent of the primary course management system.

The final chapter in this section steps outside of the online classroom and addresses the need for instructional support for non-traditional students enrolled in online writing classes. Although online writing centers have become increasingly common in recent years, online writing tutors often lack specific training to effectively work with the non-traditional student populations that online courses often appeal to. "Communicating with Adult Learners in the Online Writing Lab: A Call for Specialized Tutor Training for Adult Learners" identifies the special needs of non-traditional adult learners and offers suggestions for administrators of online writing centers to improve the effectiveness of their tutors for this specific population.

PART THREE: MOOCs

The focus of the final two chapters of this collection is on how MOOCs (Massive Open Online Courses) have begun to alter the scope of the online writing instruction and how they will continue to do so (in one way or another) in years to come. First, "MOOC Mania? Bridging the Gap Between the Rhetoric and Reality of Online Learning," addresses the concerns and controversy that MOOCs present to online education. While there are those who argue that MOOCs are a fad, fading quickly from the arena of higher education, this chapter provides a persuasive look at how the experimental MOOCs of today are refining effective digital pedagogies for application in both academic and corporate worlds.

The final chapter of this collection builds upon the foundation established in "MOOC Mania?" and embraces the idea that this form of instruction is one that will continue to evolve in meaningful ways. These authors begin by arguing that (until recently) online writing instruction was based largely on the foundation of the conventional face-to-face classroom and that novelty of digital writing (as a genre) needs to be more fully embraced by the academy. Demonstrated through the creation of an unconventional MOOC design, "Writing at Scale: Composition MOOCs and Digital Writing Communities," explores how an online course that fully embraces the digital realm in which it lives alter the future of online writing instruction in a meaningful way.

We hope that *Applied Pedagogies: Strategies for Online Writing Instruction* proves to be a practical text for writing instructors and administrators seeking ways to employ the best instructional strategies possible for today's diverse, dynamic, digital writing courses. While the scope of online learning and its place within higher education is continually evolving, it is our hope that this text offers you the tools to adapt to the online writing classrooms of today and anticipate needs of your students in the digital contexts that are yet to come.

PART ONE

Course Conceptualization and Support

1
RETURN TO YOUR SOURCE
Aesthetic Experience in Online Writing Instruction

Daniel Ruefman

The controversy surrounding the online writing classroom is something that I have been well aware of, ever since I began studying them as a graduate student. One of my mentors at that time informed me of just how online writing instruction was creating a culture of academic mediocrity. At the time, he had never seen a study that indicated definitively that online instruction was more effective than face-to-face, though some studies at the time indicated that students were achieving outcomes in the online classroom at a comparable rate with those in more conventional classrooms.

During the 2009–2010 academic year, I found myself engaged with a series of case studies that would ultimately form my dissertation. The goal was to gain a better understanding of the pedagogical practices implemented by first-year writing instructors in face-to-face, online, and hybrid courses. Over the course of this investigation, I quickly realized the online course I was observing was using far less technology than the instructors who taught in the other two settings (Ruefman 2010). While instructors in the face-to-face and hybrid classrooms freely used a variety of web-based technologies, like YouTube and Second Life, the instructor in the online course provided directions for course activities in the form of cumbersome paragraphs supplemented with PDFs and Word Documents (figure 1.1). Essentially, the instructor whose class existed only because of web-based multimodal technologies created a monomodal, text-heavy course that used these technologies less than the other instructors sampled for these case studies.

Following the defense of my dissertation, I constantly revisited the original case study and began to wonder if these findings were limited to this single instructor or whether they were indicative of a larger trend in online writing instruction. As I continued this line of inquiry, much

DOI: 10.7330/9781607324850.c001

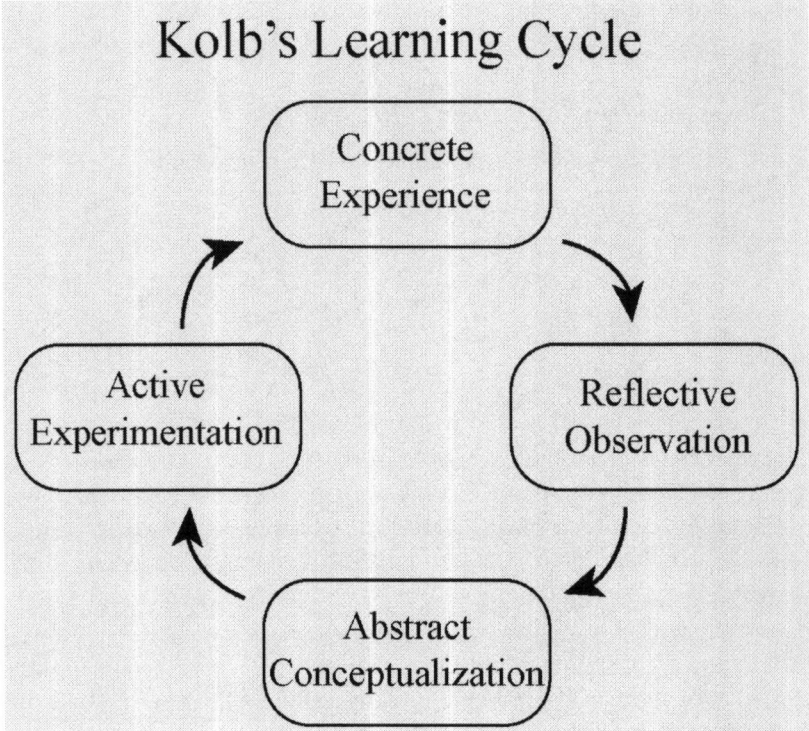

Figure 1.1. Depiction of a simplified version of Kolb's learning process as described in his seminal work, Experiential Learning (Kolb 1984)

of what I found mirrored those original findings. Most of the sampled instructors facilitated text-heavy, monomodal courses that embodied a highly transactional pedagogical model. Modules often contained large passages of text and typed course materials that were uploaded on the course management systems (CMS).

These one-dimensional courses are simply not compatible with the way the human brain is wired to learn. Over the millennia, the human brain has been wired to respond to external sensory stimuli; sight, sound, taste, touch, and smell were the primary way that we learned about the world. Scientific discovery is propelled by experimentation and the observations made are often based upon what the scientists see, hear, taste, feel, or smell. When educational environments are devoid of sensory stimuli, they become sterile and inaccessible to many students.

KOLB'S EXPERIENTIAL LEARNING THEORY
AND AESTHETIC EXPERIENCE

Before it is possible to comprehend the importance of aesthetic experience in online education, an understanding of the terminology is required. *Aesthetics*, in contemporary terms, often refers to concepts of pleasure or artistic beauty. Further exploration reveals that the term is actually derived from *aesthetikos*, a Greek word that translates as "capable of sensory perception" (Uhrmacher 2009). An aesthetic learning experience is therefore not one that is deemed as "pleasurable" or "beautiful," but it is one that is made tangible by the senses—sight, sound, taste, touch, or smell.

Sir Ken Robinson is an educational scholar who has previously touched on the need for aesthetics in American public education. In his presentation entitled "Changing the Paradigm," he explains that "aesthetic experience is one in which your senses are operating at their peak, when you are present in the current moment, when you are resonating with this thing that you are experiencing, when you are fully alive. An anesthetic is when you shut your senses off and deaden yourself to what is happening" (Robinson 2010). By creating one-dimensional, text-heavy online courses, writing instructors are fostering anesthetic, sterile experiences that require students to shut their senses off, depriving them of the learning tools gifted to them by the nature of human biology.

To further understand the role that aesthetic experience plays in learning, it is vital to refer to David A. Kolb's experiential learning theory. Kolb explains that experiential learning is rooted in the concept that "ideas are not fixed and immutable elements of thought but are formed and re-formed through experience . . . knowledge is continuously derived from and tested out in the experiences of the learner" (Kolb 1984). For him, knowledge stems from a process of active experimentation, whereby the learner continually tests what they know and amends their understanding based on the results.

Learning can be best understood as a cycle. It consists of four different stages: (1) concrete experience, (2) reflective observation, (3) abstract conceptualization, and (4) active experimentation. For Kolb, learning is best thought of as a cycle, that has no definitive beginning or end. Depending on the learning style of the student, their preconceptions, beliefs, or experiences will often cause them to resume their learning process at a different stage of the cycle, but ultimately all four stages must be encountered to truly build knowledge.

To better illustrate the learning process, consider the way you learn a new word. You first encounter that term through one of your senses.

Perhaps someone uses it in conversation and you hear it. Maybe you see the written term while reading a book or article. The sensory input serves as a tangible, concrete experience that jumpstarts the learning process. Following that initial experience, a period of reflective observation will usually follow, where your experience is committed to memory. In this process, you begin to store the experience for future recall, remembering how the word looked or how it sounded in that initial context. Once committed to memory, you will transition to a stage of abstract conceptualization where you use the context clues to attribute meaning to the new term you are trying to understand. At this time, you recall things that you have already learned, meaning prefixes, suffixes, root words, and the other words that were mentioned or written around the new term. This is where critical thinking skills enable you to begin theorizing what the new term might mean and you begin to strategize ways that you might use this word in the future. Finally, the cycle proceeds to active experimentation where you put your plan into motion by using the new term in conversation or in your own writing. Often, this use of the new term will lead to another concrete experience. Perhaps feedback from your audience informs you that the term was misspelled or pronounced incorrectly, and that information is processed, building upon the previous lessons to establish a more refined concept of the new word.

Although there are different learning styles that impact how individuals move through these four stages, most true learning seems to conform to the process summarized by Kolb. The reason why is actually found in the more recent work of biologist, James E. Zull. Zull's book, *The Art of Changing the Brain*, maps many of the mind's structures, illustrating why Kolb's learning process seems to work so well. Zull (2002) argues that humans are simply biologically wired to learn in this way. According to Zull, if we examine the structures and functions of the human brain, we can observe that Kolb's learning process mirrors the organization of the brain's structures.

There are four regions of the cerebral cortex that Zull draws our attention to—the sensory cortex, temporal integrative cortex, frontal integrative cortex, and motor cortex. He goes on to state that "the sensory cortex receives first input from the outside world in form of vision, hearing, touch, position, smells, and taste. This matches with the common definition of concrete experience" (Zull 2002). In short, Zull is tracing the most basic components of Kolb's learning cycle, beginning with a sensory rich, concrete experience. When sensory stimuli are received by the brain, these impulses are concentrated in the sensory cortex, located toward the rear of the brain (encompassing portions of the parietal, occipital, and temporal lobes).

Upon receiving the initial sensory input, the human brain immediately begins processing the information. The first step in doing so is to form a memory of the event. This occurs when "the back integrative cortex is engaged in memory formation and reassembly, language comprehension, developing spatial relationship . . . In short it integrates sensory information to create images and meaning" (Zull 2002). Here, Zull matches the functions associated with the back integrative cortex with those that occur during reflective observation (e.g., recalling relevant information, reliving past experiences, creating insights, and analyzing past associations). As the mind moves into this reflective process, neural activity shifts from the rear of the brain to the more centrally located temporal lobe and the information is stored in the hippocampus.

Once a memory is formed, neural activity shifts forward again, this time to the frontal integrative cortex. This region of the brain is responsible for "short-term memory, problem solving, making decisions, assembling plans for action, making judgments, directing the action of the rest of the brain, and organizing actions and activities of the entire body" (Zull 2002). Essentially, the frontal integrative cortex is the center of reason, where critical thinking takes place. These abilities are well suited for abstract conceptualization, where the working memory is reorganized and manipulated to develop working hypotheses and strategies for testing those hypotheses.

Finally, after the frontal integrative cortex has engaged with the short term memory, resulting in an abstract hypothesis, the final stage of the learning cycle involves "active experimentation," where the learner puts a plan into action to test a theory (Kolb 1984). Zull traces this activity to the motor cortex, stating that this region "triggers all coordinated and voluntary muscle contractions made by the body, producing movement. It carries out plans and ideas originating from the front integrative cortex, including the actual production of language through speech and writing" (Zull 2002). In short, Kolb explains that experimentation must take place to develop true knowledge, to validate or refute the hypothesis developed by the learner. This process involves "conversation of ideas into physical action or movements of parts of the body, [including] intellectual activities such as writing, deriving relationships, and talking in debate or conversation" (Zull 2002). As the motor cortex is engaged, a shift in neural activity is observed moving back from the frontal lobe, to the more centrally located border of the parietal lobe, as the learning process completes one cycle, but active experimentation often produces more sensory stimuli, there by moving back to a concrete experience and jumpstarting the cycle again.

Understanding Zull in relation to Kolb is vital to understanding how the brain has been wired to learn, as the proximity of the structures of the brain that are responsible for activities associated with learning are often adjacent to, or overlap one another, making it easy for signals to be sent from one portion of the brain to another. Considering the structures of the brain as they relate to the learning cycle also highlights the transitive nature of sensory experience, as it was described previously in Robinson's work.

The importance of aesthetic learning experience in all educational settings is undeniable. Robust, sensory rich environments and engaging activities that bring students into contact with one another, as well as with the subject matter, is how true learning occurs. However, many online writing courses still adopt a transactional approach to learning, presenting most—if not all—information to students in the form of typed PDF and Word Documents. This sort of passive learning is simply not compatible with the way the human mind processes information.

Aesthetic learning experience is of universal importance for all students, but in an increasingly digital age, dynamic sensory experience is particularly important to the writing classroom. After all, true literacy in the twenty-first century requires readers and writers to continually code-shift between linear (textual) and nonlinear (graphic) components of written texts (George 2002, 16). Writing instructors must encourage their students to create multimodal texts in which the written word is supported by graphic and aural components. In the words of Takayoshi and Selfe (2008):

> Whatever profession students hope to enter in the 21st century . . . they can be expected to read and be asked to compose multimodal texts of various kinds, texts designed to communicate on multiple semiotic channels, using all available means of creating and conveying meaning . . . If composition instruction is to remain relevant, the definition of 'composition' and 'texts' needs to grow and change to reflect peoples' literacy practices in new digital communication environments. (3)

Essentially these scholars are arguing for the inclusion of aesthetic writing assignments that require students to compose documents uniting photographs, animated clips, videos, and audio files with written words to communicate a message in a variety of rhetorical contexts. This allows instructors to tap digital writing skills that students are already adept at using, ultimately increasing student engagement. Moreover, these are the contemporary writing skills demanded by the twenty-first century workplace, which makes these writing courses more relevant.

Given that online writing classes exist wholly within the digital environment, it would seem reasonable to consider them as prime territory for engaging students with web-based, multimodal texts. This class format creates easy access to a variety of media, including video clips, podcasts, blogs, games, and a wealth of web-texts. Furthermore, screen casting, video-editing software, and hosting sites (e.g., Vimeo and YouTube) make it easy for instructors to create their own multimodal resources to engage students more fully. The benefits of doing so was recently captured by a study from Texas Woman's University that examined the impact of personalized, instructor-made videos on student engagement in the online classroom. The study suggested that 88 percent of students who were enrolled in online courses where instructors created their own multimodal texts indicated that those materials enriched the course content; furthermore, students who viewed instructor-created videos expressed a better understanding of who their instructor was and an increased willingness to engage them with comments and questions (Rose 2009). While creating such resources takes time, it is worth it to meet students on a familiar plain.

CONTEXTUALIZING THE PROBLEM

During the 2013 Minnesota Writing and English (MnWE) Conference, I had the opportunity to discuss pedagogical strategies with online instructors, many of whom were adjunct faculty, from a variety of two and four-year institutions. After reflecting on many of these issues, several of the individuals engaged in this discussion admitted that the online courses they had been teaching, or were preparing to teach, were consistent with the monomodal examples I had shared with them during my presentation. One of the participants commented, "I don't teach this way in my face-to-face classes, so why am I teaching this way online?"

Fault does not lay entirely with instructors. The commodification of education has forced the composition classroom to adopt an outcome-based, corporatized model of efficiency. Economic viability is an imperative to most colleges and universities, public, private, and for-profit alike. Institutions increase the number of courses taught by instructors, overload students in each section, and condense academic calendars, limiting the time necessary for instructors to develop an effective pedagogical strategy, specific to the students in each course. This business model breeds a culture of academic mediocrity, as the most efficient means of providing information to students is in the form of text-heavy, skill-and-drill activities, that allow students to demonstrate their level of proficiency with each of the course aims outlined in the syllabus. Often, many educators simply lack the time to develop the instructional resources that effectively engage their students in multiple modes.

Another issue that arose from the conversation with the MnWE instructors that may lead to the perpetuation of a monomodal style of instruction is the overwhelming presence of monomodal online courses themselves. Some of these first-time instructors based their course design on the examples offered by colleagues. Without time to consider their own pedagogical strategies, these instructors emulate what they have seen others doing, perpetuating the less effective, less engaging experience.

MULTIMODALITIES AND AESTHETIC EXPERIENCE

To understand how to create a more aesthetic learning environment online, it is important to understand the role of multimodal texts and technologies. Multimodal texts have long been defined as "texts that exceed the alphabetic and may include still and moving images, animations, color, words, music, and sound" (Takayoshi and Selfe 2008). While monomodal courses communicate in only one mode of communication—written, alphabetic language, multimodal texts and technologies utilize more than one method to communicate with the audience. For example, video clips may often provide visual stimuli that is accompanied and supplemented by audio. Multimodal texts offer the audience information through two or more sensory perceptions that, together, provide a more aesthetic learning experience for the audience.

Today's digital age offers a proverbial buffet of multimodal texts and technologies that instructors can use to supplement learning. YouTube videos, PowerPoint and Prezi presentations, video games, and interactive websites represent only a few of the options available to an instructor short of time. By engaging two different senses at any given time, these types of resources are capable of fostering more concrete experiences throughout a given course than written documents and correspondence alone could provide. However, simply incorporating these resources is not sufficient. It is necessary to consider how materials complement one another to build a more complete understanding of the course material.

All multimodal resources must be consistent with the print media that is already included in the writing courses. When used appropriately, multimodal texts serve to supplement and reinforce the content of existing course materials. Although instructors may find some open-source, multimodal materials compatible with their aims, occasionally these materials can cause some confusion if their content differs in any significant way from the information provided in the instructor-made PDFs or Word Documents. For example, in one of my own online writing courses, students were asked to read an essay written by a fairly popular contemporary American author. After searching the web, I located a video of the author reading his essay at a public reading a few years prior. Thinking that this reading would add a dimension to the experience of my students, I embedded the video on the CMS. I had not noticed that the reading was actually of an earlier version of the essay, and several phrases were omitted and revised in the draft of the printed essay that I had included as a PDF to my students. These subtle changes created major reading comprehension issues, particularly for those students who chose to read along with the author. Instructors looking to incorporate multimodal materials should review those materials carefully to ensure that all information is up to date and compatible with the other documents used to facilitate the class. However, whenever possible, I find that the best course materials are those created by the instructor.

Developing concrete, sensory experiences in online courses is important to present information to students, but it is also important to establish a sense of community. A recent study, conducted at Texas Woman's University, examined the impact of personalized, instructor-made videos on student engagement in the online classroom. Although the findings were based on a limited sample and are not widely generalizable, the study indicated that 88 percent of students who were enrolled in online courses where instructors created their own multimodal texts indicated that those materials enriched the course content; furthermore, students who viewed instructor-created videos expressed a better understanding of who their instructor was and an increased willingness to engage them with comments and questions (Rose 2009). Although it often takes time to create these personalized materials, doing so demonstrates a commitment to your students. Specialized delivery of lectures and personalized feedback allows you to lead by example. Students often emulate the tone of their instructors in both online and face-to-face classrooms. Engaged instructors provide a basis upon which students can model their own interactions with the material and with one another.

STRATEGIES FOR FOSTERING AESTHETIC LEARNING EXPERIENCE

As established previously, aesthetic learning is facilitated through multimodal concrete experiences. When we think about the learning cycle emphasized by Kolb, it is clear that all learning builds upon the foundation of prior experiences of the learner. Providing experiences to online students in a way that allows them to absorb information through more than one of their senses, should provide a more thorough understanding of that information. Although it is true that no two courses (or students) are identical, there are a few strategies that could be universally beneficial to instructors seeking to create a more aesthetic experience in their online courses by providing direction, reinforcing content, and offering constructive feedback.

Providing Direction

Any assignment (whether in an online or face-to-face course), begins with the instructions provided to the students, detailing goals and objectives of the tasks set before them. In a face-to-face course, it is common practice to provide written instructions for major assignments that correspond with an explanation of the assignment that is provided during scheduled class time. When transitioning to online courses, instructors often provide those same written instructions to their students, but often overlook the oral explanation that they would normally provide during scheduled class time. On those occasions, the online course lacks aesthetically.

Supplementing written instructions with audio or video components is particularly important in online courses. Many college students today are resistant to reading intensive tasks and exhibit some challenges with reading comprehension (Worley 2011). When instructions are presented through multiple modalities, more complicated or confusing directions can be clarified and questions may be answered preemptively. This strategy can be helpful when addressing terminology and theories that are key to the discipline, but it can be equally beneficial to students as they interpret instructions related to course activities. Instructors teaching online can provide similar explanation by using screen capture software (e.g., Screencast-o-Matic, Jing, or Camtasia) to walk students through tasks outlined in the CMS and annotate the text with additional information that they would normally provide to face-to-face classes.

Providing multimodal instructions to students using these audio-video techniques can be difficult for some instructors, depending upon the CMS that is adopted by their home institutions. While some systems include a YouTube Mashup function, which enables you to embed web-based videos within modules in the same CMS, others only enable instructors to add hyperlinks to external web-texts. In these cases, the best means of delivering this content may require instructors to build a parallel blog that houses information on a free hosting sight outside the CMS (e.g., Wordpress, Weebly, Jimdo, etc.). Screen capture videos with audio commentary may be uploaded to a video host site, like YouTube or Vimeo, and can then be embedded within the individual blogs. While there is the option of including a hyperlinked list of videos directly within most CMSs, a list of links is not as engaging as the embedded videos. Furthermore, this format more closely resembles the online experience that students have become accustomed to. Compartmentalizing these multimodal components within pages that mirror the setup of modules on the CMS is also a way that demonstrate continuity between the two systems.

Reinforcing Content

Once assignments are laid out for the students, there comes a question of how to best make course content accessible. Many scholars, like Karen Worley, have observed that today "the purpose of education is to produce learning, not deliver instruction. Faculty must strive to create a positive learning environment that enhances student learning and meets the needs of all adult learners" (Worley 2011). Students, particularly those who are digital natives, are accustomed to accessing information quickly through a variety of media, and Worley (2011) explains that they often harbor an expectation to continue to do so in the classroom environment. In online courses the technology used shapes that environment, given that these classroom communities occupy no physical space. The very technologies that are used by a tech-savvy society have a role to play in online learning, and it is up to instructors to incorporate technology in a purposeful way that is conducive to a more independent learning style.

As stated previously in this chapter, emerging research indicates that many online writing courses are particularly text heavy in their design, at a time when students are learning to read differently than ever before. Still, reading remains vital to learning and the goal of instructors should be to create an environment in which assigned readings are made accessible to their students. This can be done, once again, by supplementing readings with digital media that parallel or reinforce the concepts illustrated in those primary texts. Assembling multimodal theme-sets that are centered on a core text will allow students an opportunity to re-experience the content of that text aurally and visually. Moreover, by juxtapositioning materials effectively, students are able to unpack key concepts in a way that prepares them for critical analysis (Richison, Hernandez, and Carter 2006). For example, logical fallacies may be a topic with which students may wrestle in any writing class—online or face-to-face (see table 1.1). To introduce the concept to students, instructors may include a reading from the course text-book. The introduction to Gary Goshgarian's book, *Exploring Language*, includes a great discussion of some of the most common logical fallacies and provides a few basic examples of how those logical fallacies may be used. However, it may still be difficult for students to observe precisely how logical fallacies operate in different rhetorical contexts. To help students to broaden their understanding of the concept, the instructor may also present supplemental web-texts from publications, like the *Writing Commons*. This web-based, open-text resource includes a series of web-texts that define a variety of logical fallacies (some of which are also addressed in Goshgarian's book). However, many of these web-texts include embedded YouTube videos that demonstrate how logical fallacies are employed by politicians and corporations through advertising. To go a step further, there are several vlogs produced by non-profit organizations which provide animated videos and lectures that delve more deeply into the topic, relating logical fallacies specifically to argumentation and critical analysis.

Offering Constructive Feedback

Most instruction in the contemporary writing classroom occurs not through pedagogical materials, but from the feedback prompted by student writing. Students learn to write best by writing and accessible feedback from the instructor is essential to guiding that process. Even in traditional classrooms, feedback takes the form of written annotations in the margins of the page. In online courses, the review functions provided in word processing programs, like track changes and comment functions in Microsoft Word, allow instructors to annotate materials in similar ways. However, recent studies have indicated that using screen capture technologies (e.g., Camtasia, Jing, etc.) and audio feedback have helped students apply instructor comments to their own writing (Eckhouse and Carroll 2013). Audio and video feedback does not take the place of written comments, but rather, it provides an opportunity for the instructor to clarify those comments. Most content management systems today include an audio grading function in their gradebooks, allowing the instructor to explain the rationale of their feedback in

Table 1.1. Sample theme-set for logical fallacies

Primary/Core Text	*Textual*

Goshgarian, Gary. 2013. "Introduction: Reading and Thinking Critically." *Exploring Language,* 13th edition. Boston: Pearson.

Supplemental Web-Texts	*Textual/Visual*

McIntyre, M., and J. McKee. "Logical Fallacies." *Writing Commons.* Accessed January 28, 2014. http://writingcommons.org/open-text/information-literacy/rhetorical-analysis/logical -fallacies.

Purdue University. 2013. "Logical Fallacies." Online Writing Lab. Retrieved January 28, 2014. https://owl.english.purdue.edu/owl/resource/659/03/.

Supplemental Videos	*Visual/Aural*

McRae, M., and J. Hutson. 2011. "Critical Thinking Playlist." *YouTube.* Accessed January 28, 2014. https://www.youtube.com/watch?v=iSZ3BUru59A&list=PLKCy4138lUoNp7kztKVmXp goJXjVacqr-.

a way written comments might not allow. Microsoft Word also allows the embedding of audio files within a document. Thus instructors may use basic audio recording software (e.g., Windows Sound Recorder or Audacity) to create WAV or WMA files that can then be inserted as an object directly into the Word Document. While multiple files can be included in a document, it is most practical for instructors to insert a single audio file that complements the written feedback. Moreover, audio files can establish a more personalized tone that makes students more receptive to the written feedback.

CONCLUSION

The transition from face-to-face instruction to the digital writing classroom is not simply a matter of dusting off old course materials and uploading them to the content management system. True learning takes place through aesthetic experience in an environment that is conducive to the learning process, and it is the responsibility of instructors to construct that environment. As online writing courses exist only through digital technologies, it is vital to utilize those technologies to engage students in a manner that is compatible with the biological learning process—at the center of which is sensory experience. In so doing, sterile, inaccessible web-based courses can be revitalized by taking into account the single most important variable in learning—the human element.

References

Eckhouse, Barry, and Rebecca Carroll. 2013. "Voice Assessment of Student Work: Recent Studies and Emerging Technologies." *Business Communication Quarterly* 76 (4): 458–73. http://dx.doi.org/10.1177/1080569913506488.

George, Diana. 2002. "From Analysis to Design: Visual Communication in the Teaching of Writing." *College Composition and Communication* 54 (1): 11–39. http://dx.doi.org/10.2307/1512100.

Kolb, David. 1984. *Experiential Learning: Experience as the Source of Learning and Development.* Upper Saddle River, NJ: Prentice Hall.

Richison, Jeannine, Anita Hernandez, and Marcia Carter. 2006. *Theme Sets for Secondary Students: How to Scaffold Core Literature.* Portsmouth, NH: Heinemann.

Robinson, Ken. 2010. "Changing Paradigms." *YouTube.* Royal Society for the encouragement of the Arts (RSA), February 4. Accessed July 12, 2013. https://www.youtube.com/watch?v=mCbdS4hSa0s.

Rose, Katherine Kensinger. 2009. "Student Perceptions of the Use of Instructor-Made Videos in Online and Face-to-Face Classes." *Journal of Online Learning and Teaching / MERLOT* 5 (3). Accessed June 23, 2013. http://jolt.merlot.org/vol5no3/rose_0909.htm.

Ruefman, Daniel. 2010. "Examining the Influence of Multimodal New Media Texts and Technologies on First-Year Writing Pedagogies: A Cross Sectional Case Study." PhD diss., Indiana University of Pennsylvania.

Takayoshi, Pamela, and Cynthia L. Selfe. 2008. "Chapter One: Thinking About Multimodality." In *Multimodal Composing: Resources for Teachers,* ed. Cynthia L. Selfe, 1–12. Cresskill: Hampton Press.

Uhrmacher, P. Bruce. 2009. "Toward a Theory of Aesthetic Learning Experiences." *Curriculum Inquiry* 39 (5): 613–36. http://dx.doi.org/10.1111/j.1467-873X.2009.00462.x.

Worley, Karen. 2011. "Educating College Students of the Net Generation." *Adult Learning* 22 (3): 31–9. http://dx.doi.org/10.1177/104515951102200305.

Zull, James E. 2002. *The Art of Changing the Brain: Enriching the Practice of Teaching by Exploring the Biology of Learning.* Sterling, VA: Stylus Publishing.

2

WHEN THE DISTANCE IS NOT DISTANT
Using Minimalist Design to Maximize Interaction in Online Writing Courses and Improve Faculty Professional Development

Heidi Skurat Harris, Dani Nier-Weber, and Jessie C. Borgman

Online writing classes serve populations who face impediments to attending traditional college courses (e.g., rural students, working parents and caretakers, students with disabilities). Given these challenges, providing opportunities for interaction in these classes can seem like a daunting task. However, interaction in the online classroom is a key indicator of student satisfaction in online teaching and learning. According to the Noel-Levitz National Online Learner's Priorities Report (Noel-Levitz 2013), three of the top five areas of highest importance to online learners related directly to interaction: "Institutions have opportunities to improve the interaction between online faculty and students with responsiveness, timely feedback, clearly defined assignments, and the perception of the quality of instruction" (9). In addition to the Noel-Levitz surveys, the Conference on College Composition and Communication Committee for Best Practices in Online Writing Instruction (2013) (CCCC-OWI) released its position statement on effective practices for online writing instruction in April 2012. The report, based on six years of research, also highlights the need for accessible, interactive instruction for students, opportunities for interaction in faculty professional development, and support for both students and faculty that maximizes the effective use of technology.

The CCCC-OWI Principles and Example Effective Practices and the Online Learning Consortium (OLC)[1] Five Pillars for Online Instruction provide frameworks for sound design and implementation of effective online courses that can lead to greater faculty/student interaction.

DOI: 10.7330/9781607324850.c002

In this chapter, we connect elements of the CCCC-OWI Principles and Example Effective Principles and the OLC Five Pillars for Online Instruction to classroom practices that challenge online students and faculty to engage and collaborate through what we consider to be minimalist design: paring instruction down to its golden essence in designing and assigning tasks in order to maximize faculty-student and student-student interaction. In doing so, we connect specific principles to effective online practices for creating well-designed, operative learning environments in a variety of courses—from first-year composition to upper-division technical writing and rhetoric courses—that promote peer collaboration and engagement for both students and instructors.

DISTANT TEACHERS CONNECTING THROUGH EFFECTIVE ONLINE PRACTICES

As writing instructors, we understood that the principles of engagement and interaction were central to successful online learning, and later found the formal structures of the two principles' statements that provided research-based frameworks for our classroom design. Although we were not aware of the OLC Five Pillars (and the CCCC-OWI Position Statement of Principles and Example Effective Practices had not been developed), we found these frameworks for online education reflected the practice we had organically found effective in our online teaching practice. In addition, we realized that these frameworks and our practice all converged in one essential way: all called for interactive and engaging pedagogy delivered in a clear, direct manner. The CCCC-OWI Position Statement of Principles and Example Effective Practices reflects the need for effective interactive practice in Principles 3 and 4 in particular (see appendix 2.A for a full list of principles). The OLC Five Pillars includes a section on student satisfaction that requires that "students are pleased with their experiences in learning online, including interaction with instructors and peers" (OLC Consortium 2014). In addition to the emphasis on interaction, all frameworks emphasize the need for faculty to be supported in developing online courses and also for those courses to involve faculty who are using innovative technologies (see appendix for Principles 7 and 12; CCCC-OWI 2013).

In order to engage students with our course content, with ourselves, and with each other, we focused on principles of minimalist design. Our minimalist principles center around the concept that "less is more." In other words, because of structural differences in communication and interaction in online courses (i.e., faculty and students spend much more time interacting through written text or one-on-one, than they would in a face-to-face classroom), we believe that online courses should shift from a broader focus on "coverage" of a variety of types of documents and concepts to deeper focus on a more narrow range of topics and/or assignments. The key to minimalist design is to closely align individual activities and course assignments with multiple course goals or course learning outcomes. For example, if course outcomes are based on the WPA Outcomes Statement for first-year composition, a single online class activity, such as using Google Docs to complete a collaborative annotated bibliography assignment, might fulfill components of all five categories of learning outcomes: Rhetorical Knowledge; Critical Thinking, Reading, and Writing; Processes; Knowledge of Conventions; Composing in Electronic Environments (Council of Writing Program Administrators 2008). In addition, the course navigation of a minimally designed course removes unnecessary course elements and provides a clear and logical structure to minimize student confusion. This minimalist practice allows students to complete fewer assignments in a more intentionally designed space while still meeting the outcomes of the course.

The OLC recommends designing classes from the top down, working from big picture ideas and goals to lower order questions—sound pedagogy, arguably, for any instructional format, but one that lends itself well to minimalist design. First, an instructor identifies the course goals (i.e., what the course will provide to the students). Then the instructor identifies the course learning objectives, or what the student will be able to do after successfully completing the course. Finally, the instructor chooses the means of assessment, or the ways in which the student will demonstrate what he or she has learned. Only then should an instructor choose or design those tasks that will aid students in acquiring and demonstrating their learning; the tasks are not the least important component, necessarily, but they are subordinate to the goals, learning objectives, and methods of assessment, and they exist only to serve the larger purpose of learning—however that learning ultimately takes place. What matters in minimalist design is not the number of tasks students perform, but that they perform a cohesive and well-chosen set of tasks that helped them meet the goals and objectives of the course.

The following sections provide concrete examples of how two online faculty, Jessie Borgman and Dani Weber, used focused course activities and minimalist course design reflective of the principles in the OLC Five Pillars and in the CCCC-OWI Principles and Example Effective Practices documents to increase faculty-to-student, student-to-student, and student-to-content interaction in their online courses. We conclude with an argument that administrators and faculty professional development specialists should consider implementing similar practices in their professional development activities to reinforce the importance of minimalist design and to provide interactive experiences and professional support to faculty at a distance.

MINIMALIST DESIGN USING GENRE THEORY FOR ENHANCING STUDENT INTERACTION

Jessie Borgman taught two courses (English Composition 101 and English Composition 102) at a small community college in the Midwest as an adjunct faculty member. She did not receive any professional development support. While she had not seen the CCCC-OWI Principles or OLC Five Pillars before composing the courses, Borgman was intent on making quality courses that were accessible to those students who did not have the time or ability to take classes face-to-face. Borgman knew that she wanted to incorporate genre theory and minimalist course design principles to the online learning environment, recognizing that students were more likely to be successful in online courses if those courses used simple, clear navigation and course design centered around a single theme for course content: genre theory.

Online learning environments have the potential, using a minimalist and focused design, to create a flexible system that incorporates genre study. In their article, David R. Russell and David Fisher suggest that, traditionally, research has shown minimal transfer of knowledge between educational/school genres and professional/workplace genres (Russell and Fisher 2009). The research suggests that students struggle to separate the two genre systems (school and work) and therefore struggle to reproduce genres used in school settings in the workplace setting. Students who move into the workplace demonstrate a failure to work within specific contexts or social situations, not understanding the link between genre, context and rhetorical situation. Russell and Fisher then go on to suggest that

> Electronic learning environments allow teachers and educational planners to . . . create a genre system which represents activity both spatially and temporally . . . In order for students to recognize and use genres in ways that may be more likely to prove useful outside the classroom—to see genres "from the inside"—the place of genres in a genre system operating in time and space can be represented using electronic media in ways that traditional classrooms . . . cannot represent them. (Russell and Fisher 2009, 187–88)

In Borgman's first-year classes, students implemented the genre studies approach by dissecting texts—identifying the writing genre, the conventions and properties of that genre, how it works in the world, and its
trajectory and limitations. This ability to dissect genres allowed students
to understand and reproduce texts. In their book *Genre: An Introduction
to History, Theory, Research, and Pedagogy*, authors Anis Bawarshi and Mary
Jo Reiff state,

> Research into genre learning and acquisition has provided teachers with
> useful methods for situating learning and for fostering meta-cognition
> that connects new and already-acquired knowledge. In addition, research
> into genre knowledge and performance has motivated pedagogical appli-
> cations that work to facilitate the transfer of genre knowledge and writing
> skills from one writing context to another, from first-year composition
> (FYC) courses to courses in the disciplines, and from academic writing to
> workplace writing. (Bawarshi and Reiff 2010, 175)

Borgman found that, in the case of her courses, it seemed as though
the online writing course was more conducive to teaching genre awareness
because both the instructor and the students are confined to a specific,
minimalist space that requires only a few modes of communication: writing, audio, and video. The nature of her online courses forced students
to interact and communicate online, providing the perfect opportunity to
model effective communication practices in online media (genres).

Minimalist Design and Course Navigation

Borgman's minimalist course design modeled effective online composition practices by first creating a clear navigational structure in the
course management system (CMS). Making the course navigation simple, uncluttered and clearly labeled helped the students stay focused on
the content/material rather than on navigating the classroom. One way
she approached this was through simplifying the tools available to the
students in the CMS. The course menu consisted of only seven buttons:
welcome, announcements, discussion, assignments, quizzes, course files,
and grades. Thus, Borgman was able to focus on the affordances of the
CMS in order to create a navigational structure that clearly led students
through her simplified assignment sequence.[2]

Borgman also wrote simple course documents (i.e., syllabus, course
schedule, written assignments explanations) that "used straightforward, plain, and linguistically direct rather than indirect language" and
"avoid[ed] ambiguous rhetorical questions, phrasal verbs, idioms, and
metaphorical/figurative language as much as possible" (CCCC-OWI

2013, 3.1). Students were much less likely to "give up" if they had a clear picture of what was expected from the start of the course. The syllabus used a table to format sections, and chunking broke up important information. Headings on the left side of the table allowed students to easily identify instructor information, the time and "place" for virtual office hours, and grading policies, making the document easily "scannable" for students. Finally, she created a course schedule that was color coded (green = readings, orange = tasks, pink = discussion assignment) and clearly segmented in weeks that ran from Monday–Sunday.[3]

In order to keep the pedagogy as simple as the design, she shaped the major writing assignments around students' career choices and technology to assist the students in seeing how they could use what they learned in her class in their own career fields. She asked students to research the history of their career fields with an emphasis on the impact of technology on these fields. In keeping with the minimalist concept, the course had only four assignments, and each assignment built on the skills of the previous assignment while addressing multiple course outcomes. Each assignment focused on reading, writing, and technology and was approached through the lens of genre, which encouraged students to consider the rhetorical situation of each piece they produced. Thus, Borgman was able to model how she used minimalist design in her field of choice (teaching) as a means to effectively communicate with an audience (students) just as she hoped that students would do in their genre-based assignments and later in their career fields.

Minimalist Assignment Design for Increased Interaction

Borgman used minimalist instructional design to promote increased student interaction, both with texts and with each other, by alternating work weeks and discussion weeks. Work weeks allowed students time to complete reading assignments and work on writing assignments so they would be adequately prepared for the discussion weeks, which focused heavily on the assigned readings and portions of their writing assignments. In discussion weeks, the students shared their writing by posting rough drafts and participating in focused peer reviews. In a second discussion thread each discussion week, students dissected other writers' methods and genres. Students were able to "situate learning" and "connect new and already-acquired knowledge" (Bawarshi and Reiff 2010) through minimally designed tasks that required sustained engagement with the assigned readings in the discussions and interaction with the assigned readings and their own writing assignments.

By focusing on career fields and writing genres, Borgman found that, as she followed the principles of minimalist design, she was more available to interact with and assist students to develop their writing in a way that was specific to their individual career fields. She encouraged these students and was able to give more concrete feedback on their writing assignments and discussion replies, coaching the students individually through the course messaging system and email.[4] She also found that more students sought her help outside of the online classroom because they were thinking about larger connections and contexts in their writing. She spent the majority of the course modeling genre dissection through responses to students in the discussions and feedback on rough drafts, which also took place in the online discussions. Indeed, most of the modeling she did was in written form in the discussions area. Students posted their rough drafts and responded to readings in the weekly discussions, so she was able to post questions to the students that kept drawing them back to thinking about specific genres as well as how these genres functioned in their classroom. She also challenged them to think about how they could take the skills they were practicing and apply them to other writing situations. Borgman's responses helped the students learn the language of a genre-based approach, which they then applied in their responses to each other.

The OLC principle of starting with course goals and outcomes in mind in designing these online courses was the key that led to minimalist design. In Borgman's classes, she wanted students to see a clear connection between what they were writing and discussing in the class and what they wrote and discussed in their daily lives—to be able to see how their outside writing activities, from Facebook posts to emails, grocery lists, to the writing they did in their jobs, both influenced their writing in the course and were influenced by the writing they were doing in the course. In a recent *College Composition and Communication* article, author Michelle N. Cleary (2013) discusses writing transfer among adult learners in college writing courses:

> These students move, often daily, between writing at work, at school, in communities, and at home. To ignore how writing in these other contexts influences how students write for school is to unnecessarily impoverish our understanding of our students, their writing development and the possibilities for transfer. (661)

Borgman observed that the multiple discussions on genre and the first two chapters of the textbook, which she wrote for the courses, ("Genre and Context" and "College Writing and the Five-Paragraph Essay"), also appeared to give the students more "vocabulary" to discuss what they noticed about the writing they did daily or for the course. Students continually referenced the fact that learning about "genre and context" helped them to realize while the five-paragraph essay theme was prevalent in their education, they had the power to write in different genres. The students were able to "move" between their different writing contexts, as Cleary suggested, and they were able to draw applicable real-world connections between the activities they were doing in the course and the writing they were doing in their daily lives.

Considering strategies such as inclusive and accessible minimalist instruction, applying effective composition teaching and learning strategies, and migrating these practices to the online course helped shift the focus of the course (and the students' perspectives) from content management and learning tasks to community interaction and the process of becoming better, stronger writers. Borgman found out that the online learning environment was a great venue for illuminating a shift in focus and perspective because of the unique space it inhabits. She saw students develop and gain confidence in their writing abilities and found that the minimalist practices she had employed helped develop all kinds of interactions: student and content, student and student, instructor and student, student and workplace writing. Thus she confirmed her belief that the minimalist design did indeed work, (especially with the student demographic she had; they were not computer savvy) and this belief was reflected in the success rate of the course and the fact that many of the English 101 students continued with her into English 102.

RESISTING (AND EVENTUALLY EMBRACING) THE LESS-IS-MORE OF MINIMALIST ONLINE INSTRUCTION

As Dani Weber designed her first online classes as an adjunct instructor, she at first resisted the "less-is-more" philosophy behind minimalist design. However, a demanding teaching load during a summer when she was moving cross-country forced her to re-think her previous assumptions about online course design. In Summer 2010, Weber taught three summer classes for a small, rural, state university. The first course, junior-level Technical Writing, was a course designed by Heidi Skurat Harris that Weber copied and directly implemented with no instructional changes. The second course, sophomore-level Argumentation, was a course Weber had taught twice as a face-to-face course. The third class, a junior-level special topics course on Constructions of Corporate Identity, was a new course delivered in a new medium. All of these classes were created and implemented simultaneously, within a matter of weeks, during a summer in which her temporary living situation did not provide reliable Internet access as she transitioned into a new job.

Initially, Weber worried that "less is more" would equate to the students completing a lesser amount of work in online classes while officially fulfilling the same course requirements and receiving the same credit as students in face-to-face classrooms. Ultimately, however, Weber realized that she was asking of students not that they perform less work, but that they complete fewer tasks—an important distinction. Working her way through redesigning the Argumentation class to move online and creating the new Constructions in Corporate Identity class required her to match learning tasks to learning objectives. Weber came to think of the shift to minimalist design not as "less," but simply as different, much the way a drawing that conveys an image in a few well-chosen strokes is not necessarily a lesser work of art than a lavish, detailed oil painting.

The process of redesigning around minimalist principles taught her two important strategies: (1) breaking instruction into smaller units, and (2) refocusing the design on providing course content that met course goals, as opposed to simply having online students complete the same set of tasks required in the face-to-face classroom. Following Hewett and Ehmann's (2004) recommendation for a "principle-centered approach" (5), Weber used focused course design to figure out how "less" can be "more" when online instruction provides that narrower-but-deeper instructional focus that relies above all on sound pedagogy, strong content, and personalized instruction.[5] This corresponds to a decrease in complexity of design that leads to an increase in student engagement and interaction.

In Weber's class, Harris's pre-designed shell for the Technical Writing class provided a model of the top-down course design method advocated by OLC, which focused on student interaction. The Technical Writing course was arranged in three units, with each unit subdivided into individual weeks. The first assignment included a group project with peer reviews, drafts of a group report, peer review of and individual reflection on the group project. The second assignment of the course was an individual service-learning project that included a proposal, progress report, peer review, and a final report with reflection. The final unit of the course was a portfolio in which students were asked to demonstrate how they had met the learning outcomes for the class using examples from previous assignments in the class while communicating clearly and effectively. This technical writing class met numerous standards for online classes[6]: instructions were clear, assignments were clearly tied to measurable outcomes of course learning objectives, and learning objectives aligned with overall course goals. As well, the course included group work, a wealth of student interactions that helped build a strong learning community, and several opportunities for substantive student reflection on various aspects of their work and on course content. Although she was new to online course design, Weber was thus able to transfer principles she was learning from Harris's pre-designed course shell (PDS) to the design of the two additional courses.

Using Minimal Design Models for Maximum Course Redevelopment

As Weber struggled to fit the components she had used successfully in her face-to-face Argumentation course, she used the model of the PDS for the Technical Writing class to cope with the structural differences in communication and interaction in the online class. A crucial difference between face-to-face classes and online classes, for example, was the number of tasks instructors could ask students to accomplish. Students would need to both become familiar with the technology and communicate primarily in writing in order to be successful in the class, elements that Weber had not needed to address as explicitly in her face-to-face courses.

In addition, Weber's wanted to ensure that peer-to-peer interaction, which was key in achieving face-to-face course goals and in mastering the language of analytical approaches that students could then apply in their responses to each other, was a centerpiece of her online classes. For example, in her face-to-face Argumentation classroom, Weber used informal mini-debates to prepare students to write their own formal arguments, examining one controversial issue each class period that was presented by teams of four, two students arguing on each side of the debate. The class analyzed each argument for effectiveness, credibility, and validity by examining claims, sub-claims, evidence, appeals, counterarguments, concessions, and underlying values and assumptions. In the face-to-face class, students mapped out their analysis on a physical blackboard. This worked well in the face-to-face classroom; every topic engendered lively debate, and by the end of this preliminary activity students were well versed in argumentative terms as well as in the analysis of traditional argument. An identical or even similar activity, however, seemed unsuited to the virtual blackboard of the online classroom, particularly in a threaded forum where the discussion would be asynchronous, laborious, and overly complex.

To keep the peer interaction while addressing the inadequacies of the CMS, Weber redesigned her first two assignments, which had asked students to work with partners on opposing teams, first researching an issue, then creating and presenting an argument for their side. In the face-to-face class, students had listened to and analyzed each argument, as a group, before moving on to write a formal argument paper. Combining these assignments Weber began instead by asking students to write, individually, a more formal piece on a topic of their choice. After the introductory week and brief readings on definitions and terms, students posted a three-page argument to the discussion board. Lively debates began the week after as students analyzed each other's work using guiding questions and criteria to respond to each other's ideas and claims, identify elements of argument used, and point to gaps in logic or a lack of evidence. The online format, which was already a familiar forum for many of them who already used social media and other Web 2.0 affordances to engage in online debate, proved ideal for this assignment. The simplified design thus provided a way for students to not merely complete a task but to engage with each other in meaningful, although not always unemotional or detached, ways. Ultimately, this streamlined assignment structure enabled students to efficiently analyze the structures of, and tease out the same kinds of weaknesses or flaws in, each other's arguments that it had taken students in the face-to-face class several steps to achieve.

For Weber, further analysis of differences in design between face-to-face and online courses helped her to identify several other principles that seemed particularly important to effective online instruction, principles that she included (although not perfectly) as she created her new online Constructions of Corporate Identity course. Course material each week, text and video, was followed by required postings on the Discussion Board; as in the Argumentation class above, all of the writing students did was available through the CMS, where student-to-student interaction was an integral part of the course. This made visible to all, in writing, how students processed material that was at times emotionally difficult as well as intellectually challenging—the processing itself became part of the learning endeavor. As online classes thus became less teacher-focused, and as the teacher role shifted from "front woman" to facilitator, social presence took center stage as a key component of minimalist design in the online learning environment.

Student interaction that took place solely through asynchronous writing activities, however, proved insufficient to fully develop that social presence, which remained crucial both as an element of the course and as an absence that at least some students felt keenly as they compared the online environment Weber had created to the relative ease of

seated class discussion. This was especially true after challenging readings or viewings in the class on Constructions of Corporate Identity. In
her post-assessment of her classes, for which she solicited end-of-term
student feedback using specific and detailed questions on course content, management, and design, Weber realized that she had not adequately fulfilled one critical principle of effective design, particularly in
the Constructions of Corporate Identity class: the need to provide sufficient student-to-student interaction. Student reflections greatly helped
her understand what she could do to improve the course if she taught
it again. One student wrote, "I thought that the structure for this class
as an online, discussion and reading-based communication worked well.
However, I feel that a sense of community or activism may be better
inspired in an on-campus setting. Sometimes I felt slightly alone among
my friends and family." Another stated, "I thoroughly enjoyed this class.
Part of the reason why I was frustrated at times was because it made me
think about who I am, what defines me, how I want to live, and why I buy
the things I do. This experience is invaluable." A final comment, however, revealed a response Weber had not sufficiently considered while
designing the course:

> I felt like a brutally wrung-out dishrag after watching every film and I
> couldn't really convey my sense of helplessness in writing as I think I could
> to a classroom of my peers. If this class is only to ever exist online, it might
> be helpful to require a "phone conference" between each student and
> the professor to discuss ideas, analysis, and frustrations about American
> consumerism and corporate culture.

Such a class in particular, Weber concluded, would benefit greatly
from occasional synchronous class discussion (through the CMS platform or other online meeting space), or from short video responses
posted by each student after viewing the material, to better create the
interactive social presence[7] crucial to both online and face-to-face learning communities. Enabling and increasing student interaction through
the simplicity of minimalist design, therefore, seems particularly effective for online classrooms in which instructors must re-envision their
approaches to creating and promoting student learning, engagement,
and retention.[8]

Both Borgman's and Weber's students needed to learn and practice
specific vocabularies and genres of writing in order to be effective in
their online courses and in their future careers. In these courses, success directly related to (1) models for appropriate communication in
specific genres, (2) clarity of and choice in content, (3) simplicity of
navigation and design, (4) interactions with peers, and (5) instructor

engagement.[9] Online access[10] also proved as vital to instructor satisfaction as it frequently does to student satisfaction; faculty access is often unquestioningly assumed, without recognition that faculty working under real world constraints can face technical difficulties similar to those of their students. Despite their status as adjuncts juggling multiple courses (and in Weber's case during a challenging cross-country move), both faculty members worked hard to maintain regular communication with their students, checking in every 48 hours at most to answer email, and attempting to provide weekly feedback on discussions as well as assignments. Ultimately, minimalist course design provided the time and space for them to be more present in their online classes.

The lessons that we take away from designing and redesigning our courses around minimalist principles and interaction do not end at the boundaries of the virtual classroom. Indeed, administrators and individuals tasked with providing faculty professional development can use these lessons, as well as the principles from the OLC Five Pillars and the CCCC-OWI Principles and Example Effective Practices report to create strong online faculty professional development opportunities, especially for their faculty at a distance.

ENGAGING INSTRUCTORS TO ENGAGE STUDENTS: MINIMALIST DESIGN AND INTERACTION IN ONLINE FACULTY PROFESSIONAL DEVELOPMENT

While faculty need to be aware of how minimalist design impacts students' ability to navigate and successfully complete a course and promotes student and faculty interaction, Borgman's and Weber's experiences as contingent faculty struggling to design effective online courses indicates the need for faculty professional development and mentoring through this process. Both Weber and Borgman indicated that professional development (or in Borgman's case, a lack thereof) influenced their ability to design effective online courses. For Weber, faculty support proved to be the crucial component in her ability to (*a*) truly grasp the concept of minimalist design as it applied to online classroom design, and (*b*) to successfully identify and implement that design in a way that adequately considered the unique features of the online classroom. This faculty support took place in two ways: first, an initiation into the online world using a tested and proven pre-designed course shell (PDS), and second, frequent direct communication with Harris, the knowledgeable—and accessible—online educator who had designed the Technical Writing course shell. This experience provided a good example of the kind of faculty support, training, and professional development that is often crucial for a successful shift into online environments.[11] Adequate support in understanding online course preparation and design certainly proved indispensable to Weber as she began exploring the online universe.

Both the CCCC-OWI Position Statement (Principle 12) and the OLC Five Pillars indicate the importance of faculty satisfaction in order to have quality online courses and programs. For both new and seasoned online faculty, learning and implementing new technologies can be overwhelming. Just as students who encounter online courses might have difficulty with new systems of navigation in addition to new concepts, faculty may struggle with learning new systems and technologies in addition to creating effective pedagogies. Thus, a few key principles for professional development can help administrators, instructional designers and faculty professional development specialists produce quality professional development experiences.

MODEL ONLINE PRACTICES IN FULLY ONLINE PROFESSIONAL DEVELOPMENT OPPORTUNITIES THAT ASSIST FACULTY IN UNDERSTANDING EFFECTIVE, MINIMAL COURSE DESIGN

If faculty will be teaching online, professional development should involve a substantial online component that models effective course design.[12] One example of this sustained online course experience occurs in Harris's professional development workshops, where faculty meet at first face-to-face to discuss online course design. The faculty members then adjourn to become "online students," completing a segment of the professional development workshop fully online. Harris intentionally creates a series of activities which faculty must navigate through an overly (and unnecessarily complex) online course design (e.g., multiple tabs leading to confusing content, large blocks of written text, poorly written or overly wordy instructions, etc.). In addition, faculty are asked to complete poorly constructed small group projects which include examples of busywork that do not reflect course goals. As a final insult, Harris limits her interaction with faculty members, not answering emails, participating in discussion boards, or responding to student inquiries.[13]

Understandably, when online faculty members return to discuss their experiences, they express astonishment with the difficulty of navigating particular areas of the course and frustration at completing activities that they felt were "pointless" with little or no guidance from Harris.

Modeling ineffective and confusing course design and asking faculty to complete activities NOT relevant to the purpose of the workshop, while at first inciting anger, have led to opportunities to reflect on how incorporating complex activities or collaborative activities disconnected from course goals can frustrate students.

When faculty can experience these hurdles, and see how minimalist course design as described above can minimize these hurdles, implementing similar designs will be easier. However, only reviewing these designs and discussing them face-to-face is not as effective; only when online faculty face some of the hurdles that online students face in elaborate, poorly constructed courses with minimal support can they begin to truly understand the need for minimalist and interactive online courses.

TECHNOLOGY SHOULD BE IMPLEMENTED SELECTIVELY TO ENCOURAGE UNDERSTANDING AND ENGAGEMENT

In both professional development opportunities and in online courses, technology should be limited and used only when it supports the class goals. Both Weber and Borgman detailed how elements such as the discussion board and email were used only as a means to promote an engaged pedagogy, not because students should be forced to interact as a means of making up for perceived deficits in moving from face-to-face to online. In addition, Borgman removed any tools that were unnecessary for students in the course to minimize confusion just as Weber removed or streamlined unnecessary tasks. Understanding the components of the CMS and what can be made inaccessible can boost the importance of those tools that are engaged.

Faculty professional development should model the use of tools that promote engagement and maximize understanding without becoming burdensome to the students. One way to do so is to focus on the minimalist design principle of using a single assignment or activity to meet multiple course goals. For example, introductory quizzes might be used to both orient faculty to the professional development workshop or course while also demonstrating how the quiz feature works in a particular CMS (and in addition helping participants understand other concepts such as adaptive release, a mechanism that allows faculty to require that students meet certain course benchmarks before releasing additional components of the course). Thus, the technology can be integrated purposefully into the design of the professional development activity, effectively serving multiple learning outcomes without being extraneous. Faculty should then go on to create activities in their own practice shells that utilize the adaptive release feature to assist students in more effectively demonstrating knowledge and navigating their own courses.

HELP FACULTY OVERCOME THEIR SKEPTICISM THAT LESS IS MORE

A common misconception in online teaching and learning is that more activities and assignments must be put in place in to make up for the fact that students do not spend three hours per week in a classroom. When additional activities are added to make up for what is seen as a deficit in interaction, students find themselves moving from assignment to assignment, completing busywork instead of engaging in purposeful interaction.

One way that faculty can experience this in professional development workshops (whether face-to-face, hybrid, or fully online) is by blending the content with the tools faculty use to discuss the content. For example, in Harris's professional development workshop, faculty discuss what they feel are best practices for online discussion using multiple tools to facilitate online discussion. Faculty are first asked to use a Google Doc to collaboratively brainstorm elements of effective online discussions in small groups.[14] They then move into discussion boards with other groups who have also completed the brainstorming activity to discuss readings related to effective online discussion practices. Finally, the faculty come back together in groups to revisit their original document, using Google Hangouts or another synchronous discussion tool to identify which of the best practices they identified as a small group related to the whole class discussion in which they participated. The concluding activity for faculty is to write individual reflections about their experiences with these tools that promote discussion and interaction, identifying how their teaching will change as a result of their experiences in the discussion unit. Thus, the design of the unit, the content of the unit, and the technology used in the unit all further the course goals connected to the CCCC-OWI Example Effective Practices 2.4, 3.8–3.11, and 4.1–4.6. Thus, a single course sequence effectively addresses more than eleven individual learning outcomes in a faculty professional development workshop/course based around the CCCC-OWI Principles and Example Effective Practices Document.

In closing, our experiences as online faculty and professional development specialists reinforce that an online educational experience does not need to be complex to be complete. Using minimalist design, modeling best practices, and focusing on interaction in our online classrooms has not only bridged the distance between content and course delivery in our own classes, it has bridged the physical distance between us as we teach in Indiana, Pennsylvania, and Arkansas. As the three of us came together to present at a national conference and to write this chapter, we were amazed at how, while we were distant from each other, in many ways we were joined by the shared principles of minimalist course design and creating interactive experiences for our students. Since meeting and presenting, we have spoken to numerous online writing instructors who have also realized that, while they might be at a distance from each other and their students, they are connected by the best practices and principles that join all educational endeavors, face-to-face or online.

APPENDIX 2.A

Committee on College Composition and Communication Principles and Example Effective Practices for Online Writing Instruction

Accessed at http://www.ncte.org/cccc/resources/positions/owi principles

Overarching Principle

OWI Principle 1: Online writing instruction should be universally inclusive and accessible.

Instructional Principles

OWI Principle 2: An online writing course should focus on writing and not on technology orientation or teaching students how to use learning and other technologies.

OWI Principle 3: Appropriate composition teaching/learning strategies should be developed for the unique features of the online instructional environment.

OWI Principle 4: Appropriate onsite composition theories, pedagogies, and strategies should be migrated and adapted to the online instructional environment.

OWI Principle 5: Online writing teachers should retain reasonable control over their own content and/or techniques for conveying, teaching, and assessing their students' writing in their OWCs.

OWI Principle 6: Alternative, self-paced, or experimental OWI models should be subject to the same principles of pedagogical soundness, teacher/designer preparation, and oversight detailed in this document.

Faculty Principles

OWI Principle 7: Writing Program Administrators (WPAs) for OWI programs and their online writing teachers should receive appropriate OWI-focused training, professional development, and assessment for evaluation and promotion purposes.

OWI Principle 8: Online writing teachers should receive fair and equitable compensation for their work.

OWI Principle 9: OWCs should be capped responsibly at twenty students per course with fifteen being a preferable number.

Institutional Principles

OWI Principle 10: Students should be prepared by the institution and their teachers for the unique technological and pedagogical components of OWI.

OWI Principle 11: Online writing teachers and their institutions should develop personalized and interpersonal online communities to foster student success.

OWI Principle 12: Institutions should foster teacher satisfaction in online writing courses as rigorously as they do for student and programmatic success.

OWI Principle 13: OWI students should be provided support components through online/digital media as a primary resource; they should have access to onsite support components as a secondary set of resources.

OWI Principle 14: Online writing lab administrators and tutors should undergo selection, training, and ongoing professional development activities that match the environment in which they will work.

Research and Exploration

OWI Principle 15: OWI/OWL administrators and teachers/tutors should be committed to ongoing research into their programs and courses as well as the very principles in this document.

Notes

1. Online Learning Consortium (2014), formerly the Sloan-Consortium.
2. This practice also reflects in the CCCC-OWI Example Effective Practice 3.1, which encourages faculty to "use straightforward, plain, and linguistically direct rather than indirect language." While online faculty do not often consider language use in functional structures (such as buttons in a CMS shell) use of simple, direct language in these areas is vital to helping students navigate online courses effectively.
3. These design features relate to CCCC-OWI Example Effective Practice 3.2: Online written instruction should take advantage of the opportunities of the word processing system, text editor, html creator, and the CMS to mirror the types of online writing students most often read. These include writing [in] shorter, chunky paragraphs" and "using formatting tools wisely to highlight information with adequate white space, colors, and readable fonts."
4. Borgman's focused feedback and interaction with students reflects CCCC-OWI Example Effective Practice 3.8: "teachers should maximize their use of the online environment for explaining assignments and answering questions, holding small group or whole class meetings, showing examples, responding to student texts, and encouraging student writing in as many forms as may be pertinent to course goals. Students and faculty often use writing to connect for guiding tasks, sharing and critiquing assigned texts or student writing, and evaluative commenting.
5. A strategy echoed in OWI Principle 4: "Appropriate onsite composition theories, pedagogies, and strategies should be migrated and adapted to the online instructional environment."
6. As outlined, for example, in the 2011–2012 edition of the Quality Matters Rubric and in the California State University's Chico Rubric, a detailed framework of standards for "high quality learning environments" (Chico 2011–2012).
7. As identified by Garrison, Anderson, and Archer (2000).
8. Moreover, when Weber later adapted the Technical Writing class to a face-to-face venue and was able to add several additional activities, she was surprised to discover that students in the face-to-face classroom ultimately performed no better overall than had those in the online class; the two classes received similar average course grades, and many students in the face-to-face class (perhaps for many different reasons) seemed slightly less engaged with their service learning projects than the enthusiastic, mostly non-traditional students in the online class. Arguably, the different demographics of the two classes may have also been an important aspect of varying student engagement.
9. All these factors are various components of successful online classes identified by the Online Learning Consortium, or OLC.
10. Universal access is the first principle in CCCCs Effective Practices of Online Writing Instruction.
11. The need for faculty professional development and support is reflected in CCCC-OWI Principles 3, 4, and 7.
12. Or, in lieu of these experiences, provide course models, such as the PDS Technical Writing course, for faculty to review as they implement their own courses. Ultimately, however, faculty "should retain reasonable control over their own content and/or techniques for conveying, teaching, and assessing their students' writing in their OWCs [online writing courses]" (OWI Principle 5).
13. Harris also includes well-designed components of the course to contrast with poorly designed elements, and faculty members participate in well-planned, intentionally structured activities that model effective minimalist online course principles.

14.   While Google Docs is not necessary to complete this step in the task, this application is useful for this particular activity because it allows participants to collaboratively edit a document while also chatting to the side of the document, thus collaborating in both drafting and discussion.

References

Bawarshi, Anis, and Mary Jo Reiff. 2010. *Genre: An Introduction to History, Theory, Research, and Pedagogy*. West Lafayette, IN: Parlor Press.

Chico. 2011–2012. "Welcome to the Rubric for Online Instruction." *csuchico*. California State University. December 14, 2013. http://www.csuchico.edu/roi/.

Cleary, Michelle N. 2013. "Flowing and Freestyling: Learning from Adult Students about Process Knowledge Transfer." *College Composition and Communication* 64 (4): 661–85.

CCCC-OWI (Conference on College Composition and Communication Committee for Best Practices in Online Writing Instruction). 2013. "A Position Statement of Principles and Example Effective Practices for Online Writing Instruction (OWI)." March. http://www.ncte.org/cccc/resources/positions/owiprinciples/.

Council of Writing Program Administrators. 2008. "WPA Outcomes Statement for First Year Composition." *wpacouncil*. Council of Writing Program Administrators, July. Accessed December 11, 2013. http://wpacouncil.org/positions/outcomes.html.

Garrison, D. Randy, Terry Anderson, and Walter Archer. 2000. "Critical Inquiry in a Text-Based Environment: Computer Conferencing in Higher Education." *Internet and Higher Education* 2, no. 2–3: 87–105. Accessed December 14, 2013. http://dx.doi.org/10.1016/S1096-7516(00)00016-6.

Hewett, Beth L., and Christine Ehmann. 2004. *Preparing Educators for Online Writing Instruction: Principles and Processes*. Urbana, IL: NCTE.

Noel-Levitz. 2013. "2013 Adult and Online Learners Satisfaction and Priorities Report." *noellevitz*. Noel-Levitz. Accessed December 11, 2013. https://www.ruffalonl.com/student-retention-solutions/satisfaction-priorities-assessments/student-satisfaction-inventory.

Online Learning Consortium. 2014. "The Five Pillars." *OLC*. Online Learning Consortium. Accessed October 30, 2014. http://olc.onlinelearningconsortium.org/5pillars.

Russell, David R., and David Fisher. 2009. "Online, Multimedia Case Studies for Professional Education: Revisioning Concepts of Genre Recognition." In *Genres in the Internet*, ed. Janet Giltrow and Dieter Stein, 163–92. Amsterdam: John Benjamins; http://dx.doi.org/10.1075/pbns.188.07rus.

3
SHIFTING INTO DIGITAL WITH-OUT STRIPPING YOUR GEARS
Driver's Ed for Teaching Writing Online

Leni Marshall

Imagine: for many years, you have been driving an old Oldsmobile—not flashy, but everyone gets where they need to go. One morning, you find it replaced by a 1965 Thunderbird convertible, fully refurbished, paint gleaming in the sun. You have heard legends about this car, dreamed about driving one. Excited, perhaps a little nervous, but confident in your driving skills, you slide behind the wheel—and stop cold. *A stick shift?* Some of your friends drive these, and you have watched educational programs about standard transmissions, but you never have driven one. What happens next?

As many teachers have learned, in-person and online classes have analogous differences. Some of the strengths and weaknesses of each information delivery vehicle depend on the medium; others are more user-based. Even for composition instructors with decades of experience, teaching a writing-intensive general education course using an online classroom management system (CMS) means a significant adjustment. Faculty members may have incorporated CMS elements into their in-person classes, putting syllabi, assignment sheets, and handouts online, using the CMS's gradebook, and having students exchange peer review drafts and comments in the discussion boards, but that is not the same as teaching a course wholly online. For some instructors, teaching a composition course fully online is an unwelcome mandate, while other instructors anticipate a greater freedom of schedule and institutional recognition for providing an additional learning method for the students. When a faculty member is scheduled to teach online, what happens next?

The answer to that question varies widely, depending on the department and the institution. For instructors new to online teaching, some

DOI: 10.7330/9781607324850.c003

colleges require attendance at training sessions, which range in length from a few hours to several months. Some instructors begin teaching online with no instruction or practice other than their classroom experience. Faculty members who have had CMS training are nearly unanimous in their desire not to return for more (Chisholm 2006; Salaway, Caruso, and Nelson 2007). In a room of composition teachers, the suggestion of CMS training usually creates an audible, collective groan as the room's occupants flash on memories of stultifying or frustratingly technical training classes led by individuals who spend most of their time working with computers, rather than people.

This chapter considers the educational value of training writing instructors and students in the technical and the pedagogical possibilities of online classes, demonstrating the consequences that instructors' engagement in constructive learning experiences have on instructors' and students' classroom experiences. Along the way, readers may find ideas that help them reconsider the design of some online course components.

TRAINING À LA MODE

As best this author has been able to ascertain, no studies have been done about how to maximize faculty learning in CMS training courses, but instructors know that learners tend to be able to retain and apply information better when they have instruction, models, and practice. Some or all of those elements are missing from most online teacher training options. There is no data on the number of institutions that require online instructors to take a class online before they teach one. Only 60 percent of schools that offer online courses also offer training in using the online course management system (Mupinga and Maughan 2008, 18). For many schools, online teacher training focuses on the technical aspects of the CMS, as evidenced by the majority of data-driven research about faculty professional development in online courses focusing on the effectiveness of a particular information technology program (Marek 2009, 275–56; see also Hardy and Bower 2004; McIntyre 2011; Welker and Berardino 2005, 46; Wiesenberg and Stacey 2005, 397, 399); usually, the instructional facilitators are Information Technology staff, people who know the CMS reasonably well but are less likely to be skilled in teaching about online pedagogy.

Faculty members want instruction in pedagogy. They "worry about losing the benefits of face-to-face interactions and seek to understand new instructional design methodologies that maintain the level of interaction and relationship inherent in face-to-face classroom environments" (Taylor and McQuiggan 2008, 35; see also Marek 2009, 278–79, 284, 286). The majority of instructors say they would not demand recompense for the time they spend learning about "best practices" pedagogical techniques and how to employ those methods in their online courses (Tallent-Runnels et al. 2006, 116–17). Most teachers understand that CMSs and traditional classrooms are to education as a standard transmission and a manual transmission are to vehicles; drivers need similar but not identical skills to help their passengers move forward smoothly. Creating an online class that merely translates an in-person class into a CMS is one of the least effective ways of teaching online (Berge 2002; Hardy and Bower 2004; Steinbronn and Merideth 2008): "teaching online requires a different pedagogy from that of the traditional classroom, as well as a unique set of skills" (Hardy and Bower 2004, 47). When faculty learn to use online classrooms as a new kind of educational environment, rather than just as an extension of the traditional classroom, they add not only another *location* for learning, but another *mode* of learning to their teaching repertoires (Welker and Berardino 2005). The pedagogical differences and the impact on learning, as well as the implications for an instructor's career, can be substantial.

WHAT IS THE DIFFERENCE?

Instructors who have information about online pedagogical methods can be more effective in helping their students achieve the course goals. For example, consider student participation in online discussion boards. These locations, including the nomenclature, seek to replicate class discussions. However, in online classes, when instructors post in the discussion boards, it tends to shorten discussions even when the instructor posts a question, but students feel that they get more out of the class and instructors are rated higher for both their content knowledge and their enthusiasm (Mazzolini and Maddison 2007). This information can impact how an instructor chooses to design and manage the online classroom discussion boards and chat rooms. Designing for the online environment without that pedagogical information will lead an instructor to retain and utilize the information differently—and potentially less effectively.

One of the key differences is the "transactional distance" between the educator and a student. Both parties have learned to communicate in the classroom using instantaneous interpersonal feedback. The psychological and communication distance between teacher and learner in an online course room create potential barriers (Dennen, Darabi, and Smith 2007, 66). Teachers can create a two-way information flow to bridge that distance. Online, students are more dependent on the faculty members because the faculty members create every element of the online setting, giving them control over the learning environment in ways that they don't have in most face-to-face classes. Because the teachers will not necessarily be present in the online classroom when the students are, even before students are enrolled in the course, the instructor needs to have anticipated the questions and concerns that students may have, designing the course to respond to those needs (Lee and Busch 2005, 114). Also, in face-to-face classes, faculty members tend to communicate informally when explaining how an assignment helps students reach the learning goals. Often, instructors overlook this informal communication when designing online courses, which may detract from students' learning experiences (Boyd 2008, 232–33, 240; Tallent-Runnels et al. 2006, 101). Students may complete an assignment to earn the points, but without understanding why they are doing the activity, they learn less and respond less positively to the experience (Boyd 2008, 232–33). Technology needs to have meaning in the classroom; according to students, all too often, teachers will use a technology without having a particular pedagogical reason to employ it (Salaway, Caruso, and Nelson 2007, 15–16, 86–88). These beliefs lead to an even greater gulf between teachers and learners, frustrating teachers who strive to create stimulating learning environments. Designing the course in a way that impels students to engage in bridging the transactional distance requires a clear yet pithy framing of the course elements.

IMPROVING STUDENT LEARNING VIA PEDAGOGY

In composition courses, the connections between the course materials and the elements of an online environment are particularly apt. The fifth category of the Council of Writing Program Administrator's (WPA's) outcome statement is "composing in electronic environments." This outcome "makes the links between writing learning in technology a crucial pedagogical priority" (Corbett 2011). Learning about online teaching allows instructors to match the course design to their pedagogical goals.

Currently, online teachers report that the top reason why they choose a particular instructional method or strategy is technical resources. "Student considerations in learning" comes second (Steinbronn and Merideth 2008, 273). CMSs open a new world of possibilities in technical resources, so creating a learning-rich online classroom environment can begin with the learning goals rather than with the limitations of information and resources. The quality of online education rests on instructors' facility and comfort level with the available tools (Kearsley and Blomeyer 2003). Having experience as an online learner adds to teachers' understanding of the student experience and leads to better online pedagogy (Cowham and Duggleby 2005, 16; Kearsley and Blomeyer 2003; Straumsheim and Lederman 2013). Without that background, instructors are not as aware of the potential challenges and are less engaged in proactively creating solutions that improve the educational experience.

Having explained the concept of audience to scores of students, composition teachers are likely to create course materials that take into account what their students know, want, and need, and those specifics vary by student demographics. For example, a larger percentage of students at state colleges select online classes than do students at a university, and the majority of online learners are thirty- to thirty-five-years-old and white, a demographic that has been fairly consistent over time (Tallent-Runnels et al. 2006, 111, citing two studies). Among those students, learning styles can vary quite widely (cf. Tallent-Runnels et al. 2006, 110, citing one study), yet some elements of online instruction may apply to most online learners.

For example, students learn more when watching a video than they do during an online lecture with still pictures, but when embedding an animated video in a course, adding on-screen text that mirrors the narrative sound track does not improve information retention, and adding sidebars of information that is potentially interesting but "conceptually irrelevant" decreases student learning (Tallent-Runnels et al. 2006, 117, citing two studies). The online environment can improve student learning by providing course content in multiple formats: an annotated video and a transcript of the annotation with descriptions of the video, or both audio and visual reviews of the course materials (Corbett 2011). Students feel that the course offers a "value added" element when it includes an expert guest lecturer, who might, in an hour of time, hold a synchronous chat or respond asynchronously to questions and comments students have posted to a discussion board (Hardy and Bower 2004, 50; Lewis and Abdul-Hamid 2006). Including a guest lecturer fulfills several other "best practices" recommendations, supporting the higher level of student participation when the course design includes "dramatic tension from week-to-week," as well as helping to "create a sense of engagement, foster the sharing of information, and promote individual gratification" (Tallent-Runnels et al. 2006, 111, citing one study). Cultivating student engagement in the online classroom necessitates developing a new set of skills and practices.

Innovative assessment and classification rubrics contribute to instructors' capabilities. To "assess the thinking levels of discussion prompts and responses" in online courses, Tallent-Runnels and colleagues created a "Bloom-esque" taxonomy. They "found that unguided discussions fell into the middle level (organize, classify, apply, compare, and contrast) of the taxonomy, [and] they suggested that more direct guidance from the course instructor might have encouraged development of higher levels of thinking in the responses (synthesize and evaluate)" (Tallent-Runnels et al. 2006, 103). They suggest that instructors could contribute additional data to the discussion and ask follow-up questions to help students reach those higher levels of thinking.

Some of the elements of success in traditional classrooms become even more important when teaching online. For instance, online classroom experiences improve for both students and faculty when the instructor has a semester-long plan for the course (Stone and Chapman 2006, 1371; Welker and Berardino 2005, 47), a plan that aligns learning goals, learning activities, feedback, and evaluation (Berge 2002, 84; see also Salaway, Caruso, and Nelson 2007, 16; Tallent-Runnels et al. 2006, 116; Wiesenberg and Stacey 2005, 389), as well as the technical proficiency to implement the plan (Tallent-Runnels et al. 2006, 116). In short, "when instructors are not trained . . . [s]tudents may suffer" (Lee and Busch 2005, 109). Learning to teach online, faculty members can improve the outcomes for their online students and strengthen skills that benefit their students in the traditional courses.

NEW EXPECTATIONS

In a CMS, the elements that constitute *instructor presence* are widely divergent from those elements in more traditional classroom settings. Much is made in the literature about the importance of instructor presence in the classroom—presence is generally considered key to successful teaching, successful student learning, and student satisfaction (Durrington, Berryhill, and Swafford 2006; Lewis and Abdul-Hamid 2006, 83; Mupinga, Nora, and Yaw 2006, 188; Perry and Edwards 2005, 2; Sahin 2007, 5; Salaway, Caruso, and Nelson 2007, 13; Steinbronn and Merideth 2008, 271; Stone and Chapman 2006, 1371); however, almost no research records how instructors understand what *presence* means (Stone and Chapman 2006, 1370). In some ways, the students have higher expectations of instructor presence in an online course than they do in a traditional class. Throughout their years of learning, students have come to understand that whenever they are in the classroom, a teacher will be there with them. Students in asynchronous online courses could be in the classroom at any point during the day, leading to an implicit expectation of 24/7 instructor presence.

Intellectually, students know that the teacher is not always logged in, but they rate courses higher when they "feel" that the instructor's presence coincides with their own (Dennen, Darabi, and Smith 2007, 77). Fortunately, to give students a sense of presence and provide timely, responsive comments does not require instructors to live near their computers or smart phones for the duration of the course. Students respond positively when an instructor posts a photo, "speaks" to the students via audio feedback (Dennen, Darabi, and Smith 2007, 67; Stone and Chapman 2006), reminds students of upcoming due dates, offers little hints in the midst of a challenging unit, and provides immediate feedback on quiz questions—even though instructors may have created those elements months in advance, and every student who has the same quiz answer receives the same response. Students experience those interactions as individualized instruction, which they equate with instructor presence (Dennen, Darabi, and Smith 2007, 68; Stone and Chapman 2006, 1373–74). As in regular classes, giving summative comments at the end of a discussion and bundling answers to student questions can give students the feedback they need to stay engaged.

Students are not necessarily expecting or even wanting high levels of interaction with the instructor (Dennen, Darabi, and Smith 2007, 68, citing one study), but if they have a question or request feedback on their performance, they want the matter resolved quickly, and in the online world, *quickly* equates to minutes, not hours; even an overnight delay can make the response feel overdue (Boyd 2008, 232; see also Tallent-Runnels et al. 2006, 101). Thus, instructor presence "should be focused on proactive response regarding learner needs for course information and *in situ* response to learner queries and needs as they arise" (Dennen, Darabi, and Smith 2007, 68, citing one study; see also Gahungu, Dereshiwsky, and Moan 2006). As instructors develop their expertise in teaching online, they can improve the students' and their own experience of the course by managing expectations (see below) and by designing the learning environment to proactively address learners' needs (Dennen, Darabi, and Smith 2007, 68; see also Boyd 2008, 227). Teachers can address student anxieties about working in a novel class environment and improve student engagement in the course and the institution by responding quickly to queries and offering a rapid turn-around for qualitative and quantitative feedback on coursework (Dennen, Darabi, and Smith 2007, 67–68; Lewis and Abdul-Hamid 2006, 90; see also Stone and Chapman 2006, 1373). To expand writing students' learning experiences online, faculty members may need to rethink their understanding of *presence*. In traditional classrooms, this instructional element comes as a given and is limited by the number of waking hours in a day. Online, *presence* becomes another instrument in the pedagogical toolbox. Too much of it stifles student engagement; too little of it, and students feel abandoned (Boyd 2008, 241). Instructors can learn how to deploy this teaching tool as a positive element of students' learning experience.

In online classes, students "need more support and feedback from their instructor than would be required in a face-to-face course" (Stone and Chapman 2006, 1371). Students say that they expect "24 hour confirmation of receipt of assignments . . . and e-mail . . . 79% of the students expected the assignments . . . to be graded 'immediately' and if that is not possible, 'at least in two business days,' but not later than the 'following week'" (Boyd 2008, 231–32; Mupinga, Nora, and Yaw 2006, 186). If an instructor plans to follow a different time frame, that can be stated in the syllabus—and then the instructor will want to follow through by staying within that time frame all semester long (Durrington, Berryhill, and Swafford 2006). Some online faculty talk about yielding to demands to be online three times a day and to provide written feedback on all students' papers within five days of submission (Lewis and Abdul-Hamid 2006, 91; Perry and Edwards 2005, 1375). In the twenty-first century, many traditional-aged, "digital native" college students are used to mere infinitesimal lags in computer response time. Perhaps it is understandable that these students would anticipate a similar e-based immediacy in their online courses, with instructors reacting as if they were merely regurgitating preprogrammed responses. Luckily for faculty members, such expectations tend to be malleable.

Many composition students are relatively new to online learning, so a significant part of constructing their positive learning experience rests on the proactive management of student expectations (Boyd 2008, 232, 241; Dennen, Darabi, and Smith 2007, 77; Durrington, Berryhill, and Swafford 2006; Gahungu, Dereshiwsky, and Moan 2006; Lewis and Abdul-Hamid 2006, 89; Mupinga, Nora, and Yaw 2006, 185; Welker and Berardino 2005, esp. 47, 50; Young 2006). These management efforts can include expectations that the faculty member has for students (Gahungu, Dereshiwsky, and Moan 2006; Lewis and Abdul-Hamid 2006, 89; Welker and Berardino 2005; Young 2006), such as that students will have some basic proficiency with the technology, that they communicate, and that they spend a certain amount of time on coursework each week (Mupinga, Nora, and Yaw 2006, 185; also Welker and Berardino 2005, 47, 50). Some teachers want their students to build an environment of trust and support or to demonstrate "skillful critique and inquiry skills" (Wiesenberg and Stacey 2005, 391–92); those requirements and information on how to achieve those skills can be detailed in the online classroom. Students perceive that there are more opportunities to engage with instructors in online classes than there are in traditional courses (Boyd 2008, 231). By providing explicit guidelines, faculty members aid students in understanding their roles in the brave new world of online learning (Tallent-Runnels et al. 2006, 111, citing one study). Student expectations can then focus on other aspects of the course, a change that many students experience as positive.

Faculty members' feelings about online instruction tend to be more complex. Teacher satisfaction ties in with student satisfaction and with students achieving the learning goals, but it also is closely linked with time management. In-person teaching has become more omnipresent in all aspects of instructors' lives, as students' papers may cover the coffee table and student e-mails appear in instructors' mailboxes at all hours of the day. And most studies find that online teaching creates an even greater demand on faculty time. The amount of increase varies by study; statistics range from a 14 percent increase (Tomei 2006) to a 300 percent increase (Wiesenberg and Stacey 2005) in time commitment (other qualitative support for this idea: Hardy and Bower 2004; Mupinga, Nora, and Yaw 2006; Salaway, Caruso, and Nelson 2007; Turgeson 2006; Welker and Berardino 2005, 33, 40–42; Young 2006, 67; and there is one study that suggests the time commitment is less: Mupinga and Maughan 2008, 18.) There is a solid body of evidence that "teachers often feel resentful and overburdened when asked to teach online" (McIntyre 2011, 10, citing five studies). Most estimates suggest that developing an online class requires more than twice the time commitment as creating an in-person class (Lee and Busch 2005, 110, citing one study; see also Tallent-Runnels et al. 2006, 114). At institutions that have staff support for online course development, faculty members' design schedules become "dependent on information technologists, graphic designers, and other support staff" (Bozarth 2006, 3). In the first semester of online teaching, up to 90 percent of instructor time is in designing the online course environment (Hardy and Bower 2004, 49). Once the design is done and the course is live, "The feeling that one never gets a break from the course since it is always on" seems constant, no matter what the class size, and is a complaint of students as well as faculty members (Welker and Berardino 2005, 46). Course design, managing expectations, and setting clear limits can make a significant difference in the experience of online courses. Because time management is such an important component in faculty and student lives, the time commitment continues to be a critical pedagogical component in the online as well as the in-person classroom.

WHO IS TRAINING WHOM?

Students do not necessarily have the most sophisticated and well-researched ideas about online learning, but they have definite opinions about it, and those opinions shape their educational experiences. Most students understand technology as learning-neutral. That is, 60 percent of students agree or strongly agree that technologies have a positive impact on their educational experience (Salaway, Caruso, and Nelson 2007, 80; see also Steinbronn and Merideth 2008), but they also note that faculty underuse, overuse, inappropriate use, and overdependence is still too frequent and creates a classroom environment that frustrates, rather than encourages, learning (Salaway, Caruso, and Nelson 2007, 15–16). Another potential frustration is that students might enroll in online classes for convenience of time management (Mupinga, Nora, and Yaw 2006, 185), yet online classes are more time intensive for students as well as for faculty.

Students say that they appreciate the ways in which online courses give them more control over course pacing (Tallent-Runnels et al. 2006, 116) and a different mode of engagement in class discussions (Boyd 2008, 236), as well as the ways that those discussions support their idea generation, revision work, idea clarification, and project focus (Boyd 2008, 237). The instructor actions that students report improve their online experience include providing prompt feedback on assignments, participating in class discussion, encouraging non-course-related interactions, and assigning collaborative learning activities (Boyd 2008, 226; Tallent-Runnels et al. 2006, 101; see also Dennen, Darabi, and Smith 2007, 75). The collaborative elements of online instruction also alleviate the isolative elements of distance learning, which, if unchecked, can lead to "demotivation and dropout (Cowham and Duggleby 2005, 17–18). "Interactions that maintain whole-class presence and communication seem to be valued by students over those that meet isolated individual needs. Further, constant contact seems preferable to in-depth contact" (Dennen, Darabi, and Smith 2007, 77). Composition courses can incorporate all of these components in ways that students find engaging, but most data about students' perceptions of online courses is not specific to writing courses.

Boyd's research compares how well in-person versus online courses support the learning goals in composition courses. Most evident is the connection between the course communications taking place in writing and the goals of the course, which is to improve student writing through activities such as practice. In engaging with other students via discussion boards, students "craft their thinking within dialogic exchanges" (2008, 239). This helps students do a better job understanding their audience and targeting their writing for that group. Having readers who take their writing seriously makes students more thoughtful in their writing. Online composition assignments can help students see how writing not only *expresses* ideas but can assist them in *arriving* at interesting ideas. Composition students in the online environment take "more responsibility for their learning and . . . [do a better job connecting] the course material to their own lives" (Boyd 2008, 237, 239). The online environment is particularly pedagogically suitable for composition classes.

Instructor competencies that students say contribute to beneficial learning experiences include teachers' abilities to "adapt to student needs, use meaningful examples, motivate students, and facilitate effectively" (Young 2006, 70–71). Unfortunately, in a list of twenty characteristics of online teaching, students generally give online instructors the lowest score in their ability to motivate students, second to bottom in their ability to "adapt to student needs," and third from the bottom in their ability to "facilitate effectively" (Young 2006, 68–71). Online instructors can take those factors into consideration when designing course content and online activities, keeping in mind that for students, finding that the course has "personal relevance is the strongest predictor of student satisfaction." (Sahin 2007, 5; see also Young 2006, 74). Learning about the *why* of student enrollment in online courses, as well as about the online class elements that students appreciate, helps instructors configure their course designs, incorporate proactive communication elements, and frame the class activities in ways that students understand and value.

ANOTHER LEARNING EXPERIENCE

Much like their instructors, students strongly feel that they do not want or need additional training for online coursework (Salaway, Caruso, and Nelson 2007; Welker and Berardino 2005), yet students are more successful in a class if they have attended training for the CMS (Wiesenberg and Stacey 2005). Although 74 percent of students report that they do not need more computer training (Salaway, Caruso, and Nelson 2007), 93 percent of online learners express a need for technical help with computers during the semester (Mupinga, Nora, and Yaw 2006, 187). Many faculty members who teach online and who write about teaching online also say that students' learning is negatively impacted by technology-related communication breakdowns (Gahungu, Dereshiwsky, and Moan 2006; Wiesenberg and Stacey 2005, 390; Young 2006, 67;) and that students need more training and speedier responses from the IT staff when there are technology glitches (Welker and Berardino 2005, 46). Moreover, "the more the students experienced technical problems, the lower they rated their instructors" (Tallent-Runnels et al. 2006, 114). Having more data about student reactions to technological snafus can help writing teachers preempt these events by learning in advance the ways to help students navigate through an institution's information technology infrastructure for support.

One course's instructors inadvertently studied this topic in a class in which half the students were on campus and half were solely distance learners. Those students who were able to attend an in-person training about the technological aspects of taking an online class were more successful and had a more positive learning experience than those students who were not able to attend the in-person training (Wiesenberg and Stacey 2005, 391). Even when schools offer trainings or user manuals, most students prefer that the professor who is using the CMS teach them about it rather than having IT professionals teaching it (Young 2006, 67; see also Salaway, Caruso, and Nelson 2007, 52). One easily avoidable mistake: instructors tend to overestimate students' comfort levels with CMS technology (Salaway, Caruso, and Nelson 2007, 16; see also Gahungu, Dereshiwsky, and Moan 2006); students have commented on how those faculty assumptions significantly disadvantage nontraditional and lower income students, who often have even less exposure to technology than their younger or more affluent counterparts (Salaway, Caruso, and Nelson 2007, 87). Even with the potential for such oversights, having the teachers doing the technical as well as the content instruction seems to be key to improving student understanding of and appreciation for the CMS environment.

TRAINING THE TRAINERS

Most faculty members appreciate the potential of this instructional medium and want to learn how to use it well. "We tend to teach the way our favorite professor taught" (Marek 2009, 275). Few of the instructors currently teaching writing online received online instruction from their favorite professors, but many faculty members became teachers because they enjoy learning. In learning to teach online, these people can become students again, as the new medium "prevents teachers from teaching in their familiar ways and [makes them] rethink their teaching practices" (McQuiggan 2007). In addition to *presence,* online instruction encourages people to redefine terms such as *learning, content coverage,* and even *teaching* itself (Bozarth 2006, 6). In essence, online pedagogical elements "challenge [teachers'] assumptions about learning," which can be particularly interesting (and engaging!) because the transition is happening in an educational paradigm that is highly resistant to change (Boyd 2008, 238). In other fields, one of the elements that creates a barrier to faculty adaptation of online teaching is their reluctance to transition to a learner-centered environment. Faculty in composition courses have been creating learner-centered courses at least as far back as the early 1970s, which means that this field tends to be one of the early adapters, despite the challenges of teaching writing-intensive content online.

In learning about online pedagogy, one advantage writing instructors have as adult learners is that they tend to be motivated and engaged (cf. McQuiggan 2007). However, "many educators find it difficult to invest time and effort into analyzing the available theory and research. Quickly and easily deriving practical online teaching approaches suitable to individual circumstances and skill levels . . . can be difficult" (McIntyre 2011). To create a constructive and engaging learning opportunity for instructors, researchers suggest things ranging from having the IT staff design a mock classroom, which instructors could tour through for ideas (Steinbronn and Merideth 2008), to "constant . . . training "(Gahungu, Dereshiwsky, and Moan 2006), to "adequate compensation and incentive structures" (Mupinga and Maughan 2008, 18) for online instructors, to a twenty-three-week course with two instructors for each fifteen to twenty students (Cowham and Duggleby 2005, 19), to a period of apprenticeship (Wiesenberg and Stacey 2005, 398), to having a "centralized team approach that ideally includes . . . [the] subject matter expert or author; graphic designer; a web developer; programmer; and instructional designer" (Wiesenberg and Stacey 2005, 389)—a pedagogically-sound option that nevertheless might cause even the most supportive deans to pause in their considerations of the cost/benefit ratio.

Researchers studying the pedagogy of teaching about online learning frame some of the challenges of this education as stemming from the institutional structure and its dealings with educators:

Universities have a real obligation to stop running training courses in systems and telling academics how to do things. Universities need to . . . see staff development as a genuine developmental exercise, in which time, and resources, and money are put into helping staff innovate, become sophisticated internet users in their teaching[. Institutions need] to appreciate that there will be an intangible return on that freedom . . . [as] academics then help other academics to become sophisticated, even expert, in these fields. (McIntyre 2011)

Optimally, teaching about online pedagogy would take place via a structured learning opportunity in which there were "explicit assessment criteria that the learner is required to provide evidence of having achieved" (Cowham and Duggleby 2005, 22), and a team of expert teachers providing individualized instruction that incorporates best practices while showing respect for learners' experiences, helping learners develop applicable skills in a supportive environment, and advancing the learners' results through the efforts of expert support staff: this is the environment of faculty members' dreams (Cowham and Duggleby 2005, 16–18, 22–24; Kearsley and Blomeyer 2003; Marek 2009, 278; McQuiggan 2007; McQuiggan 2012; Tallent-Runnels et al. 2006, 113, 116). *Cost* is an obvious downside, but there are no disputes about whether the investment would create higher-quality online instruction.

SUPPORTING PROFESSIONAL DEVELOPMENT

The amount of support from the administration for faculty learning to teach online varies widely. In far too many institutions, "distinct lines have emerged between student and faculty desires for quality learning, and administrators desires for the profitable economic model seen in online course delivery," and colleges are being penny wise and pound foolish by investing a lot of money into the technologies and relatively little money into helping instructors use the available technologies effectively (Marek 2009, 276–77; see also Cox et al. 2011, 808; McIntyre 2011, 10; Patrick and Dawley 2009, 7; Tomei 2006). Administrators are concerned with online course quality and student learning (Durrington, Berryhill, and Swafford 2006, 190) and play a fundamental role in making online learning a success. When they call for more online teaching presence, faculty members can help them learn the importance of professional development in accomplishing these goals.

Although 79 percent of university and college administrators report that faculty training is the top issue in campus computing, investments in online education were rated effective by only 47 percent of respondents to Educause's 2013 survey, (Straumsheim 2013). Faculty can help create an institutional environment that supports high quality online instruction by advocating for these practices; institutions can provide incentives for faculty to participate in online teaching, as well as adequate opportunities for instructional training (Hardy and Bower 2004; Lee and Busch 2005, 114; Marek 2009; Tallent-Runnels et al. 2006; Welker and Berardino 2005, 46; Wiesenberg and Stacey 2005, 397, 399). Also, when an institution reconfigures the possibilities for student educational experiences by adding online courses to its offerings, it needs to restructure its faculty evaluation policies. Administrators may be surprised to learn that instructors "rank redesigning and rethinking faculty roles as *the* highest priority" in their preparation to teach online (McQuiggan, 2007; emphasis added). Adequate training, reliable technical support and infrastructure, and formal institutional recognition are the three most important factors influencing faculty members' willingness to contribute to a university's online course offerings (Lee and Busch 2005, 109; Tallent-Runnels et al. 2006, 114). Without those elements, the significant changes that the digital revolution brings to the academy may happen in the absence of—and in a way that ignores—the pedagogical experience and significant knowledge base of the faculty (Marek 2009, 279; see also 285–86). Maintaining this intellectual gap can have significant consequences for the institution's reputation and its fiscal stability.

As members of the administration learn more about the importance of training for quality online instruction—particularly for instructors in fields such as composition, which impacts so many students—they may also come to realize that even experienced teachers have significant learning curves in developing expertise in the new pedagogies. In a three-hour or even a three-day workshop, instructors can do little more than achieve a level of basic competency in online pedagogy; it takes "an average of four years and may take a further five years to achieve expert status" (Boyd 2008, 234, citing one study; see also Corbett 2011). Given the long training curve for approaching expertise in this area, in addition to the pedagogical and practical aspects of online teaching, writing instructors also can educate themselves about the ways in which online teaching is going to impact their academic careers.

1. Anecdotally, most hiring committees respond positively to instructors who have online teaching experience. Many faculty members, both new and advanced, feel some pressure to engage with online pedagogy (Turgeson 2006). Given those institutional pressures, faculty members

might assume that an institution will have tenure and promotion criteria that recognize or even promote excellence in teaching online (Lee and Busch 2005, 110, citing one study); however, many, if not most, institutions have not made that change (Boyd 2008, 227). This situation makes online instruction particularly risky for contingent and adjunct faculty and teaching assistants, who are more likely than tenure-track instructors to get enmeshed in "aggressive distance education initiatives that limit faculty agency and operate on a market model" (Chisholm 2006). Furthermore, with online learning, intellectual property rights are very much in question.

2. At most institutions, when an instructor posts content in a CMS, that content becomes the property of the institution. This is in direct contrast to the AAUP statement on copyright, which suggests that "prevailing academic practice treats the faculty member as the default copyright owner of course materials created independently for traditional academic purposes" (Chisholm 2006). Also, the work that an instructor does within a CMS is difficult to share with colleagues. Faculty members may encounter bureaucratic hurdles if they try to collaborate with other teachers to develop online course content, even when they are at the same school. For online courses, receiving informal feedback from mentors, sharing assignments with colleagues, and documenting innovative pedagogies may prove challenging, a particular disadvantage for instructors who are on the job market. On the other hand, people who are higher up the ladder at the instructor's institution may be able to do a close reading of anything posted in the course. The work is both invisible and hyper visible; every word is available for administrative review (Chisholm 2006; Lewis and Abdul-Hamid 2006, 95). The increase in work time in teaching online and the decrease in intellectual property rights combine to create a situation that is, at the very least, imbalanced, and can be exploitive. Even while recognizing the significant opportunities and benefits that informed, competent online pedagogy can add to student learning opportunities, instructors need to educate themselves to keep from undermining their own success even as they support students' educational achievements.

A SMOOTH START

The pillars of quality for online teaching—learning effectiveness, cost-effectiveness, institutional commitment, access, faculty satisfaction, and student satisfaction—apply to learning about online pedagogy as much as they do to online courses. The hope is that this article provides data-driven evidence supporting the importance of both teacher- and student-based education in online learning. Learning to teach writing online is like learning to drive a stick shift. Without instruction or practice, new drivers may be a menace to themselves and others, especially when the route involves hills and stops, and the vehicle can end up significantly worse for the wear. With a bit of training for yourself and your passengers, though, you can learn enough to make a smooth start from a red light heading up a steep hill, comfortable and effective in your new environment. Good luck, drive safely, and have fun!

References

Berge, Zane L. 2002. "Active, Interactive, and Reflective eLearning." *Quarterly Review of Distance Education* 3, no. 2 (Summer): 181. Professional Development Collection. Accessed December 25, 2008.

Boyd, Patricia Webb. 2008. "Analyzing Students' Perceptions of Their Learning in Online and Hybrid First-Year Composition Courses." *Computers and Composition* 25 (2): 224–43. Accessed July 9, 2103. http://dx.doi.org/10.1016/j.compcom.2008.01.002.

Bozarth, Jane. 2006. *Classroom Trainer Resistance to E-Learning: Literature Review.* Raleigh: North Carolina State University. March; Accessed July 9, 2013.

Chisholm, Julie K. 2006. "Pleasure and Danger in Online Teaching and Learning." *Academe* 92 (6): 39–42. Accessed December 25, 2008. http://dx.doi.org/10.2307/40253523.

Corbett, Steven J. 2011. "Technology and Teaching Writing." *Inside Higher Ed*, July 25. Accessed December 30, 2011.

Cowham, Terry, and Julia Duggleby. 2005. "Pedagogy and Quality Assurance in the Development of Online Learning for Online Instructors." *Journal of Asynchronous Learning Networks* 9 (4): 15–27. Accessed July 21, 2013.

Cox, Bradley E., Kadian L. McIntosh, Robert D. Reason, and Patrick T. Terenzini. 2011. "A Culture of Teaching: Policy, Perception, and Practice in Higher Education." *Research in Higher Education* 52 (8): 808–29. Accessed July 9, 2013. http://dx.doi.org/10.1007/s11162-011-9223-6.

Dennen, Vanessa P., A. Aubteen Darabi, and Linda J. Smith. 2007. "Instructor-Learner Interaction in Online Courses: The Relative Perceived Importance of Particular Instructor Actions on Performance and Satisfaction." *Distance Education* 28 (1): 65–79. Accessed July 9, 2013. http://dx.doi.org/10.1080/01587910701305319.

Durrington, Vance A., Amy Berryhill, and Jeanne Swafford. 2006. "Strategies for Enhancing Student Interactivity in an Online Environment." *College Teaching* 54 (1): 190–93. Accessed December 25, 2008. http://dx.doi.org/10.3200/CTCH.54.1.190-193.

Gahungu, Athanase, Mary Dereshiwsky, and Eugene Moan. 2006. "Finally I Can Be with My Students 24/7, Individually and in Group: A Survey of Faculty Teaching Online." *Journal of Interactive Online Learning* 5, no. 2 (Summer): 118–42. ERIC. Accessed July 9, 2013.

Hardy, Kimberly P., and Beverly L. Bower. 2004. "Instructional and Work Life Issues for Distance Learning Faculty." *New Directions for Community Colleges* 128 (2004): 47–54. Accessed December 25, 2008. http://dx.doi.org/10.1002/cc.174.

Kearsley, Greg, and Robert Blomeyer. 2003. "Preparing K–12 Teachers to Teach Online." *~gkearsley*. Sprynet.com, June. Accessed July 9, 2013.

Lee, J. A., and P. E. Busch. 2005. "Factors Related to Instructors' Willingness to Participate in Distance Education." *Journal of Educational Research* 99 (2): 109–15. Accessed July 9, 2013. http://dx.doi.org/10.3200/JOER.99.2.109-115.

Lewis, Cassandra C., and Husein Abdul-Hamid. 2006. "Implementing Effective Online Teaching Practices: Voices of Exemplary Faculty." *Innovative Higher Education* 31 (2): 83–98. Accessed December 25, 2008. http://dx.doi.org/10.1007/s10755-006-9010-z.

Marek, Kate. 2009. "Learning to Teach Online: Creating a Culture of Support for Faculty." *J of Education for Library and Information Science* 50, no. 4 (Fall): 275–92. EBSCO. Accessed July 19, 2013.

Mazzolini, Margaret, and Sarah Maddison. 2007. "When to Jump in: The Role of the Instructor in Online Discussion Forums." *Computers & Education* 49 (2): 193–213. Accessed December 25, 2008. http://dx.doi.org/10.1016/j.compedu.2005.06.011.

McIntyre, Simon. 2011. *Learning to Teach Online.* Sydney: College of Fine Arts at the University of New South Wales; Accessed July 9, 2013.

McQuiggan, Carol A. 2007. *"The Role of Faculty Development in Online Teaching's Potential to Question Teaching Beliefs and Assumptions." Online Journal of Distance Learning Administration 10, no. 3.* Education Source; Accessed July 13, 2013.

McQuiggan, Carol A. 2012. "Faculty Development for Online Teaching as a Catalyst for Change." *Journal of Asynchronous Learning Networks* 16 (2): 27–61. Accessed July 9, 2013.

Mupinga, Davison M., and George R. Maughan. 2008. "Web-Based Instruction and Community College Faculty Workload." *College Teaching* 56 (1): 17–21. Accessed December 25, 2008. http://dx.doi.org/10.3200/CTCH.56.1.17-22.

Mupinga, Davison M., Robert T. Nora, and Dorothy Carole Yaw. 2006. "The Learning Styles, Expectations, and Needs of Online Students." *College Teaching* 54 (1): 185–89. Accessed December 25, 2008. http://dx.doi.org/10.3200/CTCH.54.1.185-189.

Patrick, Susan, and Lisa Dawley. 2009. "Redefining Teacher Education: K–12 Online-Blended Learning and Virtual Schools." *Redefining Teacher Education in a Digital Age,* December 6–8. Accessed July 9, 2013.

Perry, Beth, and Margaret Edwards. 2005. *"Exemplary Online Educators: Creating a Community of Inquiry." Online Submission, April 1.* ERIC; Accessed December 25, 2008.

Sahin, Ismail. 2007. *"Predicting Student Satisfaction in Distance Education and Learning Environments." Online Submission, April 1.* ERIC; Accessed December 25, 2008.

Salaway, Gail, Judith Caruso, and Mark Nelson. 2007. "The ECAR Study of Undergraduate Students and Information Technology, 2007." *Educause.* Educause. edu. Accessed July 15, 2008.

Steinbronn, Peggy, and Eunice Merideth. 2008. "Perceived Utility of Methods and Instructional Strategies Used in Online and Face-to-face Teaching Environments." *Innovative Higher Education* 32 (5): 265–78. Accessed December 25, 2008. http://dx.doi.org/10.1007/s10755-007-9058-4.

Stone, Sophia J., and Diane D. Chapman. 2006. *"Instructor Presence in the Online Classroom." Online Submission, February 1.* ERIC; Accessed December 25, 2008.

Straumsheim, Carl. 2013. "Survey Shows IT as a Service Dominates Top Priorities Among University IT Officials." *Inside Higher Ed.* Insidehighered.com, October 17. Accessed December 9, 2013.

Straumsheim, Carl, and Doug Lederman. 2013. "Teaching to Teach." *Inside Higher Ed.* Insidehighered.com, November 22. Accessed December 9, 2013.

Tallent-Runnels, Mary K., Julie A. Thomas, William Y. Lan, Sandi Cooper, Terence C. Ahern, Shana M. Shaw, and Xiaoming Liu. 2006. "Teaching Courses Online: A Review of the Research." *Review of Educational Research* 76 (1): 93–135. Accessed July 16, 2013. http://dx.doi.org/10.3102/00346543076001093.

Taylor, Ann, and Carol McQuiggan. 2008. "Faculty Development Programming: If We Build It, Will They Come?" *EDUCAUSE Quarterly* 31, no. 3: 28–37. ERIC. Accessed July 13, 2013.

Tomei, Lawrence. 2006. "The Impact of Online Teaching on Faculty Load: Computing the Ideal Class Size for Online Courses." *Journal of Technology and Teacher Education* 14 (3): 531–41.

Turgeson, DeMil. 2006. "UW-Stout Faculty and Instructional Staff Members Use of Computer Technology in Their Courses Survey—Executive Summary." Master's thesis, February 24.

Welker, Jan, and Lisa Berardino. 2005. "Blended Learning: Understanding the Middle Ground Between Traditional Classroom and Fully Online Instruction." *Journal of Educational Technology Systems* 34 (1): 33–55. Accessed December 25, 2008. http://dx.doi.org/10.2190/67FX-B7P8-PYUX-TDUP.

Wiesenberg, Faye, and Elizabeth Stacey. 2005. "Reflections on Teaching and Learning Online: Quality program design, delivery and support issues from a cross global perspective." *Distance Education* 26 (3): 385–404. Accessed December 25, 2008. http://dx.doi.org/10.1080/01587910500291496.

Young, Suzanne. 2006. "Student Views of Effective Online Teaching in Higher Education." *American Journal of Distance Education* 20 (2): 65–77. Accessed December 25, 2008. http://dx.doi.org/10.1207/s15389286ajde2002_2.

PART TWO

Fostering Student Engagement

4

LOST IN CYBERSPACE
Addressing Issues of Student Engagement in the Online Classroom Community

Tamara Girardi

I recently had a conversation with one of my former graduate program professors about online learning. She was awed by my interest in teaching online courses and admitted that she neither had the time nor the motivation to learn an entirely new way to teach. This professor has been teaching in the face-to-face (F2F) setting for a couple of decades, and I can speak from experience that she is quite good at it. I wasn't surprised that she anticipated the online learning environment would differ from the F2F environment; on the contrary, I'm often amazed when faculty members believe the teaching approaches that work in the traditional classroom are likely to work online as well.

In other words, the fallacious assumption is that since some faculty have been teaching for decades F2F, they have numerous approaches, lectures, and activities stocked up for online interaction. And what could be better than teaching in their pajamas, lightening their course loads during the year, and spending summers on the beach but still earning a paycheck? Such benefits are certainly present in online teaching, but there are significant pedagogical differences that must be recognized. In addition, these differences may require a greater time commitment and yield less impressive results than instructors who are new to online learning might anticipate.

When I began teaching online at a local community college in 2007, my students often enrolled in a combination of some F2F classes and some online classes. They took whatever fit into their schedules. That often meant two or three classes at the campus and two or three classes virtually. It seemed in those early years that students attempted to diversify their schedules in terms of online or F2F classes because they were apprehensive about taking a full course load of five online classes. Why?

DOI: 10.7330/9781607324850.c004

Because they're hard. At the time, both students and faculty were learning about the online environment, and really still are. According to the anecdotal evidence from my students and my colleagues, many of the online instructors were copying and pasting their lectures, assigning the students to read pages from the book, and grading an essay or major project at the end of the semester. There was little email communication, nonexistent discussion board interaction, and a situation in which the students were teaching themselves the material. So, yes, for the students, it was hard. It was because of these early experiences with online teaching that I found the utmost importance in eliciting feedback from students. My intention was to uncover their unique needs and affective concerns, and as a result, I have learned a great deal about online students. For this reason, I plan to discuss some of my attempts at innovation and student engagement in this chapter. Furthermore, I would love to hear about your experiences, so that all of our students might benefit.

FOUNDATIONAL PRINCIPLES FOR THE NARRATIVE

The narrative in this chapter is supported by three foundational principles. First, developing an online community is paramount to student engagement. Second, additional efforts at engaging students are necessary in the online environment compared to the F2F classroom. And third, online faculty must carefully analyze, select, implement, and assess what tools best create an online community and engage students in the online environment.

To begin, let's address the first principle regarding developing an online community. "Social presence is something we rarely consider in the face-to-face classroom. When students see one another within a physical space, we simply assume that presence will occur; students will develop a sense of who their colleagues are simply by being around them" (Palloff and Pratt 2007, 30). However, students in online classes have often reported a sense of isolation, "a factor often ignored by many educators, but one that may make the difference between a successful and an unsuccessful online learning environment for many students" (McInnerney and Roberts 2004, 73).

Therefore, efforts must be made by the instructor to create a sense of community and minimize student frustration with the quality of much desired human interaction (McInnerney and Roberts 2004). As Abigail Scheg (2014) points out, "studies demonstrate increased student academic success, dedication to coursework, and interest in overall education when online classrooms are not just groups of individuals but a learning community in which each student is personally invested and valued" (29).

The second aforementioned principle of the importance of extra effort in building an online learning community is closely connected to the first as the Rena Palloff and Keith Pratt reference above illustrates (Palloff and Pratt 2007). While teaching online saves hours spent commuting to and traversing a physical campus, additional time must be spent on fostering a learning community. Because the term "community" has often coincided with a geographic location, the definition in an online classroom has proven a bit more elusive for scholars and instructors. However, in recent years, "online learning communities" have become a major research focus. For instance, technology could be instrumental in forming the community students innately desire, or using it in the classroom could prove prohibitive, depending on prior expertise. To offer one example of a theory that illustrates the potential variation in technological skill of students, Don Tapscott (2009) identified eight "norms" associated with the Net Generation, or students he defined as born between 1977 and 1997. The norms are "distinctive attitudinal and behavioral characteristics that differentiate this generation from their baby-boom parents and other generations" (74). Therefore, one classroom comprised of learners from several different generations creates additional challenges in terms of building an online community. Some scholars, such as Alvin Wang and Michael Newlin, have argued for synchronous discussion opportunities to build community (Wang and Newlin 2001) while others such as J. E. Aitken and Leonard Shedletsky advocated for asynchronous tools such as email and discussion boards (Aitken and Shedletsky 2002). Student demographics provide complications in terms of community; additionally, many online students fall into Tom Brown's (2011) underprepared category because of affective concerns such as being single parents, working full time, returning to school after several years or decades, and so on. Therefore, these students log on at different times of day, different days of the week and come from various generations and backgrounds. They have different expectations for the course and for their interaction with each other. In other words, building an online community is not a simple exercise, but it is a worthwhile one.

Finally, online instructors must be flexible in terms of analyzing, selecting, implementing, and assessing tools that might facilitate the aforementioned goals of developing an online learning community and engaging online students. In my F2F classrooms, I find myself tweaking a few details here and there from semester to semester. Online, though, is where I find the greatest change in my courses; I am more frequently altering lectures and innovating techniques. Mostly I find these changes are influenced by feedback from students; if several students are having difficulty understanding a specific set of written directions, it becomes clear that text is not working as it should, for example. Flexibility is imperative as is the openness to continually assess current approaches and implement new ideas all the while keeping a few core concepts in mind. First:

> Technology does not teach students; effective teachers do. A virtual learning space that is effectively created by a competently trained instructor can deliver on the promise educators make to their students. It can help us deliver our content to a growing number of learners over a widely diverse geographical area. (Whitesel 1998, 1)

As Cynthia Whitesel suggests, online instructors should always remember that their unique skills and ideas are what's best in terms of teaching students. Technology is a tool, one of many, online instructors have at their disposal. In that regard, instructors, not technology, should guide the course content.

> Instructors need not get carried away with the many applications and options of a course management system (CMS) (i.e., blogs, wikis, discussion boards, tools, assignments, tests, quizzes, group work, and many more). Just because a CMS offers ten, twenty, or thirty ways to present information to students does not mean that all of these methods need to be utilized in a single course. (Scheg 2014, 26)

I learned the lesson Scheg offers above through course assessment via a student evaluation, which I discuss in more detail later in this chapter. The main idea, though, is that it is all too easy for ambition to overrule logic and instinct. Online instructors, I believe, should attempt new approaches in the classroom, but they should always anticipate a process of careful analysis, selection, implementation, and assessment will follow those attempts all the while realizing scholarship on some approaches might be severely limited. Technology is in constant flux. Because of this, reflective practice may be an educator's greatest asset to understanding and implementing various technologies in the classroom.

However, reflective practice should include soliciting insight from students. For example, "[b]efore beginning a unit that utilizes Twitter, educators should realize that although nearly 80% of teens are using social media sites, there is no telling which sites a particular group of students is using—unless teachers ask" (Girardi 2013, 266–67). Student feedback is often limited in college courses to the end-of-semester student evaluations. While the data collected on these evaluations is certainly relevant, the form of assessment does little to facilitate mid-semester improvements for the particular student population in a given course. To reiterate, although there are many factors to consider as part of any pedagogy, the discussion on the following pages depends on the theoretical foundations of the need for developing online student communities, increase student engagement efforts in online environments (compared to their F2F counterparts), and reflect and assess practices to gauge the potential for student engagement and success.

INTRODUCTORY PHONE CHATS

Engaging students does not necessarily require utilization of the most cutting edge software or Web 2.0 technologies. For an online forum where there is little synchronous interaction and even less verbal or F2F interaction, a simple phone conversation could be highly influential at developing rapport between the instructor and the students. With that in mind, one of the first posts in the Content folders of my online courses each semester is the following:

> With online classes, interaction between the instructor and the students can be limited. I actually prefer to interact with you all regularly. I want you to be comfortable talking with me about any issues you have in the course. To begin that dialogue, I will hold phone chats.
>
> In each phone chat, there will be up to two students and the instructor. Students should select a time that works for them, email the instructor requesting the time, and the instructor will respond to the email to confirm or offer a slight change to the requested time. At the assigned time (or within ten minutes before or after it), the instructor will call the student(s) and conduct the phone chat. The chats will last roughly 10–15 min.

Admittedly, these chats can be overwhelming for me. There have been times when I'm talking one-on-one with students for three hours straight, then have less than an hour break before starting another three-hour marathon. Although some students complain that they are too busy for the full two weeks that time slots are available, most students have been grateful, and at times, pleasantly surprised, regarding the increased interaction with their instructor. In fact, several career online students (students who take all of their college courses solely online) have revealed to me that they have never spoken to a professor outside of the CMS. Can you imagine the only interaction you have with an instructor throughout your entire college career being conducted through email or a discussion board? Some students have never even interacted with their instructors synchronously. For this reason and others, I believe that this assignment, although overwhelming for me at times, is worthwhile for my students.

Initially, the chats were designed to be one-on-one, similar to conferences many instructors have in F2F classrooms. However, I soon realized that I was often repeating myself—addressing how to succeed in an online course and the specific assignments in our course. As a result, I felt students could benefit from the interaction, not only with me, but with another student as well. In addition, doubling the number of students per chat meant reducing the number of chats by half. The alteration addressed the time commitment, which again could be prohibitive. Therefore, I transformed the chats from one-on-one to three-way telephone conversations. I have also considered conference calls, and I may attempt this approach of conferencing with up to four students in the future.

Regarding other logistics, I often schedule a block of times in the first few days of class. The times range from late morning, early afternoon, and late evening. The majority of my students seem to choose the evening times, between 7:00 PM and 9:00 PM. When I email students to remind them about the start date for the course and what book(s) they should secure for the first day of class, I also describe the phone chats and ask them to schedule times as soon as possible. Therefore, the chats can be scheduled before the course even begins, which could positively influence the number of students who participate. In other words, if I waited until the course started, then until all the students logged in, then until they emailed me to schedule a time, and I emailed them back to confirm, too much time could pass for the chats to be as successful as I had originally intended.

During the chats, I often begin by saying that I hope the conversation will open a dialogue between the students and me. In addition, I ask whether they've taken online courses before and if they have any concerns about the course content after having reviewed the syllabus. Often times, the students who have never taken online classes before are a little anxious. We discuss that, and we discuss logging in regularly to ensure they will not fall behind in the course. For the students who have taken online classes, we discuss how this course is structured— where the assignments are, how to access them, how to submit them, etc. Then, we move on to discussing the course content. Most of my courses are Advanced Composition courses in which the students write one fifteen-page argumentative, research essay and then transform that essay into a multi-genre research presentation that is dynamic, often using Facebook, PowerPoint, or Prezi. The length of the essay causes some apprehension, and we discuss how the assignments throughout the semester are designed to create a foundation for writing the essay. Students also voice concern over what a multi-genre project is and how they might plan for it. So we discuss that as well. Although these are the specifics for one of my composition courses, I believe students have varying frustrations and apprehensions with all subjects. Therefore, instructors in other disciplines could determine how best to engage students through the medium of an introductory phone chat in their particular courses.

In my experience, the average chat is ten to fifteen minutes long. Most of the conversation focuses on encouraging students and building their confidence both in their abilities as student-writers and in their relationships with me, an instructor who will challenge them but hopefully appears approachable as well. Faculty who require student-teacher conferences in the F2F classroom are likely to understand and embrace the time commitment of introductory phone chats, or midterm phone chats, essay preparatory phone chats, or any other chat the instructor sees fit. Due to the success of my introductory chats, I have often considered requiring a second chat at some point in the semester, but I cannot speak to that experience just yet.

SYNCHRONOUS CHATS

Several semesters have passed since I last hosted synchronous chats with my students because I have been teaching more F2F courses and the online courses I still teach at another college do not have a synchronous chat technology I am skilled at using. I fully intend to teach myself the new technology to incorporate synchronous chats, but realistically, that may take some time. Furthermore, I find that minimizing the number of technologies in any one course is appropriate, and I'm currently working with some of the other technologies discussed in this chapter in my online courses.

That said, I have had success with synchronous chats and therefore choose to discuss the approach here. First of all, to combat criticism that online courses are asynchronous, so requiring synchronous chats is unfair to students who enrolled for that asynchronous atmosphere, I say this: I do not require the chats, and students have shown their interest by participating in high numbers. To explain further, I often survey my students at the beginning of the course to determine the best day and time for the majority of them. If there is a fairly even split, I vary the chat schedule throughout the semester to accommodate all of the students at one point or another. Regarding participation, although the chats are not required, I have often had roughly 60 percent to 70 percent participation. To be fair, I should point out that I offered five extra credit points to any student who participated in the synchronous chat. The extra credit could have certainly influenced the students' interest, but nevertheless, they "attended" the chat and participated, which was the overall goal.

In any case, students often cited the chats as their favorite part of the course in surveys and student evaluations. Several showed appreciation during the chats for feeling like they were in an *actual* classroom. The reason they had that feeling, I suppose, was due to the structure of the chats. For instance, I often hosted chats to discuss the topic of thesis statements. These single sentences in student essays often prove to be one of the most frustrating and elusive assignments of the semester. Therefore, I would host synchronous chats that were very similar to lessons in a F2F classroom. I would welcome all of the students into the portal and then use the whiteboard or the chat area to type a lecture to the students. During the beginning of the chat, the students mostly read the "lecture." As a side note, some more recent tools in course management systems allow you to speak into a microphone or even video yourself lecturing for this portion. Either of these would be great updates to my approach. However, at the time that I started these chats, a basic chat room was all I had to work with.

Nevertheless, I posted the lecture and then asked the students questions. I asked them to offer their essay topic ideas and potential thesis statements. We critiqued and brainstormed until we found the exact words to represent the student's intentions with his or her essay. We discussed how their newly revised thesis statements could provide logical organizational patterns for their essays. We concluded the chats with Q&A, both on the topic presented for the chat and on any other questions about the course and assignments. While the chats were not required, they were recorded; any students who could not attend the chat *were* required to view the recording and participate in a follow-up discussion board that I treated similarly to the Q&A portion of the synchronous chat.

Although I have not recently used synchronous chats in the online classroom, I have been considering alterations to my previous approach discussed above. As technology changes, so do our opportunities to better teach our students and to protect our time as well. Therefore, I believe one viable alternative to the approach above is for instructors to audio or video record themselves teaching a particular lesson, such as thesis statements, and then to post that podcast or video clip. Students could listen to or view the clip prior to the chat, so that each semester, the instructor would only spend the time interacting in the chat room with the students. In addition, the chat time could be reduced from one hour to thirty minutes, which could potentially accommodate a greater number of students. A second alternative would be for instructors who teach several sections of the same course to combine those sections for synchronous chats. Therefore, instead of hosting two or three chats on the same topic with ten or twelve students each, instructors would host one synchronous chat with thirty-plus students.

DISCUSSION FORUMS

Since I began teaching online in 2007, my pedagogical approach to the Discussion forum has likely transformed more than any other tool in the course management systems I've used. Initially, the Discussion Board, although aptly named, seemed like another location for me to have students submit assignments. In fact, if I recall, I required students to submit assignments through the drop box, email, the discussion board, and a shared files feature in our community college's online portal. Then I received a wise evaluation from a student who said that there were too many ways to submit homework. "Why couldn't it be simpler?" the student asked. Good question, I thought.

So I have aimed to simplify things over the years. If the assignment is one that I would have the students submit directly to me in a F2F classroom, the submission method is the drop box. If the assignment is one used to spark small group or whole class discussion in the F2F classroom, then students submit it via the discussion forum online.

In one way, I view the discussion forum as a bulletin board. Students visit it, post things, read things, and then come back to it later to see if anyone posted a response to their posts. This would represent the asynchronous approach. However, recently, I have been logging in more regularly to stay ahead of grading, and I also log in to the Discussion forum during my office hours (although students are also encouraged to contact me via phone or the pager tool in Desire 2 Learn [D2L] at this time). Some of my students are logged in then as well, so the discussion has become more synchronous. Instead of a bulletin board with minimal interaction, the Discussion forum seems more of, well, a discussion.

In other words, I could start off a discussion by posting a few questions and asking students to reply to my questions and reply to each other (I usually require three replies to classmates per topic, but many students reply more frequently than that). Then, I reply directly to students, commenting on their posts. I consider this more of a bulletin board approach. Or, I could post a couple of questions to start the discussion and check back often to steer the discussion differently. This approach more closely represents discussions in a F2F classroom. I might say, "Student X, that's an interesting point. I think you have appropriately summarized the purpose of thesis statements, so let's move on. What is the purpose of body paragraphs and what do you include in them?" Then students who log in after this exchange has occurred respond to the latest question instead of the initial question that started the discussion. To do so, these students must read the earlier posts to ensure they are offering new information rather than repeated previously posted ideas.

A second example comes from a recent online Introduction to Literature course, in which I had a very vibrant group. Several of the roughly fifteen students responded to *each* of their classmates' posts. This made for busy reading on my part, but it also sparked great conversation. When we were discussing Langston Hughes's poetry, we were able to incorporate themes of nationalism, patriotism, and changing American attitudes regarding work, race, motivation, and more all because one student raised an issue in his or her comment in our New Historical Analysis forum of Hughes's work. I read the posts fairly quickly after they were published and posted further questions for other students logging in. As a result, the discussion was one of the most effective and fruitful that I have led in the last several years online.

I suppose the lesson here, then, is that a balance is necessary for several reasons. The bulletin board approach is effective for students to think about new ideas and complete assignments. The reading for the instructor is minimal in comparison to the approach that mimics F2F instruction. However, the F2F approach, which requires the instructor to log in at least once, if not twice, daily and steer the discussion to new topics and ideas, is incredibly valuable, according to informal student feedback, to student learning. Of course, it is more intensive for the instructor.

SOCIAL NETWORKS

My view on social networking in the classroom has transformed in recent years. I do believe tools such as Twitter and Facebook are valuable, but they must be clearly understood and appropriately used. For instance, Twitter is excellent at creating a chaotic, synchronous or asynchronous discussion atmosphere; additionally, it can be used to connect students to other students, experts, industry professionals, and more. I have used Twitter in F2F literature courses to encourage deeper discussion of works, discussions in which no student can sit quietly and listen without contributing. I'm aware of the pedagogical debates regarding participation, including silent participation, but I won't go into them here. My point is that all students can participate *at the same time* using Twitter. In fact, when I used the social network in a group of eight literature students F2F, the room was quieter than it had been the entire semester, but each second new tweets were appearing in the Twitterstream that served as a visual record of our discussion. In other words, all of the students and I were "talking" at once, which made for a chaotic but rich exchange of ideas.

Second, Facebook has been excellent for posting photos during visual rhetoric lessons and for my students to use in developing course projects. For instance, my Technical Communications students have created Facebook pages for nonprofit organizations or as informative resources on topics of their choice for semester projects. In addition, as previously mentioned, my Advanced Composition students have created Facebook pages for their multi-genre research projects. They posted several genres—quotes, pictures, cartoons, videos, poems, articles, websites, songs, etc.—that supported their research claims, and they also created opportunities for interaction with both students in the course and their friends and families.

I have used these two tools in several different ways, and this is what I have learned. Twitter is much better for synchronous chats, especially with traditional students who have grown up with technology constantly around them. These students easily engage the hectic discussion forum of constant updates, general tweets for the whole group, tweets directed to one or two students specifically, etc. These students are often able to conduct several conversations simultaneously, which is the value of Twitter. Admittedly, there are some security issues with the tool as the discussion is open to anyone who has a Twitter handle. To combat this issue, I encourage my students to create Twitter handles for a literary character they adore. At times, the students have tweeted in the character's voice, but mostly, they use the character as a sort of cover identity and engage the discussion just as they would in the F2F classroom, as themselves. On the other hand, Twitter has not proven as effective when the chat is not a scheduled, synchronous chat. Different than Twitter, Facebook has proven particularly valuable for presentation-type assignments, assignments that incorporate various genres, and assignments that include images and videos. The same privacy issues apply, and students should be cautioned to consider what they want friends and family to see. Finally, many academic institutions have begun developing social network policies, and it is wise to research those and/or seek permission before assigning the use of a social network in class.

EMAIL CHECK-INS

Reports at the turn of the millennium identified 60 percent to 80 percent attrition rates of minorities studying at community colleges (Nora n.d.). Recently, a study reported that 20 percent of community college students will not return for a second year (Schneider and Yin 2011). "The research has shown over and over again that community college students who enroll in online courses are significantly more likely to fail or withdraw than those in traditional classes" ("The Trouble with Online College" 2013). According to this research, the portrait of online learning is dim, but statistics are not necessary for many of my colleagues or me; we see online students disappearing from our course management systems regularly each semester. These disappearing acts are often followed by emails detailing computer woes, illness, or family crises. Occasionally, students who disappear never return, and I'm left to wonder about computer woes, illness, and family crises.

I have come to the conclusion that I should reach out to these students for several reasons. First of all, I care about their learning. I want them to succeed. Second, as a student I experienced frequent illness due to allergies; likewise, I experienced significant loss with the death of both of my parents. During these times, I clearly recall both high school teachers and university professors reaching out to me. They asked how I was doing, if there was anything they could do to help, if I was feeling well enough to complete the work that week. My coursework was always important to me, but there were certainly affective concerns throughout my academic career that challenged my ability to think and study effectively. I expect that my students are no different, and scholarship supports this observation. Brown (2011) recommends seeking students out when engagement or academic performance does not meet instructor or institutional expectations because "frequently they won't come to us because very often underprepared students have difficulty recognizing that a problem exists" or "asking for help seemed to violate their notion of what it meant to be strong, independent, and self-reliant."

Early in the semester, the email check-ins are broader. For instance, here is an email I send to my students as we near the end of the second week in the course:

Hi, Class.

I hope you are all doing well. As we enter the third week of class, I want to urge you to check the Gradebook and review your grades. Several of you have received 0s for Dropbox items, and I want to be sure you realize you are missing assignments. All assignments are detailed in the week's Content area, so if you have received a 0, you can access more information about the missed assignment there.

Also, as per the syllabus, you can make up work up to two weeks past the due date. Please contact me if you have questions about specific assignments.

When students persist in missing work and/or do not respond to the email above, I send a second email that is more strongly worded but also shows concern:

Dear [student's name],

I'm writing because I am concerned with how far behind you are in [course name]. The class has started working on more in-depth assignments to prepare for the semester project, and I believe in order for you to be successful in the course, the time to make up work is now. Please email or call me if you have any questions or would like to discuss some personal concerns that might be preventing you from participating in the class as you would like.

BEYOND TECHNOLOGY: EXPECTATION VERSUS EXPERIENCE

While the approaches described in this chapter have facilitated engagement and student learning throughout my online teaching career, I must admit implementing various technologies is not enough. According to Robert McCabe (2000), more than one million academically underprepared students enter higher education every year. These students are in need of developmental programs and educational services. In addition, college classrooms, online classrooms included, are filled with underprepared students such as veterans, first generation learners, international students, multicultural students, students with disabilities, transfer students, single parents, and returning adult students (Brown 2011). Implementing technologies that are readily available to these students, such as those above, could empower and engage them. However, some technologies could also frustrate students who are unfamiliar with them.

In other words, engagement in the online classroom must extend beyond technology. As retention in my online community college classes dwindled semester after semester, I became concerned that my teaching was primarily to blame. And while I have by no means concluded my teaching is immune to critique, research has shown that attrition rates at community colleges are particularly problematic. Roughly "one fifth of full-time students who began their studies at a community college did not return for a second year. These students have paid tuition, borrowed money, and changed their lives in pursuit of a degree they will likely never earn" (Schneider and Yin 2011). With so much at stake for students, fostering academic engagement is even more important. One recommendation I find particularly valid for the online classroom comes from Brown, who suggests that to be successful in engaging students, instructors must bridge the gap between student expectations and their experience. According to a survey Brown conducted of college faculty between 2001 and 2009, 69 percent of participants disagreed or strongly disagreed with the statement: "Students usually have a realistic understanding about the demands of academic work and what is required to be successful." Eighty-six percent of students entering college believe they are academically prepared for success, yet 60 percent of incoming community college students require at least one development course upon enrollment (Brown 2011). What does this mean? Student and institutional expectations are far from aligned.

I opened this chapter by arguing that the approaches necessary to engage students online vary from those that have been successful at engaging students in the F2F classroom. While I believe there are certain pedagogical variations, particularly with the use of technology, some successful strategies of academic engagement in the traditional classroom could benefit online learners. For instance, midterm grades, progress reports, supplemental instruction, peer support, study groups, and peer mentoring programs facilitate academic engagement and success (Brown 2011). Institutions often require a selection of these measures, but instructors are free to determine what approaches they'd like to implement independently. To offer an example, a colleague of mine creates a discussion forum where her students can interact with other students the first week of class and choose a support partner. Then, throughout the semester, partners motivate each other however they feel is best: by phone, text, Facebook, email, the CMS, or F2F. My colleague has reported success with this approach.

Personally, the claim that instructor and student expectations are not aligned seems particularly relevant. By surveying my students throughout the semester, I have heard from them when their expectations do not align with their experiences. Quite often, the expectations were that online courses should somehow be simpler than F2F courses, and online learners were surprised to learn my course was significantly challenging. Therefore, a potential cause of student disappointment and attrition is a lack of alignment between expectations and experience, both for the instructor and for the students in a given course. To combat this, I suggest an honest discussion to discover, reveal, and share expectations in the first week of the course. First, let me address the aspect of discovering expectations. I'm not sure that expectations are immediately clear to students and instructors when they enter a classroom. General expectations might be obvious: to pass, to get a specific grade, to learn for the student or to help students learn for the instructor. Yet, those expectations are not specific enough to affect change in the classroom or as Brown suggests, to bridge the gap between expectation and experience. Therefore, it is imperative that I assess my own expectations. What do I expect from my students? I expect them to log into the online class several times each week. I expect them to read discussion board posts from other students and to revisit the discussions after they post to read any feedback they've received. I expect them to make the class a priority despite their busy schedules and other responsibilities. I expect them to want to learn, to want to become better writers. I expect them to reach out to me when they are having difficulty. I expect them to access resources such as the textbook, writing websites, and college offices when they have unanswered questions. I expect them to treat their classmates, themselves, and me with respect. I expect them to understand that learning is a partnership, and both the students and I have to be dedicated for the best potential learning to take place. I'm sure I expect other things, but my brainstorm yielded these expectations. They are significantly more specific than: I expect my students to want to learn. But what about the students' expectations? What do they expect from the course? And quite simply, how can I address those expectations in the course if I don't know what they are?

As the various discussions in this chapter illustrate, engaging students in an online learning community is a complex endeavor, and this chapter only skims the surface of research and scholarship on the topic. For those instructors who have taught online and those who are considering the medium, these issues are not only heavily debated, but they are also difficult to measure. In astounding numbers, students are choosing online courses in place of traditional F2F options, but their expectations are perhaps flawed and their resources are often limited. The populations of online students are underprepared, as is the trend in all college classes, but connecting to these underprepared students in ways that effectively engage them in the online environment can leave instructors lost in cyberspace, struggling to help students who may not respond, but instead continue to struggle. The approaches discussed here are those that have proven successful for me in some ways; yet, they may not be ideal for other instructors for various reasons. That said, I leave you with this: developing an online community is key for student engagement. To achieve this, online instructors should be open to the likelihood that efforts to build such a community will be more intensive and vary from those in traditional F2F classes, and finally, since the technology through which we teach online courses changes so rapidly, online instructors should embrace reflective practice as well as scholarly research to make the best decisions possible for the student population before them.

References

Aitken, J. E., and J. Shedletsky. 2002. "Using Electronic Discussion to Teach Communication Courses." *Communication Education* 51 (3): 325–31. http://dx.doi.org/10.1080/03634520216512.

Brown, Tom. 2011. "Helping Underprepared Students Succeed: How to Influence Student Engagement, Learning and Persistence." Innovative Educators Webinar, March 3. http://www.innovativeeducators.org/category-s/158.htm#underprepared.

Girardi, Tamara. 2013. "Working toward Expert Status: Love to Hear Students Go Tweet, Tweet, Tweet." In *Social Software and the Evolution of User Expertise: Future Trends in Knowledge Creation and Dissemination*, ed. Tatjana Takšéva, 259–72. Hershey, PA: IGI Global. http://dx.doi.org/10.4018/978-1-4666-2178-7.ch015.

McCabe, Robert. 2000. "An Interview: Robert McCabe." *National CrossTalk: A Publication of the National Center for Public Policy and Higher Education* 8 (4). http://www.highereducation.org/crosstalk/ct1000/interview1000.shtml.

McInnerney, Joanne M., and Tim S. Roberts. 2004. "Online Learning: Social Interaction and the Creation of a Sense of Community." *Journal of Educational Technology & Society* 7 (3): 73–81.

Nora, Amaury. n.d. "Reexamining the Community College Mission." *American Association of Community Colleges.* Accessed November 23, 2013.

Palloff, Rena M., and Keith Pratt. 2007. *Building Online Learning Communities: Effective Strategies for the Virtual Classroom.* San Francisco: Jossey-Bass.

Scheg, Abigail G. 2014. *Reforming Teacher Education for Online Pedagogy Development.* Hershey, PA: IGI Global. http://dx.doi.org/10.4018/978-1-4666-5055-8.

Schneider, Mark and Lu (Michelle) Yin. 2011. *The Hidden Costs of Community Colleges.* Washington, DC: American Institute for Research. http://dx.doi.org/10.1037/e537212012-001.

Tapscott, Don. 2009. *Grown Up Digital: How the Net Generation is Changing Your World.* New York: McGraw Hill.

"The Trouble with Online College." 2013. *The New York Times,* February 18.

Wang, Alvin Y., and Michael H. Newlin. 2001. "Online Lectures: Benefits for the Virtual Classroom." *T.H.E. Journal* 29 (1): 17–24.

Whitesel, Cynthia. 1998. "Reframing Our Classrooms, Reframing Ourselves: Perspectives from a Virtual Paladin." *The Technology Source Archives at the University of North Carolina.* Raleigh: University of North Carolina School of Public Health. http://technologysource.org/article/reframing_our_classrooms_reframing_ourselves/.

5

A RHETORICAL MANDATE
A Look at Multi-Ethnic/Multimodal Online Pedagogy

Mary-Lynn Chambers

On the first day of a new semester, the traditional face-to-face teacher walks into the classroom and is immediately given the chance to assess the ethnic identities of his or her students. This quick visual assessment is easy in a face-to-face classroom; however, it is a greater challenge in an online class. Along with the visual impression that happens in a traditional classroom, verbal exchanges also occur between teacher and student, and these exchanges can provide the opportunity to identify the student's learning style. In a face-to-face classroom, the visual and verbal elements come easily and aid in the formation of a critical pedagogy that will promote learning for those particular students. This same process needs to be a part of the development of online pedagogy; however, the steps in that process vary from the traditional approach. When considering the development of an effective pedagogy, research has demonstrated that "an interaction exists among cognitive processes, basic learning skills, and the cultural and social contexts in which they develop" (John-Steiner and Smith 1979). The cognitive process and learning styles of the students are typically considered when constructing an appropriate pedagogy. However, the cultural make-up of the online class also needs to be considered in order to effectively reach the students who are sitting under the instructor's tutelage. An instructor who longs to increase the agency of his or her students in an online class must consider the needs of each student and these needs are not only based in the learning styles of the students but also the cultural aspects that impact their cognitive process.

In order to better understand the pedagogical challenges facing online instructors, it is important to first acknowledge the historical development of online learning within American academia. In 2007, 70 percent of American colleges and universities used Blackboard (Bb) as

DOI: 10.7330/9781607324850.c005

their system of choice for online classes (Bradford et al. 2007). Since Bb dominates the online educational scene, it has been chosen, for this discussion, to be the representative online educational venue. The design of Bb was originally engineered by three white males: Stephen Gilfus (Gilfus Education Group 2012), Matthew Pittinsky (The Education Guy 2007), and Michael Chasen (Zipkin 2009). In 1997, Gilfus and Cane developed a software product that would power online education at Cornell University (Gilfus Education Group 2012). The student body at Cornell University was over two-thirds white when Gilfus and Cane were researching and developing their online course software (Cornell University 2012). However, the focus of the software broadened from Cornell University to the general American university population when Gilfus and Cane joined Pittinsky and Chasen, two white males, and together these four white males worked to design and implement Bb (The Education Guy 2007; Zipkin 2009). At the time Bb was being designed, the American university population was 74.7 percent white (Hansen 1998). Thus, Bb was designed by white males for a predominantly white audience.

Before considering the defining characteristics of the varied cultures that are potentially part of an online class, it is necessary to understand two terms that will be used throughout this chapter: field independent and field dependent. Field-independent students are less socially oriented and more achievement oriented. They are comfortable with a competitive element within the classroom. These students are able to discern parts from the organized whole, and they are more analytical in their approach to problem solving. These students are task-oriented, focused, disciplined learners. They depend more on internal rather than external cues, and they prefer more formal learning environments like an online class where written Standard English (SE) is the form of communication used. Field-dependent students depend on cues and structure from their environment. They make the learning process contingent on their experiences in their environment. They prefer a casual setting because they are more socially oriented. This group relies heavily on external stimuli to motivate them (Mestre 1997; More 1987; Wooldridge and Haimes-Bartolf 2006); thus, a multi-modal approach to online learning that provides external cues is helpful for these students.

Moving on to student demographics, there are some defining characteristics that make up a typical "white" European American audience. This particular people group is culturally comfortable receiving instruction through written Standard English (Bennett 1998; Kynard 2007; Ornstein and Levine 1982). Also, research has demonstrated that the

European American "White" people group is made up of linear, field-independent learners, which means they can isolate facts as needed, and they are able to manage well with instructions and feedback that are provided in a written form in an online classroom setting. European Americans also value independent work and are self-motivated rather than group motivated, which is conducive to the traditional way online learning operates (Mestre 1997).

Online Bb classes that take the traditional approach of disseminating information through the use of written SE, appear to be set to a "default 'White' position" (Lockard 2006, quoted in Anderson 2006), and this position is "White" because of the use of the accepted language of American academia, SE, presented in the commonly used written form (Crawford 2004; and Bernard et al. 2004). Crawford (2004) acknowledges that in America, SE is the academic language of choice used within academic domains. Also, within the traditional implementation of Bb, written SE is the mode of communication used by most instructors (West, Waddoups, and Graham 2007) along with "the students [who] must use written forms of expression to interact" (Bernard et al. 2004). Those students who are comfortable communicating in written SE could potentially be privileged over those students who are not comfortable with that form of communication. There are minorities who do not connect well with the written form of communication or their dominant dialect/language is not SE, and these ethnic minority students, if not considered within the development of the online pedagogy, could be marginalized.

The design of new technology, such as Bb, is determined by its creators; and the computer industry in the 1980s, when Bb emerged, was dominated by white males. Gruber (1999) concludes that the ingrained values of the white male designers determine the whiteness of the online class setting. Gruber challenges online education with the charge that the "dominant belief system [within online education] reinforce[s] the marginalization of nondominant groups by privileged groups"; thus, the minority students' growing representation in an online setting (Rovai 2003) needs a pedagogy that will not marginalize them through the sole use of written SE, but rather they need a pedagogy that will increase their agency with the consideration of their learning styles based in their cultural context.

In order to develop a rhetorically based, culturally responsive online pedagogy, instructors must go beyond mere awareness of cultural diversity to acquire data concerning the cultural particulars of specific ethnic groups and determine how the cultural dynamics impact the student's learning style. In this chapter, we will consider the following four ethnic groups: Asian American, Native American, Mexican American, and African American. The first three groups identify another language than English as their dominant language spoken in the home or within their social community. The fourth group, which is the African American group, identifies the African American Vernacular English (AAVE) as their dominant dialect. Thus, within all four people groups, there is a segment of their population who do not claim English as their dominant language or dialect resulting in an academic challenge when SE is the educational language implemented within the classroom setting. Also, in this chapter there will be a specific focus on impeded agency for these four student groups when their culturally based learning styles are not considered by their online instructors. Rita and Kenneth Dunn, the developers of the Dunn and Dunn Learning Style Model, "define learning style as the way in which each learner begins to concentrate, process and retain new and difficult information" (Dunn and Dunn 1993). Over the course of a decade, forty-two experimental studies were conducted revealing that "students whose learning styles are accommodated would be expected to achieve 75% of a standard deviation higher than students whose learning styles are not accommodated" (Griggs and Dunn 1996). Hence, it is vital for online instructors to investigate the culturally based learning styles of their minority students in order to design an online class where these students are able to experience agency.

The first group of minority students to consider is the Asian American group. Asian Americans consist of three main people groups: South Asia including Bangladesh, India, and Pakistan; Southeast Asia including Laos, Thailand, Vietnam, and the Philippines; and East Asia including China, Hong Kong, Japan, Korea, and Taiwan. This extensive collection of nationalities has people who now call the United States their home. Although they are American or immigrants who are assimilating into the American culture, there are some members in this category identified as Asian Americans who still identify their native language as their dominant language and SE as their second language (Griggs and Dunn 1996). Therefore, for the bilingual Asian American student, instructions provided in written SE will not be as easily understood and could potentially hinder their agency. Hence, additional modes of communication to enhance the educational experience need to be considered by the online instructor. Also, statistical analysis indicates that an English language learners' learning style often differs from European American English speaking students (Reid 1987), and this has proven to be somewhat true for Asian American students and even more so true for Native

Americans, Mexican Americans, and African Americans as you will see further on in this chapter.

The cultural influence on Asian American students has implications for online instructors during the pedagogical process. The Asian American people group is a vast category, and the approach to learning varies with each culture within this category. For example, Korean students approach the learning process very differently from the Chinese students. It is important to identify the cultural specifics concerning your students before making shifts in your pedagogical approach. The important application from this research included in this chapter is that there are pedagogical shifts that need to take place if an online instructor's sole approach is a Eurocentric, text-based approach to disseminating information to an online class. Within the Asian American people group, Griggs and Dunn (1996) identify a number of cultural characteristics including accepting roles, valuing family, and committing to learning and academic achievement. High expectations coupled with family commitment motivate the Asian American student population to own their own educational experience. Griggs and Dunn (1996) in their article "Understanding Learning Style" explained that Asian Americans ranked very high in the category of analytic skills, which is correlated with field independence. Field independence indicates the student's ability to process information without the need for environmental cues; also, individualized learning scenarios work well for field-independent students. This learning style usually means that a student is able to experience agency through written instructions without a multi-modal approach that incorporates the verbal and visual elements. This minority group, overall, preferred structured lectures and they are confident with written communication that allows them to engage in copious note taking (Park 1997). Also, the research of Stanley, Rohdieck, and Tang (1999) revealed that Asian American students prefer independent work over group work; however, they do need their online instructors to assume a more aggressive approach regarding teacher/student contact since they are generally hesitant to contact the teacher. Therefore, research indicates that the Asian American group is similar to the SE speaking European American group since both generally experience agency when written SE is the form of communication used in an academic setting (Bennett 1998; Kynard 2007; Ornstein and Levine 1982).

When considering the research done regarding the minority group of Asian Americans, there are a few pedagogical conclusions that can be reached. In order to improve the Asian American students' agency, the online instructor needs to provide clear written instructions that incorporate opportunities for student note taking. Furthermore, if group work is part of the course, then determine the best way to incorporate an individual component within a group assignment. Since these students generally work better independently, it could be that an online instructor might assign a grade to each student's individual component, then assign another grade to the group submission. This way these Asian American students who prefer individual work have an opportunity to work within their learning preference. Also, when working with this group of students, the multi-modal approach might need to be incorporated if the students are not responding to emails (Stanley, Rohdieck, and Tang 1999; Zhenhui 2001). In contrast to the Asian American group of students, Native American students require a different pedagogical approach.

There are around 175 different Native American languages spoken in the United States today. These Native American languages are spoken in about thirty of the fifty states. Some states have one indigenous language represented, like Hawaiian in Hawaii, Cherokee in Oklahoma, and Choctaw in Mississippi. About 11 percent of these languages are being taught in the traditional manner through parents or grandparents in the home setting. On the other hand, about 30 percent of Native Americans don't formally teach their native language to their children, although these adults do speak the language in the home, and their children are exposed to the language as a result. This group of students, who are formally taught or informally exposed to the native language spoken in the home, identifies their native tongue as their first language and SE as their second language (Krauss 1996).

Native American students' learning style is inter-connected with their culture, and these indicators warrant careful attention when developing an online pedagogy for a multi-cultural online class that has Native American students on the roaster. Within the Native American community, impressions are formed by careful scrutiny of faces, livestock, weather, etc., and through visual discrimination they imitate the behavior of others (Swisher and Deyhle 1987). This visual learning within their culture is carried over into the classroom setting. More (1987) conducted interviews with teachers and parents of Native American students and discovered that in general the Native American students' cognitive ability increased through visual processing, especially when imagery is included. On the other hand, More (1987) cites a relative weakness in their verbal coding and understanding. The research done by Swisher and Deyhle (1987) supports More's findings regarding Native American's desire for visual rather than verbal instruction; also, Swisher and Deyhle's research added insight into the Native American student's preference for learning through observation. Hilberg and Tharp (2002) added to the list of components that are part of their learning process by citing a Native American student's need for collaboration and their typical desire for a reflective style of processing information.

When considering Native American students' learning styles, More (1987) suggests that bilingual Native American students will appreciate the inclusion of a visual component when an online instructor is introducing new information in an online, academic setting. Also, included in the pedagogy for an online class that contains Native Americans, it would be prudent to prioritize frequent and effective use of imagery to help these students remember and understand concepts; in other words, an image rather than a dictionary definition would be more effective with this people group. Finally, the online instructor of Native American students needs to recognize that dialogue regarding information is helpful for these students; thus, a discussion board venue that allows the student to collaborate and reflect is important for student agency to occur. Therefore, pedagogical consideration for Native American students should include a holistic approach with visuals that allows for observation, collaboration, and reflection (Hilberg and Tharp 2002) in order to support the students' achievement that would otherwise be hindered with a pedagogy that only incorporates written SE communication and that only promotes an individualistic approach to learning. Many bilingual Native American students appreciate a multi-modal approach to online communication with the specific use of visual images along with the opportunity for dialogue; also, research has revealed that the Mexican American people group provides indicators regarding their need for a multi-modal component to be included in online pedagogy.

Although there is a large Mexican American population in the United States, when considering culturally sensitive online pedagogy, the student population of Mexican Americans to be considered involves students who speak Spanish in their home and social settings. Ofelia Garcia (2010) in her research on ethnolinguistic diversity explains, "According to the U.S. Census, 80 percent of U.S. Latinos over five years of age are very fluent in English." However, the 20 percent of Mexican American students who are classified as "speaking English less than very well" is almost 2 million. The magnitude of this number alone is reason to address this bilingual segment of the US population. It is important to acknowledge that it "takes between five to seven years to develop academic proficiency in standard academic English," yet most Mexican American bilingual students stay in a special language program for only one year (Garcia 2010), which results in many of these online Mexican American students struggling with agency issues when written SE is the only mode of communication used by the online instructor.

The Latino or Mexican American people group is the fastest growing minority group in the United States (Fry and Gonzales 2008); thus, they are a minority group that must be considered when writing a culturally sensitive online pedagogy. The Mexican American people group has a strong society connection (Gonyea 2010), with a specific focus on family commitment that results in other-directedness. Also, within the Mexican American culture there is an emphasis on the cooperation in the attainment of goals (Griggs and Dunn 1995). As an online instructor, these cultural identifiers are important to keep in mind when developing a culturally influenced pedagogy. When there is the potential that Mexican Americans could be a part of the online class roster, then there should be diversification within the traditional approach to online learning that only utilizes written SE as the instructional form of communication. Mexican Americans need to be given cooperative learning opportunities that are suited for field-dependent students. Field-dependent learners are usually good at seeing the big picture; however, they need personal relevance to help them engage in assignments given (Mestre 1997). One way to help secure agency for Mexican American online students is to require peer interaction, which is a helpful element for field-dependent learners. Unlike European American students whose approach to learning values individualism (Griggs and Dunn 1996), many bilingual Mexican American students prefer group work where they are able to pick up on the cues provided by their classmates (Mestre 1997). Also, these students are contextual learners (Rivera 2011) who need practical situations that have societal connections (Gonyea 2010).

There are several pedagogical implications for online instructors once instructors recognize the potential for Mexican Americans to be part of their online class roster. It is important, as an online instructor, to remember that this student population "draw[s] creatively from their linguistic and cultural systems in innovative combinations . . . [that incorporate the use of] different modalities of communication" (Garcia 2010). Also, as field-dependent learners, Mexican Americans will enjoy more group-oriented activities where cooperative learning opportunities are well structured. Once there is an acknowledgment that "Latino students' needs and learning styles tend to differ from those of the mainstream [student] population" (Mestre 1997), then it is easier to recognize that online instruction and feedback that is presented in written SE will not be as effective with Mexican Americans as communication that includes both oral and written elements (Mestre 1997), that utilizes examples that relate to the Mexican American culture (Gonyea 2010), and that provides practical "real life" situations (Rivera 2011). Thus, practical, culturally sensitive group assignments that provide opportunities for verbal and visual interaction should be a consideration when planning the strategies for teaching Native American students. This kind of approach will allow for peer-oriented learning (Griggs and Dunn 1995) and a stronger community experience (Gonyea 2010) within the online class, which will help to increase the Mexican American students' agency. Mexican Americans are a strongly represented people group within academia along with African Americans; thus, the language style and cultural implications of African American students must also be considered in the development of an online pedagogy.

African American students are not identified as bilingual but as bidialectal (DeBose 2007), and the foundational work of Smitherman (1977, 2007) regarding their language development serves as an excellent reference when considering the role of the African American Vernacular English (AAVE) on the cognitive process of those students who claim AAVE as their first or dominant dialect spoken with family and friends. Smitherman (2007) asserts that "there [are] stylistic patterns [of Black communication that] are the sole property of Black folks," and regarding black "style," she is referring to "patterns of Black communication combine[d] with Black verbal rituals." Call response, tonal semantics, and nonverbal cues are three of the defining elements in AAVE. Smitherman (2007) defines call response as "the speaker's solo voice alternat[ing] or . . . intermingle[ing] with the audience's response." Smitherman (2007) concludes that the "printed page obviously cannot reflect the Call-Response pattern," and this conclusion also applies to the screen page of Bb. Tonal semantics is detailed by Smitherman (1977) in her foundational book *Talkin and Testifyin* and can be summarized as "verbal power [that is] achieved through the use of words and phrases carefully chosen for sound effects." Further on in her book, she adds that tonal semantic is a reference "to the use of voice rhythm and vocal inflection to convey meaning in black communication." Smitherman (1977) explains that it is not just what is said in African American communication, but it is also how it is said that results in the communication of information to the listener. Nonverbal cues are a reference to body language and movement. Smitherman (2007) highlights black performance, explaining that the African American communication style is filled with "nonverbal gesticulations," which is the third element of African American communication that I label as nonverbal cues. Therefore, the use of written SE as the only mode of communication in an online setting would challenge the agency of an African American student who needs call response, tonal semantics, and nonverbal cues to be a part of the online communication process.

Since there are differences between the communication styles of those speaking AAVE and those speaking SE (Bennett, 1998; Hecht, Jackson, and Ribeau, 2003), it is also vital to acknowledge the cultural characteristics of the African American community and the impact those characteristics should have on the development of online pedagogy for these bidialectal African American students. In his article "It's Not a Colorless Classroom: Teaching Religion Online to Black College Students Using Transformative, Postmodern Pedagogy" Arroyo (2010) references research done by Boykin (1983) who identified nine black cultural learning styles (BCLS). These nine BCLS are: spirituality, harmony, movement, verve, affect, communalism, expressive individualism, orality, and social time perspective. These nine elements within African American culture provide indicators that African American students whose dominant dialect is AAVE are field-dependent learners who incorporate external cues including movement and who value community in the learning process. It is important to note that movement relates to nonverbal cues and orality relates to tonal semantics. Arroyo (2010) goes on to say that "empirical studies of white and black students support the notion of learning style differences by race, showing how failure to properly attend to them impacts student grades." Also, Durodoye and Hildreth (1995) acknowledge that conflict can occur when African American students must perform an academic exercise that is not facilitative to his or her learning/communication style. On the other hand, power and agency occur when a student has the ability to "give effect to their wishes" (Anderson 2006) by completing an exercise without frustration because the process was facilitated through their own learning/communication style. Arroyo (2010) believes that these bidialectal (DeBose 2007) African American students experience "disjointedness" within the educational system; however, if online pedagogy incorporated a multi-modal approach for these field-dependent learners (Irvine and York 1995) whose culture incorporates the visual and verbal along with the value of social interaction, then agency would increase for the bidialectal African American online students.

Although all students appreciate the opportunity to benefit from hearing and seeing the instructor when feedback or instructions are given, in schools where there is the potential for AAVE speaking African American students to be a part of an online class, then the inclusion of verbal/visual elements should be incorporated into the Bb teachers' pedagogy. Also, the online class should provide a venue that allows for call response, which involves the "back and forth" where the speaker's voice is able to be interrupted with the listener's response. With this particular segment of the student population, the importance of incorporating the elements of call response, tonal semantics, and nonverbal cue in an online classroom should be mandated if the agency of the students is valued.

The twenty-first century online classroom is a multi-cultural classroom; however, many online instructors do not consider the implications of a multi-cultural classroom when they are developing the pedagogy for a particular online class. Kynard (2007) explains that white Americans have established the norm for academic communication and that the majority of online educators also embrace the traditional "white" way of communicating through the expected use of SE. West, Waddoups, and Graham's (2007) article, "Understanding the Experiences of Instructors as They Adopt a Course Management System," support Kynard's assertion that SE is the default language for online communication. Also, these authors attest to the fact that "Most instructors . . . do not understand how to teach online," and these authors go on to write that instructors do not see their colleagues implementing modes of communication other than written SE when they are teaching online; thus, these instructors default to the trend of instructing through the sole use of written SE in an online class (West, Waddoups, and Graham 2007).

If a multi-modal approach will improve the agency for the multi-cultural, field-dependent segment of an online class, then implementing venues that allow for a community based learning environment that incorporates the verbal and visual elements must be part of the pedagogy. Arroyo (2010), explains the need for a "transformative, postmodern pedagogical techniques filtered through the lens of culturally specific learning styles," and Richardson (2006) supports this transformative approach to pedagogy since improved student agency results from multimodality that "create[s] new ways of making meaning." Thankfully, there are a number of multi-modal approaches to be considered. "Screen capture" provide visual cues or demonstrations that could be particularly helpful to Native American students, and "lecture capture" allows students to hear and see the instructor giving the lecture, which is important for African American students who are looking for call response, tonal semantics, and nonverbal cues, along with the Mexican Americans who value an oral element along with the written element. Also, YouTube has instructional videos or clips that can enhance the students' learning experience by providing needed external cues, and these clips are even more effective when they contain cultural material that relates to the ethnic group being targeted in the online class. Skype meetings can allow for call response to be experienced, which African American students are looking for. Also, Skype can provide a context where field-dependent students, who are the Native American, Mexican American, and African American students, are able to ask questions or potentially receive culturally specific material aspects that will help to increase their agency. A PowerPoint presentation that is accompanied with the teachers' voice providing an instructional commentary with each slide will benefit the Asian American students who are looking for an organized venue from which they can take notes, but it also benefits the African American students who are needing tonal semantics to be a part of the educational experience. Emails and phone calls are also important to consider when looking for ways to reach the multi-ethnic community; however, there are some emerging technologies that can be incorporated into a Bb course, and that process can be investigated with the IT team at most academic institutions. Finally, many online instructors incorporate a discussion board element into their online pedagogy, but when the online class is multi-ethnic with potential field-dependent students as a part of the class roster, then creatively incorporating more significant group interaction within the discussion board experience will motivate the field-dependent students to engage at a deeper level. One suggestion would be to provide discussion options for your field-independent and field-dependent students that meets their learning and cultural styles. For the field-independent students, like the European American or Asian American students, they could participate in an independent analysis of a document and then post their summary or findings. On the other hand, there could be an option for the field-dependent students, like the Native Americans, Mexican Americans, or African Americans, where they could access a cultural related visual or image that will inspire dialogue. This dialogue could take place in a chat forum that could be incorporated into the Bb course. There is value of providing options for both the field-independent and the field-dependent students so that agency is experienced by all students. These are just a few of the many options available for online instructors who want to design an online pedagogy that is relevant for their multi-cultural classroom.

As an online instructor, it is mandatory that a multi-modal approach be incorporated into any online pedagogy when there is a potential that the class roster could contain ethnic students who are not academically engaged through the sole use of written SE. Alim (2007) explains that there is a marginalization of students whose language and literacy practices are other than SE, and this inevitably impacts their success in the classroom. If academic success for our students is the online instructor's goal, then there needs to be a learner-centered approach (Angelino, Williams, and Natvig 2007) that is specific to the changing demographics of the student population (O'Neill and McMahon 2005). Getting to know the specific learning styles of each online student can be a challenge, but understanding the general principles attached to the students' culturally influenced learning styles (Ornstein and Levine 1982) will help the online instructor become more field sensitive in the writing of an online pedagogy. Easton (2003) asserts that an "online instructor's role does require a paradigm shift regarding instructional time and space, virtual management techniques, and the ability to engage students through virtual communication." Anderson (2003) explains that "thirty years ago, the overwhelming majority of college students were white . . . Today, [however], 28 percent of students are persons of color [and] . . . these trends will only grow stronger during the next decade." It is time that all online instructors embrace the potential that their online class is a multi-cultural class; thus, a multi-modal approach to the development of an online pedagogy should be a rhetorical mandate for all online instructors who value student agency.

References

Alim, S. 2007. "The Whig Party Don't Exist in My Hood: Knowledge, Reality, and Education in the Hip Hop Nation." In *Talkin Black Talk*, ed. S. Alim and J. Baugh, 15–29. New York: Teachers College Press.

Anderson, B. 2006. "Writing Power into Online Discussion." *Computers and Composition* 23 (1): 108–24. http://dx.doi.org/10.1016/j.compcom.2005.12.007.

Anderson, E. L. 2003. "Changing U.S. Demographics and American Higher Education." *New Directions for Higher Education* 121 (2003): 3–12. http://dx.doi.org/10.1002/he .97.

Angelino, L. M., F. K. Williams, and D. Natvig. 2007. "Strategies to Engage Online Students and Reduce Attrition Rates." *Journal of Educators Online* 4 (2): 1–14. http:// www.thejeo.com/Volume4Number2/Angelino%20Final.pdf.

Arroyo, A. 2010. "It's Not a Colorless Classroom: Teaching Religion Online to Black College Students Using Transformative, Postmodern Pedagogy." *Teaching Theology and Religion* 13 (1): 35–50. http://dx.doi.org/10.1111/j.1467-9647.2009.00571.x.

Bennett, M. 1998. *Basic Concepts of Intercultural Communication: A Current Perspective*, 1–34. Yarmouth, ME: Intercultural Press.

Bernard, R. M., P. C. Abrami, Y. Lou, E. Borokhovski, A. Wade, L. Wozney, P. A. Wallet, M. Fiset, and B. Huang. 2004. "How Does Distance Education Compare with Classroom Instruction? A Meta-Analysis of the Empirical Literature." *Review of Educational Research* 74 (3): 379–439. http://dx.doi.org/10.3102/00346543074003379.

Boykin, A. 1983. "On Academic Task Performance and Afro-American Children." In *Achievement and Achievement Motives*, ed. J. R. Spencer, 324–71. Boston, MA: Freeman.

Bradford, P., M. Porciello, N. Balkon, and D. Backus. 2007. "The Blackboard Learning System: The Be All and End All in Educational Instruction?" *Journal of Educational Technology Systems* 35 (3): 301–14. http://dx.doi.org/10.2190/X137-X73L-5261-5656.

Cornell University. 2012. www.cornell.edu.

Crawford, J. 2004. *Educating English Learners: Language Diversity in the Classroom*. Los Angeles: Bilingual Educational Services, Inc.

DeBose, C. 2007. "The Ebonics Phenomenon, Language, Planning, and the Hegemony of Standard English." In *Talkin Black Talk*, ed. S. Alim and J. Baugh, 30–42. New York: Teachers College Press.

Dunn, R. S., and K. J. Dunn. 1993. *Teaching Secondary Students Through Their Individual Learning Styles: Practical Approaches for Grades 7–12*. Boston: Allyn & Bacon.

Durodoye, B., and B. Hildreth. 1995. "Learning Styles and the African American Student." *Education* 116 (2): 241–8.

The Education Guy. 2007. *Teachers College Columbia University*. TC media center from the office of external affairs. http://www.tc.columbia.edu/news.htm?articleId=6345.

Easton, S. S. 2003. "Clarifying the Instructor's Role in Online Distance Learning." *Communication Education* 52 (2): 87–105. http://dx.doi.org/10.1080/03634520302470.

Fry, R. A., and F. Gonzales. 2008. "One-In-Five and Growing Fast: A Profile of Hispanic Public School Students." *Pew Hispanic Center*, 1–29. http://www.pewhispanic.org/2008/08/26/one-in-five-and-growing-fast-a-profile-of-hispanic-public-school-students/.

Garcia, O. 2010. "Latino Language Practices and Literacy Education in the U.S." In *Ethnolinguistic Diversity and Education: Language, Literacy and Culture*, ed. M. Farr, L. Seloni, and U. Song, 193–211. New York: Routledge.

Gilfus Education Group. 2012. "Education Strategy, Research and Implementation." http://www.gilfuseducationgroup.com/stephen-gilfus.

Gonyea, N. E. 2010. "The Impact of Acculturation on Hispanic Students' Learning Styles." *Journal of Hispanic Higher Education* 9 (1): 73–81. http://dx.doi.org/10.1177/1538192709352228.

Griggs, S., and R. Dunn. 1995. "Hispanic-American Students and Learning Style." *Emergency Librarian* 23 (2): 11–17.

Griggs, S., and R. Dunn. 1996. "Understanding Learning Style." *Emergency Librarian* 24 (1): 8–13.

Gruber, S. 1999. "Communication Gone Wired: Working toward a 'Practiced' Cyberfeminism." *Information Society* 15 (3): 199–208. http://dx.doi.org/10.1080/019722499128501.

Hansen, E. 1998. "Essential Demographics of Today's College Students." *Accounting Education News* Suppl.:15–18.

Hecht, M., R. Jackson II, and S. Ribeau. 2003. *African American Communication: Exploring Identity and Culture*. New Jersey: Lawrence Erlbaum Associates.

Hilberg, R. S., and R. G. Tharp. 2002. *Theoretical Perspectives, Research Finding, and Classroom Implications of the Learning Styles of American Indian and Alaska Native Students*. Occasional Reports.

Irvine, J. J., and D. E. York. 1995. "Learning Styles and Culturally Diverse Students: A Literature Review." *Handbook of Research on Multicultural Education*, 484–97.

John-Steiner, V., and L. Smith. 1979. *"What Do We Know about Teaching and Learning in Urban Schools?"* *The Educational Promise of Cultural Pluralism* 8. ERIC.

Krauss, M. 1996. "Status of Native American Language Endagngerment." In *Stabilizing Indigenous Languages*, ed. Gina Cantoni, 15–20. A Center for Excellence in Education Monograph. Flagstaff: Northern Arizona University.

Kynard, C. 2007. "Wanted: Some Black Long Distance [Writers]: Blackboard Flava-Flavin and Other Afrodigital Experiences in the Classroom." *Computers and Composition* 24 (3): 329–45. http://dx.doi.org/10.1016/j.compcom.2007.05.008.

Lockard, J. 2006. (2000). "Babel Machines and Electronic Universalism." In "Writing Power into Online Discussion," ed. B. Anderson." *Computers and Composition* 23:108–24.

Mestre, L. S. 1997. "Designing Internet Instruction for Latinos." *Internet Reference Services Quarterly* 2 (4): 185–99. http://dx.doi.org/10.1300/J136v02n04_03.

More, A. J. 1987. "Native Indian Learning Styles: A Review for Researchers and Teachers." *Journal of American Indian Education* 27 (1).

O'Neill, G., and T. McMahon. 2005. *"Student-Centered Learning: What Does It Mean for Students and Lecturers?" Emerging Issues in the Practice of University Learning.* UCD/AISHE Readings.

Ornstein, A. C., and D. U. Levine. 1982. "Educators Respond to Emerging Social Trends with Multicultural Instruction." *National Association of Secondary School Principals* 66 (78): 78–84.

Park, C. 1997. "Learning Style Preferences of Asian American (Chinese, Filipino, Korean, and Vietnamese) Students in Secondary Schools." *Equity and Excellence in Education* 30 (2): 68–77.

Reid, J. M. 1987. "The Learning Style Preferences of ESL Students." *TESOL Quarterly* 21 (1): 87–111. http://dx.doi.org/10.2307/3586356.

Richardson, E. 2006. *Hiphop Literacies.* New York: Routledge.

Rivera, M. 2011. "Teaching Latino Students How to Adapt to Communication and Work Styles." *Hispanic Outlook in Higher Education* 21 (13): 48.

Rovai, A. P. 2003. "In Search of Higher Persistence Rates in Distance Education Online Programs." *Internet and Higher Education* 6 (1): 1–16. http://dx.doi.org/10.1016/S1096-7516(02)00158-6.

Smitherman, G. 1977. *Talkin and Testifyin: The Language of Black America.* Detroit: Wayne Street University Press.

Smitherman, G. 2007. "The Power of the Rap: The Black Idiom and the New Black Poetry." In *Talkin Black Talk,* ed. S. Alim and J. Baugh, 77–91. New York: Teachers College Press.

Stanley, C., S. Rohdieck, and L. Tang. 1999. "An Exploratory Study of the Teaching Concerns of Asian American Students!" *Journal of Excellence in College Teaching* 10 (1): 107–27.

Swisher, K., and D. Deyhle. 1987. "Styles of Learning and Learning of Styles: Educational Conflicts for American Indian/Alaskan Native Youth." *Journal of Multilingual and Multicultural Development* 8 (4): 345–60. http://dx.doi.org/10.1080/01434632.1987.9994296.

West, R., G. Waddoups, and C. R. Graham. 2007. "Understanding the Experiences of Instructors as They Adopt a Course Management System." *Educational Technology Research and Development* 55 (1): 1–26. http://dx.doi.org/10.1007/s11423-006-9018-1.

Wooldridge, B., and M. Haimes-Bartolf. 2006. "The Field Dependence/Field Independence Learning Styles: Implications for Adult Student Diversity, Outcomes, Assessment and Accountability." In *Learning Styles and Learning: A Key to Meeting the Accountability Demands in Education,* ed. R. R. Sims and S. J. Sims, 237–57. New York: Nova Science Publishers, Inc.

Zhenhui, R. 2001. "Matching Teaching Styles with Learning Styles in East Asian Contexts." *The Internet TESL Journal* 7 (7). http://iteslj.org/Techniques/Zhenhui-TeachingStyles.html.

Zipkin, Amy. 2009. "The Boss: Big Ideas in a Small Room." *New York Times,* November 14. http://www.nytimes.com/2009/11/15/jobs/15boss.html?_r=0.

6

CAN EVERYBODY READ WHAT'S POSTED?
Accessibility in the Online Classroom

Danielle Nielsen

In 2010, Babson Survey Research Group reported 6.1 million students, nearly one-third of post-secondary degree seekers, enrolled in at least one online class during the previous Fall Semester (Allen and Seaman 2011). In 2011, the US Department of Education (2011) found 11 percent of enrolled college students reported a disability, with specific learning disabilities and ADD/ADHD counting as the most common disabilities among students (Raue and Lewis 2011). University administrators and students alike praise online instruction for making education accessible to adults who work full time or have irregular schedules, to students who do not live near a college campus, and to those who have mobility problems. Noting the diversity of students who take online courses and with the understanding that the populations of students with disabilities and online learners are both increasing and overlapping, it is important to consider the accessibility of online writing instruction (OWI), both for students with physical disabilities such as blindness, deafness, and fine motor skills limitations, and those with cognitive, mental, and learning disabilities. For many students, the online environment, rather than enhancing learning opportunities, further disables students behind the screen.

Accessibility in online writing classes concerns the students' ability to read posted material, including graphics and outside websites, download handouts, podcasts, and videos, participate in synchronous or asynchronous discussions, and, especially important in online writing classes, compose. Though this article considers access through the lens of disability, the concerns raised and the solutions offered apply also to students who may not have consistent Internet or computer access, are English-language learners, or who may not be visual or verbal learners,

DOI: 10.7330/9781607324850.c006

the primary learning styles used in online writing classrooms.[1] Thus, accessibility in the online writing class addresses not just students with disabilities but all students.[2]

I first briefly outline the Conference on College Composition and Communication's 2013 position statement on online writing instruction, specifically as it concerns inclusivity and accessibility. I offer a critique of the online environment, and finally, I make suggestions about how to make classes and materials more accessible. Ultimately, I show that though the online class may look and act differently than a face-to-face course, diverse student populations can succeed in the online environment.

ACCESSIBILITY AND ONLINE WRITING INSTRUCTION

In 2013, the Conference on College Composition and Communication Committee for Best Practices in Online Writing Instruction released a position statement addressing increased student enrollment in online courses. As one of the professions' leading post-secondary composition organizations in North America, the Conference on College Composition and Communication (CCCC) regularly puts forth best practices for the teaching of and scholarship on college writing. At the forefront of this position statement is accessibility in the online writing class-room. Principle 1 states: "Online writing should be universally inclusive and accessible" (Conference 2013). By putting accessibility first, this committee calls both instructors and writing program administrators (WPA) to think first about *how* students learn in online classrooms. If students cannot read or understand the contents of the digital class-room, then a significant part of the student population is ignored, and one of the main reasons for online instruction—increased accessibil-ity—becomes null.

The committee provides for readers a clearer understanding of who uses the instructional space, reminding readers that "the needs of learners with physical disabilities, learning disabilities, multilingual backgrounds and learning challenges related to socioeconomic issues" all complicate the online writing environment (Conference 2013). Accessibility problems abound in online classrooms. For instance, stu-dents may not be able to access material—they may not be able to see, hear, or even download it. Students may not be able to participate in discussions as much as they would like because they have difficulty typ-ing, the discussion boards are difficult to navigate, or those boards do not interface well with tablets, smart phones, and assistive, or as Valerie Claire Haven calls them, "supportive," technologies ("New Strategies for Inclusivity, Accessibility" 2011). The CCCCs twelve effective practices that concern inclusivity encourage instructors to consider the diversity of the student population when they design courses. Specifically, faculty are encouraged to use multiple forms of media to post material and to consider the different types of technology students will use during the class. When instructors consider diversity and student use, it is more likely students will succeed in their online writing course.

WPAs can also use the CCCCs effective practices to guide professional development and course development opportunities for their faculty. For writing programs that have common syllabi, WPAs can ensure that the readings are available for different modalities (video, audio, and print). Making readings available in different media helps not only the online students but those in face-to-face classes as well. WPAs and campus technology and teaching staff can also help or encourage instructors to learn how to use the technology available in the course management systems (CMS) and be more aware of the types of technology that students bring to the course, so that the communication between teacher and student is clearer. When WPAs encourage and support faculty in their efforts to make classrooms more accessible, it is more likely that their instructors will do so.

ACCESSIBILITY PROBLEMS IN THE ONLINE WRITING CLASSROOM

Disabilities fit, generally, into one of four groups: visual, auditory, cognitive, and motor (Bradbard, Peters, and Caneva 2010). In "Disabilities and e-Learning Problems and Solutions: An Exploratory Study," students were asked about different problems they encountered when they enrolled in online courses. Of the 223 students with disabilities interviewed, 184, or 83 percent, had experienced problems with online instruction; at least 10 percent of the students experienced "inaccessibility of websites/course management systems, technical difficulties, poor use of e-learning by professors, difficulty connecting to websites/ course management systems, and students' lack of knowledge of how to use e-learning" (Fichten et al. 2009). Because instructors cannot affect the (in)accessibility of the CMS itself, I focus primarily on problems content causes, what the study calls "poor use of e-learning by professors." By improving the design of the course materials, instructors increase the likelihood of student success in the online environment.[3]

The following subsections describe accessibility problems in online writing instruction. Though the above disability divisions divide the sections below, these problems are also experienced by other students. In other words, the more accessible the course material is to a variety of learners, the more student-friendly online writing classes are and the more likely students are to successfully complete the course.

Students with Visual Impairments

Students with visual impairments may experience complete blindness, blindness in one eye, or have some sight yet, at the same time, they are not able to read texts without a screen enlarger or reader. Online writing instruction presents a variety of difficulties for students who use screen readers or enlargers. For example, rather than record lectures, faculty may post written notes, PowerPoint slides, or Prezis that cover important concepts. Applications like PowerPoint also require instructors to consider a second level of access beyond the accessibility of HTML because it is not a web-based platform (Edmonds 2004). We, as instructors, may also draw heavily on outside websites, bringing in resources we cannot control, and visually impaired students cannot often access these web sources, including both campus websites and non-campus websites because of designers' choices (Schmetzke 2001). Even though Section 508 of the US Rehabilitation Act requires government and government-funded websites to be accessible to those with disabilities, privately controlled websites are not required to follow the accessibility requirements, and a number of studies on website usability have shown that university websites and CMS also do not follow Section 508 requirements (Edmonds 2004). Rather than class discussions, where students follow along by listening, discussion boards, listservs, and email messages make up the bulk of student interaction in the online writing classroom. Thus, as a result of the online classroom's strengths, instruction "remain[s] primarily vision dependent, and in line with the progress in visual technologies there has been a noticeable increase in the use of graphics, images, and animations in the presentation of e-learning materials across the board" (Armstrong 2009). In other words, the more writing instruction we offer online, the more visual, not textual or aural, information we present.

In addition to using more robust visual presentations to convey information, visual rhetoric and literacy have become a larger part of writing instruction. For instance, *Understanding Rhetoric: A Graphic Guide to Writing* (Losh et al. 2014) is a first-year composition rhetoric presented in the form of a graphic novel, and the teacher's guide encourages instructor's to use discussions of visual rhetoric to understand the information. Moreover, as online instructors, we may wish to discuss visual rhetoric alongside verbal rhetoric, encouraging students to interact with and react to the visual world around them by drawing on advertisements, film and television, architecture, and even their textbooks because of the specifically visual nature of the online environment. Students in technical writing classes read and create graphs and tables and discuss document design principles, and courses on digital media nearly always require discussions of visual principles, viewings of websites, and the production of visually intricate web writing.

For some students—visual learners, those with hearing impairments, and non-native speakers—this text- and image-heavy instruction may prove helpful to the students' mastery of content because they can move at their own pace, take breaks, and often see the context of the discussion all at once. For students with visual impairments, however, these graphics are often inaccessible because "available information about persons who use assistive technology becomes quickly outdated," and "[a]ssistive technology alone does not remove all access barriers in online education" (Edmonds 2004). Most students with visual impairments use screen readers like JAWS, screen magnifiers, or refreshable braille output systems to read the text on the screen. While screen readers and braille output systems are perfect for text-based documents like a Word document, and many articles in journal databases include aural versions of the articles, these programs cannot read images. The screen reader and braille output system may be able to tell the student the title or the headings, but if the graphic does not have an alternative description, also known as "alt tags," the "assistive technologies used by vision impaired and blind students may translate this information incorrectly, or not at all, leading to incomplete, erroneous, or different interpretations of concepts presented" (Armstrong 2009). Students who use screen enlargers also experience problems because the graphics do not fit on an entire, enlarged screen. Students may not be able to see the whole image at once, relate columns in tables to one another, or understand the relationship between parts of a chart. If the students are studying visual rhetoric, they may not be able to see text, such as an advertisement, as it is presented, making it difficult to express how the design makes an argument. Writing assignments, especially those addressing visual rhetoric, commonly ask students to analyze not only the parts but also to relate those parts to the whole. A difficult prospect if the graphic is not clearly described to the student.

Graphics, pictures, tables, and logos are not the only problems that students encounter with their screen readers. Though the PDF is a nearly universally downloadable format and the required Adobe Reader is free, many scanned PDFs are saved as images. While a sighted person or screen enlarger sees text, the screen reader sees only an image, making that reading inaccessible. The technology will tell the student there is an image, but it will not convey any information about it. In other words, the technology the student uses to read cannot interpret the words on that page. We often post chapters from essay collections, scan sample assignments, and share other original print materials. If we do not convert those images into text, many students with visual impairments will not be able to read them.

Online writing instruction, especially first-year and advanced composition classes, is accessible to students with visual impairments when instructors use text-based documents and spoken lectures. As composition classes become increasingly multi-modal, as students move into technical writing courses that include charts and graphs, and as we increase attention to visual literacy and rhetoric, however, students have a difficult time reading the materials and proving competency if we are not proactive in our own course designs.

STUDENTS WITH AUDITORY IMPAIRMENTS

In many ways, the online writing environment works well for students with hearing impairments. They can read discussion board postings and participate without requiring sign language interpreters, for instance. But as instructors make lessons more diverse (a good teaching practice that allows students to draw on their strengths), those with hearing impairments may not be able to use all of the course material. Podcasts, narrated PowerPoint presentations, and YouTube allow professors to stream lectures, videos, and even provide oral evaluations on assignments. Skype and Google Hangouts allow virtual office hours during which students talk to rather than chat with instructors, giving a name, face, and voice to the person behind the keyboard. This aural/oral approach works well for those with limited sight, who learn best by hearing information, or who may have a commute that allows them to listen to lectures as they travel, but the material potentially disables students with hearing impairments.

Students with auditory impairments cannot use aural material unless it is accompanied by closed captioning, clear, thorough summaries, or provided to them in another text-based form (Lazar and Jaeger 2011, 70). For example, some instructors may hold synchronous lectures and discussion sessions through programs like Collaborate, Google Hangouts, or Skype. If students with auditory impairments do not have lecture notes before the class meeting or a sign language interpreter available to them during the lecture, they cannot participate fully in the discussion, whether it is a text-based discussion in chat after a spoken lecture or a verbal discussion using voice-over protocols. Moreover, more static audio clips like podcasts or recorded lectures may negatively affect students because those "who are deaf or hard of hearing may be unable to hear audio clips well enough to understand what is being said" (Sapp 2009). When students miss a lecture, cannot participate fully in discussion, or cannot understand audio clips, they lose out on opportunities to share their ideas with others, to think through things with the support of classmates, or to help other students. Moreover, they lose out on supplementary information instructors provide through these aural media.

As for students with visual impairments, the online writing environment can be a boon to student success. If a class is heavily text-based with few videos to watch, synchronous discussions to attend, or podcasts to listen to, few accessibility problems arise. When we as instructors vary teaching strategies and take advantage of new media, we must work to ensure that different types of media do not disable students.

Students with Cognitive Disabilities

Cognitive disabilities that can affect online writing instruction include learning disabilities like dyslexia and language processing disorders, ADD/ADHD, autism, traumatic brain injuries, and depression. The range of disabilities that classify as "cognitive" vary widely, and students' accessibility needs necessarily vary. Wendy Sapp (2009) explains that "Users with disabilities face two main issues in relation to computer-based learning materials: access and comprehension" (496). If a cognitive disability is not accompanied by a visual or hearing impairment, access to course material is generally not a problem. What can be difficult, however, is comprehension.

As explained above, online writing instruction can be heavily text based, even more so than traditional face-to-face courses, and large amounts of text can cause comprehension problems. A study conducted at the Open University of Israel (a distance-learning-only environment) found that students with learning disabilities had more problems with humanities and social science courses than did those students without learning disabilities. To remember information, students with learning disabilities "devised unusual strategies or 'tricks,' usually not written ones, to help them to remember, such as singing or chanting a text, imagining various associations, marking the text in a special way or making diagrams or sketches" (Heiman and Precel 2003). Some students, like those in the study, must hear, see, and process information more than once and in a variety of ways to fully understand. Having readings, lectures, and assignments online allows students constant access to the material, and the students can review it as much as they would like. Similarly, if teachers post lectures as videos or podcasts, students can listen to them more than once, a difficult task in a face-to-face classroom unless instructors allow students to video/audio tape class. Though these positive attributes come from the online environment, some students with cognitive disabilities learn best aurally or kinesthetically, and the heavy reading load of the online classroom makes it difficult for them to complete assignments. Students with language processing disorders, those who struggle with reading, and those who find it difficult to concentrate on and complete a task, can find the online learning environment incomprehensible or overwhelming because they might not know where to start, and they see all of the information delivered to them at once or in large modules. Though they can access the information repeatedly, this information overload may be too overwhelming.

One considerable problem for students with cognitive disabilities can be the nearly constant writing. Not only must students complete formal writing assignments, like those that accompany face-to-face classes, but students also participate in discussion board conversations. Whereas these discussions would take place orally in a physical classroom either as an entire class or in small groups where students can utilize different learning styles, in an online classroom these activities are nearly always text based. Learning disabilities like dyslexia, dysgraphia, dyspraxia, and auditory and visual processing disorders all affect students' ability to read, write, organize, and type (National Center for Learning Disabilities 2013). Students may find it difficult to understand written questions, answer questions without hearing longer explanations, asking immediate questions, or relying on body language, or read and respond to classmates appropriately.

The large amount of text students process and create in the online classroom may lead students to feel overwhelmed, hand in late assignments or just not hand in assignments at all, or produce work that is difficult to understand. Often, students in face-to-face classrooms with comprehension problems have more time to speak up, ask questions and hear verbal answers, and visit the writing center. These extra steps allow students to take more time on their writing, to hear instructions and concepts more than once, and to enlist assistance to ensure that their writing is appropriate. Formal writing assignments in the online classroom may still benefit from visiting the writing center, but when asked to contribute to discussion board posts multiple times during the week, students may feel that they do not have time to take these extra revision steps, especially when posts require students to respond to other classmates.

Students with Disabilities Related to Fine Motor Skills

The final disabilities Bradbard, Peters, and Caneva (2010) identify are those that address motor skills. A number of specific illnesses and injuries can affect students' fine motor skills, skills especially important for online classes, whether it is navigating websites or typing assignments. Disabilities that affect a student's ability to type, use a mouse, or navigate other computer hardware and software, may be short-term, like a broken arm or hand, chronic, or progressive. Many diseases that fall under the term "neuromuscular disorder" cause "physical (sometimes painful) changes in the joints, difficulty with speech, and difficulty with mobility and fine motor skills" (University of Missouri 2013). Neuromuscular disorders include ALS, or Lou Gehrig's disease, multiple sclerosis, and muscular dystrophy. Osteoarthritis and rheumatoid arthritis, stroke, cerebral palsy, Parkinson's disease, muscle weakness (often caused by premature birth), and permanent injuries such as accidents that cause quadriplegia or amputations can all affect hand movements. As more senior citizens and veterans take online courses, online writing instructors may see more students who have experienced stroke, suffer from age-related chronic illnesses, or have war-related injuries. Even though students with motor skills disabilities are not generally hindered in their ability to understand material, some students with learning disabilities and some on the autism spectrum may experience motor skill deficits.

As discussed above in the cognitive disability section, online writing courses require, necessarily, a lot of writing, often more than face-to-face writing courses. Students must type responses and formal work. Classes that are held synchronously and use the chat function for real-time conversations can be difficult for students who do not type quickly because "[o]nline conversations tend to move quickly. Students may be able to type with time and effort, but the topics will likely shift before students can type their question or comment" (Case and Davidson 2011). Students who cannot join the conversation, like students with hearing impairments in an audio chat, lose opportunities to share their ideas. In addition to class discussions over chat, students must navigate the Internet, a task that can cause problems accessing information, whether a CMS or a professor's personal website, because "[w]eb pages with a long list of hyperlinks crowded together can confuse a student with visual, cognitive, or motor disabilities" (Cook and Gladhart 2002). Often, when we create collections of material for our students, the links are close together, and people who have difficulty using a mouse may find it hard to place the mouse over the correct link to open the document or move to the webpage.

While some of these problems will exist for any online course, the extraordinary emphasis on textual production—typing—that online writing instruction requires can be overwhelming for a student, especially in courses that feature synchronous chat as a large part of the grade. Below, I offer solutions for some of these problems and demonstrate how we, as online writing instructors, create accessible spaces where all student voices are heard.

MAKING THE CLASSROOM ACCESSIBLE TO ALL STUDENTS

At this time, readers might be thinking, "How can I make sure my class is accessible when our students are so diverse, so many potential problems exist, and I might not even know who my students are?" Though the discussion above seems overwhelming, clear communication with students and proactive class design can limit problems. In addition, you may not (and in many cases will not) have students affected by a wide variety of disabilities in class, which allows you to take the time to work from the largest accessibility problems to the smallest over the course of the semester or even over many semesters. In "The Development of Accessibility Indicators for Distance Learning Programs," Sheryl Burgstahler (2006) found that schools and instructors who had statements "about the distance learning program's commitment to accessible design for all potential students, . . . about how distance learning students with disabilities can request accommodations, . . . [and] about how people can obtain alternate formats of printed materials" were most successful in meeting student needs (Burgstahler 2006). Online writing instructors should include this information in their syllabi and send a clear message that students with accessibility needs are welcomed and encouraged to contact instructors early. Letting students know that we want to work with them to ensure success can prompt students to be proactive rather than reactive. We are also made aware of any potential problems early so that we can solve them. WPAs play a vital role in ensuring their faculty members know what resources are available for students and how to route students the appropriate office or staff person on campus if it is outside of the department, and WPAs can work with faculty to draft language that promotes.

Whether students ask for assistance or not, both instructors and WPAs should seek help from instructional technology and disability services offices. Because of the online environment and students' access to campus (if they do not live near campus), students might not think they need to apply for accommodations or might not know how to do it. It is the responsibility of disability services offices to ensure that students can easily file for accommodations and that those students have access to material. Using resources provided specifically for students with disabilities is one of the most important things both students and instructors can do to ensure student access to materials. Moreover, these offices often have equipment that can help instructors caption videos or podcasts, make PDFs readable, or learn about the technology students might use.

Instructors should contact the campus instructional technology office or librarians. Instructional technology professionals should be able to help faculty members navigate the CMS and ensure the usability of class documents. In research-heavy writing classes, librarians will be able to direct both faculty and students to databases that are compatible with screen readers or that have built-in screen reader functions. In short, instructors should use campus resources, especially people who work with technology and students with disabilities.

In addition to using the resources available, consider how course design can help overcome accessibility and learning problems. One strategy that increases usability is Universal Design for Learning (UDL).[4] The Ohio State University's "Fast Facts for Faculty: Universal Design for Learning: Elements of Good Teaching" (2012) defines UDL as

> an approach to designing course instruction, materials, and content to benefit people of all learning styles without adaptation or retrofitting. Universal Design provides equal access to learning, not simply equal access to information. Universal Design allows the student to control the method of accessing information while the teacher monitors the learning process and initiates any beneficial methods . . . Universal Design does not remove academic challenges: it removes barriers to access. (1)

With UDL, teachers apply flexible strategies that allow students to learn, demonstrate competency, and become interested in learning in different ways (Center for Applied Special Technology 1999–2012). All students benefit from UDL, and the three groups of students, those with disabilities, those with little computer or Internet access, and

English language learners, for whom online learning can pose the most problems are given many options to choose from and many opportunities to succeed.

One of the first ways to increase accessibility is to create course materials that are accessible through different media. The World Wide Web Consortium (2011) (created to ensure access to and growth of the web) issues Content Accessibility Guidelines and revises them as technologies evolve. To maximize accessibility, instructors should ensure that content is, in the words of the consortium, "perceivable," "operable," and "understandable." To do so,

- Write descriptive <alt> tags for graphics. The instructor must take the time to write tags, but tags allow screen readers, slow Internet connections that do not load graphics, and non-compatible browsers to display descriptions of graphics. Tags are especially important for technical writing and visual rhetoric readings and assignments.
- Post audio files and captions or text-based lectures for those files. The audio files serve commuters, those with visual impairments, and those students who prefer aural learning. The written captions make sure that students who prefer written or verbal learning and students with hearing impairments have access to information.
- Save PDFs in readable (non-image) format. To do so, run OCR (optical character recognition) on PDFs before saving and posting them. OCR is available with most Adobe products and other free options are available on the Internet. The procedure takes little time, and it allows screen readers to access the PDF's content. In addition, OCR allows students and professors to use the "find" command.

Posting information in these three ways can improve all students' learning, regardless of their accessibility needs. In addition to these recommendations, instructors can also post documents in adjustable Word format rather than as a static PDF. Students who use screen enlargers can adjust the font type or size in the document and print it off, making it easier to read than it might be on the screen. Even though many of our students have grown up reading information from computer screens, many students prefer to read and mark up print documents rather than those that are electronic. The CCCC position statement reminds instructors that they "should determine the uses of modality and media based not only on their pedagogical goals but also on their students' likely strengths and access" (Conference 2013). By integrating different media into their classes, instructors work toward universal access.

In addition to making information available in a variety of formats, instructors can offer students a variety of ways to seek assistance. To increase accessibility during office hours, professors can encourage students to come and see them in person if they are on campus, to use Skype, chat programs like AIM or Google Chat, or even to call on the telephone rather than type out emails or use the CMS, especially if the CMS is particularly difficult for a student to use or access. Providing students a variety of ways to contact you makes it more likely that the students will reach out.

An important part of most writing classes is revision. One way students discuss revisions is through office hour discussions, another way is using the writing center. Many campuses have writing centers staffed by peers, graduate students, or faculty and staff. If the writing center offers online consultations, encourage students to use the center, especially those who may not be aware of its existence. Visiting the writing center allows students an even wider variety of assistance. Asynchronous consultations can be especially productive for those who work full time, who cannot type quickly, or require extra time processing language.

In addition to making help more accessible and encouraging students to use the writing center, either online or face-to-face, instructors can vary assignments and feedback, allowing students to choose how to complete the work. For instance, instead of synchronous chat sessions, use asynchronous methods of communication like email, discussion board posts, and listservs, which allow everyone to participate no matter how fast they type or think of responses. Asynchronous communication also prevents the "we can't find a time to meet" problem and allows students to process and revise ideas before submitting them. Online writing instructors may also allow their students to choose to submit their writing assignments, including essays and discussion board posts in different media, as typed submissions, collages, or oral compositions. Many CMSs allow users to upload podcasts or digital audio files, and students can record their compositions on their phones, computers, or MP3 players using built-in or auxiliary microphones. Providing this choice still allows students who have trouble typing to demonstrate their competency and understanding of the course materials. If an instructor is uncertain about grading spoken compositions, she could encourage students to use voice-to-text software like Dragon Naturally Speaking, which allows students to speak their essays while the program transcribes it. The program requires that the students insert punctuation and paragraph breaks as they go or after they have completed their transcription. In other words, it does not think for the student, it simply takes dictation, turning their spoken ideas into a typed essay, email, or discussion board post.[5] Using oral compositions or encouraging students to seek out supportive technologies still requires students to understand how to organize and analyze texts, complete and synthesize research, and create final documents. The documents, especially oral compositions, may simply look different. Your course objectives will determine which media and genre work best for you and your students.

Not only can instructors encourage or allow their students to use audio files to submit work, but teachers can also provide oral feedback on written work using the same MP3 recorders that students do. Students who learn best by listening rather than reading and those with vision impairments may find it easier to understand this kind of feedback. Moreover, verbal feedback may end up being both faster to assemble and complete and more comprehensive than written comments, which in turn gives the student a better assessment of his or her work. We might think of oral comments as one half of a conference with a student. You may choose to give all of your feedback orally, or divide your time between written comments for some assignments, which can help English language learning students and those who are visual learners, and oral comments for other assignments.

Ensuring that students have complete access to course material in the online classroom is an important step in online writing instruction. Because the online writing classroom is so dependent upon both visual and verbal texts, some students may not be able to use, see, or even understand different course materials. Using the lens of disability, this essay has outlined some of the accessibility problems in the online classroom and offered some solutions to those problems. Creating accessible materials and class spaces that use a variety of media helps not only students with disabilities but also students who may have unreliable Internet access, are English language learners, or are not strong verbal and visual learners. When we think of not only our own course objectives in terms of modality, but also the ways in which students come to language and the course our classes are more likely to succeed. In short, creating a diverse online writing classroom benefits all students.

Notes

1. A 2011 Federal Communications Commission (FCC) report found that 6 percent of Americans with Internet access still use dial-up connections. In rural areas, that figure rises to over 10 percent (Todd 2012). Because online programs often serve rural areas, reliable Internet connections are a concern for many students.

2. Composition scholars have done little work to explain or describe accessible online classrooms. One of the most complete monographs devoted to online writing instruction, Warnock's (2009) *Teaching Writing Online: How and Why*, includes little about ensuring accessibility, and Coombs (2010) *Making Online Teaching Accessible:*

      Inclusive Course Design for Students with Disabilities is a thorough examination, but does not address online writing instruction.

3.   Importantly, the CCCC Best Practices recommends that universities' teaching and learning centers take the responsibility to teach students how to use the technology for their online courses. As a result, instructors are free to focus on the content of their course rather than on technical difficulties. I agree with this sentiment because OWI is *writing instruction*, it is not *technology instruction*, and as such, I will not discuss "students' lack of knowledge of how to use e-learning." University technology and learning centers, orientation, and library programs, work with students across the curriculum, helping them use the tools available to them on campus. When the university, rather than individual faculty members, takes responsibility for teaching students how to use the technology, online writing instructors are free to teach the content of the course without being hindered by the course delivery system.

4.   Universal Design originally attended to architecture and engineering (developing ramps that were accessible to wheelchairs, strollers, and delivery people with large packages, light switches and door handles that could be easily manipulated without fine motor skills, and closed captioning on televisions and in movies that can be used not only by people with hearing impairments but also by those in gyms, airports, and other loud areas). In the 1990s, the Center for Applied Special Technology (1999–2012) (CAST) developed a similar concept for classrooms. CAST's goal was to make education accessible without singling out students or requiring teachers to "retrofit" their courses. Jay Dolmage (2007) defines "retrofit" as a required addition that makes an object more "usable," but at the same time, keeps those who access the retrofit invisible. For instance, wheelchair ramps placed to the side or in the back of buildings render those in wheelchairs invisible and remove them from the public space of the steps (20–23). In contrast, a classroom that employs UDL allows students to "re-map, re-create and re-write the world in which they learn," a process through which each student becomes visible (Dolmage 2007, 23).

5.   Dragon Naturally Speaking, Smart Pens (pens that record lectures while students take notes) and screen readers allow students to take control of how they receive information and move through the course. These supportive technologies do not do student work but rather enhance their learning experiences.

References

Allen, I. Elaine, and Jeff Seaman. 2011. *Going the Distance: Online Education in the United States, 2011*. Babson Park, MA: Babson Survey Research Group.

Armstrong, Helen L. 2009. "Advanced IT Education for the Vision Impaired via e-Learning." *Journal of Information Technology Education* 8:243–56.

Bradbard, David A., Cara Peters, and Yoana Caneva. 2010. "Web Accessibility Policies at Land-Grant Universities." *Internet and Higher Education* 13 (4): 258–66. http://dx.doi.org/10.1016/j.iheduc.2010.05.007.

Burgstahler, Sheryl. 2006. "The Development of Accessibility Indicators for Distance Learning Programs." *ALT-J, Research in Learning Technology* 14 (1): 79–102. http://dx.doi.org/10.1080/09687760500479753.

Case, D. Elizabeth, and Roseanna C. Davidson. 2011. "Accessible Online Learning." *New Directions for Student Services* 134 (2011): 47–58. http://dx.doi.org/10.1002/ss.394.

Center for Applied Special Technology. 1999–2012. "About UDL."

Conference on College Composition and Communication Committee for Best Practices in Online Writing Instruction. 2013. "A Position Statement of Principles and Example Effective Practices for Online Writing Instruction (OWI)." March.

Cook, Robin A., and Marsha A. Gladhart. 2002. "A Survey of Online Instructional Issues and Strategies for Postsecondary Students with Learning Disabilities." Information Technology and Disabilities 8, no. 1.

Coombs, Norman. 2010. *Making Online Teaching Accessible: Inclusive Course Design for Students with Disabilities.* San Francisco: Josey-Bass.

Dolmage, Jay. 2007. "Mapping Composition: Inviting Disability in the Front Door." In *Disability and the Teaching of Writing: A Critical Sourcebook*, ed. Cynthia Lewiecki Wilson and Brenda Jo Brueggemann, 14–27. Boston: Bedford/St. Martin's.

Edmonds, Curtis D. 2004. "Providing Access to Students with Disabilities in Online Distance Education: Legal and Technical Concerns for Higher Education." *American Journal of Distance Education* 18 (1): 51–62. http://dx.doi.org/10.1207/s15389286 ajde1801_5.

"Fast Facts for Faculty: Universal Design for Learning: Elements of Good Teaching." 2012. The Ohio State University Partnership Grant. Improving the Quality of Education for Students with Disabilities.

Fichten, C. S., V. Ferraro, J. V. Asuncion, C. Chwojka, M. Barile, M. N. Nguyen, R. Klomp, and J. Wolfarth. 2009. "Disabilities and e-Learning Problems and Solutions: An Exploratory Study." *Journal of Educational Technology & Society* 12 (3): 241–56.

Heiman, Tali, and Karen Precel. 2003. "Students with Learning Disabilities in Higher Education: Academic Strategies Profile." *Journal of Learning Disabilities* 36 (2): 248–58. http://dx.doi.org/10.1177/002221940303600304.

Lazar, Jonathan, and Paul Jaeger. 2011. "Reducing Barriers to Online Access for People with Disabilities." *Issues in Science and Technology* 17 (2): 68–82.

Losh, Elizabeth, Jonathan Alexander, Kevin Cannon, and Zander Cannon. 2014. *Understanding Rhetoric: A Graphic Guide to Writing.* Boston: Bedford / St. Martin's.

"New Strategies for Inclusivity, Accessibility." 2011. *Distance Education Report* 15, no. 16 (August 15): 1–4.

Raue, Kimberley, and Laurie Lewis. 2011. *Students with Disabilities at Degree-Granting Postsecondary Institutions.* Institute of Education Sciences.

Sapp, Wendy. 2009. "Universal Design: Online Educational Media for Students with Disabilities." *Journal of Visual Impairment & Blindness* (August): 495–500.

Schmetzke, Axel. 2001. "Online Distance Education—'Anytime, Anywhere' But Not for Everyone." *Information Technology and Disabilities Journal* 7, no. 2 (April).

Todd, Deborah M. 2012. "Plenty of Internet Users Cling to Slow Dial-Up Connections." *Pittsburgh Post Gazette*, February 15. http://www.post-gazette.com/business /businessnews/2012/02/15/Plenty-of-Internet-users-cling-to-slow-dial-up-connections /stories/201202150852.

United States Department of Education. 2011. "Chapter 3: Post Secondary Education." *Digest of Education Statistics: 2011.* Washington, DC: United States Department of Education.

University of Missouri. 2013. "Neuromuscular Disorders." *Handbook of Disabilities*, July 3.

Warnock, Scott. 2009. *Teaching Writing Online: How and Why.* Urbana, IL: National Council of Teachers of English.

National Center for Learning Disabilities. 2013. "What Are Learning Disabilities?"

World Wide Web Consortium. 2011. "WCAG 2 At a Glance: Web Content Accessibility Guidelines." December 6. http://www.w3.org/WAI/WCAG20/glance/Overview.html.

7
TAKING THE TEMPERATURE OF THE (VIRTUAL) ROOM
Emotion in the Online Writing Class

Angela Laflen

In traditional face-to-face classes, instructors make numerous adjustments to their teaching in response to the nonverbal feedback they receive from students. Students' facial expressions, posture, head movements, gestures, and other body language indicate their levels of frustration, engagement, etc., and over time instructors become adept at interpreting and responding to this nonverbal communication. The same is not true in online classes, and the absence of body language and other nonverbal communication is one of most disorienting things about teaching online. Nevertheless, despite the absence of body language, online classes have a quite distinct emotional tenor, and often a surprisingly negative one. Moreover, emotion in an online class is created and transmitted almost entirely via writing; thus, online classes provide a valuable opportunity for writing teachers to explore both the linguistic dimension of emotion as well as the rhetorical work performed by emotion in online discourse. This chapter will present a framework that allows instructors to identify and analyze students' expressions of "emotional commitment" in their online writing and will discuss how instructors can use this information to adapt online pedagogy both to avoid conflict as well as to encourage students to develop skills in expressing emotion online.

Online discussion has unique linguistic characteristics that distinguish it from face-to-face communication and give it a distinctive emotional character. Anecdotally, instructors have long observed that discussion in online classes is noticeably more negative than in face-to-face classes and more prone to conflict as well. As a result, to date, most research on emotion in online discussion has focused on the expression of hostile feelings and on ways to manage conflict. Instructors have observed that online discussion often bears characteristics of ranting, and have

DOI: 10.7330/9781607324850.c007

considered how rants or flames incite conflict, which can have a chilling effect on course discussion and create a hostile environment. More recently, though, scholars have also considered how students' less obviously emotional postings can incite conflict. Heidi McKee (2002), for example, described how seemingly "neutral" posts led to conflict in a forum focused on affirmative action: "Posts that did not seem to be violent attacks, at least to me as a White researcher, may actually perpetuate a violent 'othering' that is more destructive to interracial communication than all-capital online shouting" (415). In my own online courses and discussion forums I have observed students transmitting emotions such as boredom and disinterest to one another just as surely as they do anger or excitement.

The implication is that all posts, even those that do not bear characteristics of rants, have an emotional dimension. It is important for instructors to develop abilities in perceiving and interpreting the mood of online discussions, just as they do in face-to-face classes, in order to respond appropriately and adapt instructional techniques accordingly. And it is increasingly necessary for students to develop skills in expressing and perceiving emotion in computer-mediated communication (CMC) as part of their general digital literacy, regardless of their major or field of study. Indeed, Stuart Selber (2004), who argues that contemporary students need to develop "multiliteracies," describes understanding "the social conventions that help determine computer use" as one of the basic characteristics of functional computer literacy (45). Often, when it comes to the social conventions guiding online expressions of emotion, the result of inexpertly communicating emotion online is miscommunication, as Peter Moor, Arv Heuvelan, and Ria Verleur's (2010) study of flaming on YouTube, among others, has found. While some online ranting is the result of deliberate choice—and this might even be a distinctive online genre of communication—most studies suggest that a great deal of the conflict created online is the result of miscommunication, as writers ineffectively express their ideas or inadvertently use language that readers find offensive. For example, examining the use of emoticons in CMC, Patricia Wallace (1999) noted that users who were familiar with emoticons were more likely to catch jokes and irony online, while those who lacked experience expressing emotion with emoticons viewed CMC as a more emotionally distant medium. And Ann Bomberger (2004) noted that "many students feel more adept at oral communication than written communication. Therefore, what they write may not be exactly what they mean or their assertions may lack sufficient development" (199–200).

Lack of skill and experience expressing emotion in CMC could help to account for the heightened emotionality in online writing as well as the quality of ranting that characterizes some student posts, especially when students discuss their emotional or personal responses to course material. Moor, Heuvelan, and Verleur (2010) reached a similar conclusion in their study of flaming: "the ambiguity of messages is frustrating and invites people to express themselves more explicitly. More explicit messages from frustrated partners may become hostile and aggressive (1538). Consequently, as we equip students to fully participate in a range of digital platforms and media, it is increasingly necessary to help them understand the rhetorical dimension of emotion as well as the social conventions guiding the expression of emotion online. However, it can be a challenge to incorporate emotion productively into online discussion without simply attempting to banish emotion altogether.

In fact, banishing emotion seems to be the goal in a variety of online writer's guides that instruct writers to carefully edit their writing for signs of emotion. To be fair, these guides focus most often on avoiding emotions such as anger in online communication, because angry messages can be and frequently are professionally or personally destructive; however, it also seems safe to conclude that emotional writing of all kind is suspect in online communication, as it is also in discourse in general. In this context, the denigration of emotion in online communication extends from the traditionally low status that emotion has held and the long-standing belief that emotion and reason are opposites of one another that cannot coexist. Laura Micciche (2007) usefully summarizes the case against emotion as follows:

> To say that an argument is "merely" emotive is tantamount to saying that it is not representative, but instead personal and idiosyncratic; not thoughtful, but solely reliant on opinion . . . What we do when we argue or persuade . . . is construct a rational position *after* sifting through emotional responses. (3)

This attitude toward emotion is longstanding and has largely led to the subordination of emotion in discourse of all kind, though perhaps especially in academic discourse.

However, an "affective turn" within interdisciplinary research has begun to question this opposition of emotion and reason, to question the "depersonalized academic voice" that is celebrated in academic discourse, and to create space for the emotions of the writer. Within composition studies, recent work suggests that emotion is an important rhetorical construct in its own right that deserves critical attention. Consequently, scholars have begun to question how emotion functions rhetorically, concerned in particular with moving this discussion beyond the equation of emotion in writing with pathos. Micciche (2007) examines emotion as "emerging relationally, in encounters between people, so that emotion takes form *between* bodies rather than residing *in* them" (13). Micciche's emphasis on the relational nature of emotion has many implications for the ways that emotion might be theorized and integrated into the class-room. For example, she posits that even *"experiencing* an emotion—not expressing, perceiving, or analyzing one—may require *skill"* (Micciche 2007), suggesting, in doing so, that "emotion is central to what makes something thinkable, which is to say that the act of conceptualizing inserts emotion into thought and so into experience . . ." (Micciche 2007).

Online discussion forums are a particularly valuable site within which to consider the rhetoricity of emotion because, while online writing is frequently emotional in content and tone, this emotion is communi-cated without the use of body language or extralinguistic cues that cre-ate so much of the meaning in what is said and unsaid in face-to-face communication. As a result, online discussion forums provide a useful way to explore linguistic markers of emotion and how these operate rhe-torically in online spaces. At the same time, understanding the linguistic markers of emotion indicate a number of ways that writing instructors can help equip students with the skills they need to express and inter-pret emotion online.

THE EMOTIONAL DIMENSION OF ONLINE WRITING

Linguistics offers a useful critical framework that writing instructors can employ to identify and analyze what linguists refer to as a writer's or speaker's "emotional commitment." Emotional commitment refers to how closely a writer's or speaker's emotions are tied to a particular communication act, and linguists use markers of emotional commit-ment to determine how "involved" a writer is with a particular point of discussion. "Involvement" can range from what Sonja Kleinke (2008) refers to as the emotionally neutral point of "sincerity-based identifica-tion" to the binary opposition of "attachment" or "detachment" (411) (see table 7.1). Axel Hübler stresses that "either [attachment or detach-ment] can be said to represent the speaker's involvement equally" (Hübler 2007, 373), so indicating that a writer is expressing attitudinal detachment does not mean the writer is less involved than someone expressing attitudinal attachment; rather, this indicates that the writer has employed linguistic token features to distance him or herself from the issue under discussion.

Table 7.1. Scale of involvement

Attitudinal attachment	Neutral sincerity-based identification	Attitudinal detachment
Evaluation Devices, positively connoted		Evaluation Devices, negatively connoted
Quantity Devices, positively connoted		Quantity Devices, negatively connoted

Writers have a variety of ways to express detachment or attachment to a topic, but Kleinke's work in addition to Laflen and Fiorenza's analysis of an online course forum suggests that two specific types of "linguistic token features" are particularly relevant: evaluation devices and quantity devices. These linguistic devices (or involvement tokens) occur much more frequently in CMC than they do in either face-to-face conversation or newspaper English, and they contribute to the unique emotional character of CMC.

Evaluation devices help writers to offer positive or negative evaluations of a topic (Kleinke 2008), with negative evaluations indicating attitudinal detachment and positive evaluations indicating attitudinal attachment. Evaluation devices are perhaps the most obvious way in which writers express attachment and detachment in CMC. In considering how involved writers are with a particular topic, or their level of emotional commitment, evaluation devices are crucial since they help to locate writers on the positive or negative side of the scale of speaker attachment. Thus, evaluation devices are strongly correlated to emotional commitment, even though they should not to be taken as a claim about the writer's actual feelings. Evaluation devices refer to emotive adjectives, adverbs, verbs, and nouns. These include the following:

1. Words with negative or positive connotations in their specific context and items referring to positively and negatively connoted concepts, as in Excerpt One (below), such as *stoop, name-calling, punch-line-throwing, logical, sophisticated, jab, sympathy, love, shout, be obsessed*

2. Members of antonymic pairs (*good-bad, rich-poor, young-old*)

3. Phraseological units, which are pragmaticalized to some extent (*to sweep something under the carpet, to pull oneself out of a hole*)

The following excerpt from a student posting to a discussion forum for a course titled Presidential Election Rhetoric indicates the student's disdain for politicians' use of slander:

Excerpt One: Although I was greatly entertained(+) by the Democratic National Convention, I tried as hard as I could not to be overly dazzled(-) by Obama's natural charisma and charm(+). Instead, I try to keep a level head(+) about each candidate while remembering that these men are humans(-), not the almighty Messiah(-) who can save our country(+).

The positive or negative connotation is often context-dependent, for example in the case of "the almighty Messiah" which is an allusion that could mean a variety of things. In the context of this excerpt, its meaning as a negative comparison is clear.

Writers use evaluation devices in CMC quite differently than they do in face-to-face conversation or newspaper English. In particular, CMC is characterized by the frequent use of negative evaluations. In her analysis of a public discussion forum, Kleinke (2008) observed that "The overwhelming majority of evaluative expressions in the data (75 percent of all occurrences) are negatively connoted, expressing negative feelings and emotional detachment from either the topic or other participants and their opinions" (417). Laflen and Fiorenza's (2012) analysis of the course forum for Presidential Election Rhetoric also revealed that the majority of evaluative expressions were negative, 62 percent of all occurrences (301). Despite the fact that the course forum was *less* negative than the public forum, likely because students felt less anonymous, it is significant that both forums were overwhelmingly negative.

Another linguistic feature, the quantity device, also contributes significantly to the emotional dimension of CMC. Kleinke (2008) explains that quantity devices emphasize "linguistic expression of measure, duration, amount, frequency or order . . . adjectives and adverbs of degree . . . [and] lexical repetition . . . and sequences of punctuation marks" (417). Alone, quantity devices often do not convey either emotional attachment or detachment. However, in combination with evaluation devices they communicate the *level* of a writer's attachment or detachment. For this reason, quantity devices are even more dependent on context for meaning than are evaluation devices. Interestingly, quantity devices appear much more frequently in CMC than in face-to-face communication or newspaper English. Kleinke found that writers in her study used quantity tokens of linguistic expression of measure, duration, amount, frequency or order, and adjective and adverbs of degree "more than nine times the expected scores for British and American conversation" (417). This was even more striking in the online course analysis by Laflen and Fiorenza, which found an average of twenty-two quantity devices per post, about 3.7 times the number of devices found in Kleinke's study (302).

Anecdotally, it can be surprising for teachers to discover how frequently students use quantity devices in CMC. For example, while most students do not rely heavily on exclamation points in the written work they submit for college courses, they frequently use exclamation points in CMC to emphasize their ideas, sometimes even using a series of exclamation points for additional emphasis, as in Excerpt Two:

> Obama's speech utilized *really* good rhetoric tools*!!* It was *so* powerful that *not only* did I feel proud of our *new* president, but I felt like I was witnessing my *first* POSITIVE *part* of history in *our lifetimes!!!* I don't think he could have done *much* better . . . v:)

In Excerpt Two the repetition of punctuation and adjectives and adverbs of degree, in combination with positive evaluation devices such as *good, powerful, proud, positive,* and *better* conveys the writer's level of enthusiasm for Obama's speech. This writer also utilizes two of the iconographic means at his or her disposal to indicate emotion graphically in online text. The writer thus adds an emoticon to this posting, which represents happiness in the form of a smiley face, and uses all caps in the second sentence, which is generally understood to represent "shouting" in CMC, and could thus be regarded as indicative of degree.

In a context in which the majority of evaluation devices are negative, the frequent use of quantity devices amplifies the negative "tone" of an individual posting, as in Excerpt Three:

> I *completely* agree that this is outrageous(-)*!* These are ADULTS(-)*!!* They don't *really* consider(-) what is important to the American people(+). They *just* bash(-) on each other. *These* commericals [*sic*] make *us as Americans* look stupid(-) . . . :(

When quantity and evaluation devices are frequently used in combination, it follows that the overall affect would be a heightened sense of emotionality.

TRANSMITTING EMOTION IN CMC

Identifying token features is an important way for writing teachers to "take the temperature" of a class during online discussion. Students cannot help but express emotion via the evaluation and quantity devices they use, and these can serve as signals to instructors about how a student or class is engaging and responding to course material and allow the instructor to make subtle adjustments as they would do in response to the nonverbal information provided by body language in face-to-face courses. However, there is another reason for instructors to attend closely to these linguistic features in online courses, and that is because students not only express their own emotions via these devices but they also transmit emotion to classmates as well. In particular, it is clear that the initial posting to which others respond plays a very important role in not only identifying a focus for discussion but also setting an emotional tenor for the entire thread.

Laflen and Fiorenza's analysis of the course forum for Presidential Election Rhetoric found that students frequently took their emotional cues from one another, and often moved farther along the spectrum of attachment or detachment after the initial post. The initial subject line and post or question thus set the tone for the thread by establishing whether attitudinal attachment or detachment toward the discussion topic was appropriate. In fact, 58 percent of the discussion threads moved from a more neutral to a less neutral position, while 26 percent remained the same, only 12 percent moved from one side of the scale to another (either moving from detachment to attachment or from attachment to detachment), and 4 percent of the threads consisted of a single posting (Laflen and Fiorenza 2012). The following example illustrates what this transmission of emotion commonly looks like in an online discussion. Notice that though the students avoid conflict with one another, the thread nevertheless becomes increasingly negative in tone from post to post.

Vicki's Initial Post

SUBJECT: SHOULD CELEBRITIES STAY OUT OF POLITICS?
As this election progresses, I find myself a bit *torn*(-) on the role of celebrities in endorsing candidates. Although I'm *not in favor*(-) of celebrities *"swaying"*(-) the *citizens' vote*(+), I think it's *great*(+) that they're *inspiring*(+) people to *vote* (+). But, in the end, *who really cares*(-) what a celebrity, who may or may not *know anything*(-) about a candidate or an issue, thinks?

Alex's Reply

I *don't approve*(-) of celebrities having a *certain political approach*(-) if they're *not going to be informed*(-) of the issues themselves and if its [*sic*] just *for the money*(-). Also, if celebrities make a *big deal*(-) about certain subjects that *don't necessarily apply*(-) to them. I think politics and fame *should be separated*(+) and celebrities should *not be allowed*(-) to use their fame to *persuade voters*(-) in a certain direction.

Meg's Reply

I know the media has a *big influence*(-) on voters and celebrities in general try there hardest to *influence*(-) their fans on which way to vote.
Personally, I try to *stay away*(-) from the *Hollywood approach on politics*(-)
because I feel like *it isn't a celebrities place*(-) to talk about voting when they
probably *don't know much*(-) about politics anyway. Consider this video.
Hayden Panettiere is a *small time actress*(-) who is *barely 18 anyway*(-). The
only reason she is making this *fake public service announcement*(-) is probably from the *endorsements*(-) shes [*sic*] getting from it. Yet, tons of Hayden
fans are going to watch this video and want to take the same approach
to politics as she.

From the outset, Vicki primed this discussion thread toward the negative end of the scale of involvement by using the negative evaluation
"stay out" in her subject line. And in the exchange that followed, the
students' use of evaluation and quantity devices became ratcheted up
from post to post as the discussion moved farther along the spectrum
of detachment. Thus, while Vicki describes herself as "a bit torn" and
recognizes positive as well as negative consequences for a celebrity's
involvement in a campaign, employing five negative and four positive
evaluations (55.5 percent negative), Alex describes himself as disapproving and includes only one positive and seven negative evaluations
(89 percent negative), and Meg is most disapproving of all, using ten
evaluations, all of which are negative (100 percent negative). Not surprisingly, most readers would judge Vicki's post as exhibiting the most
neutral attitude of the three posts and Meg's post as the most strongly
detached from the issue, placing the posts on a continuum from most
neutral to least neutral that was duplicated in more than half of the discussion threads in the course.

CLASSROOM APPLICATIONS

Understanding the unique emotional characteristics of online writing
and the ways that students and instructors transmit emotion to one
another via their writing has a number of implications for online writing pedagogy. Perhaps most importantly, it indicates that there is little
writers can do to keep emotion out of their writing, since emotional
commitment is inherent in the language itself. Writing without using
evaluation or quantity devices would not be practical or desirable. What
some instructors perceive of as inappropriate expressions of emotion in
online writing is often the result of the unique linguistic character of
online writing, which clearly does differ from face-to-face conversation

and traditional writing for print. Nevertheless, miscommunication is the frequent result of students, and instructors, who are unaware of the distinctive features of online writing or how to use these in rhetorically effective ways, and they are less likely to have strategies for dealing with the emotional dimension of online discussion. In this section, I will discuss how instructors can use this information about emotion in online writing to intervene in discussion when necessary, to foster a climate conducive to discussion, and to provide opportunities for students to practice expressing and interpreting emotion appropriately.

Instructor Intervention into Discussion

Instructors can use the information that online discussion generally moves from a more neutral position toward a less neutral position and is more likely to occur on the detached side of the scale of attachment in a variety of ways. For example, in the sample thread posted above, it is clear that even though the students did not experience conflict with one another and in fact largely agreed with one another's perspectives, the "tone" of this thread is decidedly negative and becomes more so as it progresses. And after a student has posted a 100 percent negative reply there is no room for other students to move on the involvement scale in order to further detach themselves other than to ratchet up the discussion even more, often by employing additional quantity devices to amplify the evaluations. This pattern is observable in online flame wars of all types, so it is reasonable for instructors to be wary when they notice online discussion moving toward the extremely detached side of the involvement scale. Moreover, even in the absence of conflict this pattern can have a chilling effect on discussion since it gives other students very little room to maneuver, since it seems to be difficult for students to redirect a discussion by moving it back toward neutrality themselves. When instructors observe a discussion moving increasingly toward one side of the involvement scale—attached or detached—this is an important time for instructors to intervene in course discussion by posting more neutral replies that create room for other students to join the conversation. Occasional "checks" by the instructor can keep discussion from stagnating on one side of the scale of involvement and discouraging students who may wish to express a radically different opinion. Though only 12 percent of threads were able to move from one side of the scale to the other, this pattern of movement can indicate that multiple and alternate points of view are being expressed. So though it may be necessary to accept that online writing is simply more negative than face-to-face discussion, it is also important to be able to recognize when intervention is warranted and what steps to take in order to keep a discussion fluid and not simply moving toward less neutrality.

Define Topics Appropriately and Strategically

In addition to being equipped to interpret the emotional climate of a class and intervene in discussion when necessary, instructors can also actively work to create an online environment conducive to discussion. One of the most important steps that an online writing teacher can take is to attend to the way topics are defined by the instructor or other students. As Bomberger (2004) noted as well in her study of conflict in CMC, "How a topic is defined [in online discussion] can do much to set the tone of the thread" (209). In face-to-face classrooms, instructors do much to define course topics verbally during discussion and can easily reorient a class discussion that moves off-track (whether it becomes overly hostile or students "check out" of it through boredom). The patterns of transmitting emotion in CMC suggest that once a topic is defined in a subject line or initial prompt it is difficult for students to reverse direction. Consequently, instructors need to be very careful in the way they phrase initial posts or questions to students. However, rather than attempting to write without emotion themselves, it is more useful for instructors to be aware of the effects of the initial subject line and to define topics to encourage desired results. For example, if an instructor wants to engage a class that has seem unengaged with a difficult topic, it can be useful to employ strongly negative or positive evaluation devices, coupled with quantity devices, to indicate a high level of involvement with the topic and encourage students to become involved as well. I have used this technique, for example, when posting a prompt on Gunther Kress's article "Reading Images: Multimodality, Representation and New Media?," which students find a bit challenging. The subject line I have used is, "Kress implies you can be manipulated by the letter 'e'! What does he mean and can that be true?" In this topic, the negatively-connoted evaluation device "manipulated" is intended to draw students into Kress's argument, to help them recognize what is at stake in the arguments he is making and recognize their investment in them. In contrast, if an instructor anticipates that a particular topic is likely to incite conflict or naturally draw students into debate, he or she can develop a more neutral or attitudinally attached prompt, in order to at least discourage the negative extremes that might result otherwise. For example, in a class discussion about outsourcing I have used the subject line, "How is your life better because of outsourcing?" Unlike even a neutral subject line such as "Consequences of outsourcing," the positively-connoted evaluation "better" primes the discussion toward the attached side of the scale of involvement. My point here is not to convince students that outsourcing is a positive practice but rather to encourage them to approach the issue from a perspective they may not normally consider and to foster a discussion that is less extreme in its negativity and prone to conflict than if I had primed the topic with a negatively-connoted evaluation.

Students also need practice at defining topics themselves, an activity that helps them appreciate the impact of their own language choices. Frequently, students in online courses are asked to post discussion questions or initiate discussions in forums or via blogs, but rarely do they receive any instructions about the effects of different choices on the discussion that will (or will not) unfold. Rather than simply asking students to define topics without any preparation, instructors can help students understand how to foster an appropriate emotional climate. Early in the semester in my online courses, I ask students to practice developing forum prompts based on a specific topic. I ask them to draft one prompt that is highly supportive of the topic, one that is neutral, and one that is highly critical of the topic. Then I ask them to reflect on which prompt they personally find most interesting, which one would be most likely to lead to conflict in the forum, and which one they would be most likely to use. Following this activity, students have regular opportunities to serve as "moderators" for discussion forums as well. As moderator, they are responsible for posting the initial discussion prompt and then responding to the students who post replies to that prompt to keep the flow of the discussion going. Playing the role of moderator helps students observe the interplay of language in creating tone, and they can adapt and respond as necessary to keep the discussion moving forward. They also have opportunities to reflect on the experience of moderating the forum and their observations about what worked well and what they would change to improve discussion in the future.

Practice Performing a Variety of Emotions

Finally, I wish to discuss how writing instructors can foreground issues of emotion in the online classroom by providing students with opportunities to practice expressing and interpreting a variety of emotions in online writing. Although most instructors are particularly keen to avoid conflict in online discussion, I believe it can be equally problematic when students refuse to express any disagreement and do not dig into course topics or challenge one another's ideas, sometimes because they have misinterpreted advice about avoiding conflict in CMC. To address either extreme of interpersonal conflict or superficial agreement, it can be useful to give students opportunities to practice expressing a range of emotions and to consider what strategies are more and less effective for them in doing so.

After all, there are a number of ways that students can express any given emotion in their writing, and successful communication in CMC requires writers to determine how to express emotion effectively by shifting between the identities of writer and reader. As Lisa Feldman Barrett (2005) explains in relation to the performance of an emotion such as anger, "Presumably, there is no single experience of *anger*, but many . . . It is a skill to simulate the most appropriate or effective representation" (274–75). Micciche (2007) recommends focusing on emotion as a "teachable concept" (49) in the classroom by using performative and embodied strategies that allow students to conceive of emotion as something that happens "*in relation*" (50) rather than something that resides in a text or a body and can be objectively identified and analyzed. Providing students with opportunities to practice expressing different emotions helps them to recognize how emotion is mediated by language and to appreciate how subtle differences in word choice, syntax, and punctuation use can affect meaning.

I structure this activity as a type of online debate to discuss a class reading, usually a critical article with a strong point of view, and then I assign students a variety of roles to play during the debate. I ask students in one group to advocate for the article, another group of students to argue against the article, and a third group to moderate between those who agree and disagree. It should be unmistakably clear which role each student is performing, and they are instructed not to break character by indicating that they don't really agree with what they are saying. They are also warned against personally attacking other students, even those with whom they disagree, and the roles are switched throughout the semester so they each have a chance to try the different positions. It is particularly effective if students are asked to reflect on this experience periodically and to describe which roles they found easiest and more difficult, and what this reveals about emotion in online writing.

After a few attempts, students learn to become more subtle in their use of linguistic indicators to express emotion, having discovered how easily one can be mistaken for another in CMC. This is also a low-stakes activity since the students know that each of them is performing an assigned role and can safely experiment within that role as a result. Consequently, I have found that students take risks and dig more deeply into course topics and readings during these "debates" than they do during other online discussions. So the activity encourages thorough discussion even as it also helps students practice expressing emotion in CMC.

CONCLUSION

In considering the challenges of teaching language online, Susan Yue Hua Sun (2011) contends that though it is easy to recognize that face-to-face and online teaching are different from one another,

> exactly how different, and what the differences entail, is less clear. There seems to be little concerted effort in identifying and studying the new approaches and skills which online language teachers desperately need; and consequently, teacher training or professional development seldom goes beyond the technical and software-specific skills. (Sun 2011)

The same is true for teachers of writing, though I suggest that writing teachers are well positioned to address many of the differences that result from moving to a medium based so heavily on written communication.

In the absence of the familiar body language that teachers often rely on in face-to-face classes, it is helpful to have a framework such as the one offered by linguistics to evaluate "emotional commitment" with which to gauge how attached or detached students are from course topics and discussions at any time. And for writing teachers, in particular, this affords not only the opportunity to tweak course discussions and intervene before conflict arises but also provides a unique opportunity to help students develop skills in expressing and interpreting emotion online in rhetorically effective ways, skills that are increasingly necessary as work and communication of all kinds move online.

References

Barrett, Lisa Feldman. 2005. "Feeling is Perceiving: Core Affect and Conceptualization in the Experience of Emotion." In *Emotion and Consciousness*, ed. Lisa Feldman Barrett, Paula M. Niedenthal, and Piotr Winkielman, 255–84. New York: Guilford.

Bomberger, Ann M. 2004. "Ranting about Race: Crushed Eggshells in Computer-Mediated Communication." *Computers and Composition* 21 (2): 197–216. http://dx.doi .org/10.1016/j.compcom.2004.02.001.

Hübler, Axel. 2007. *The Nonverbal Shift in Early Modern English Conversation*. Amsterdam: John Benjamins Publishing Company.

Kleinke, Sonja. 2008. "Emotional Commitment in Public Political Internet Message Boards." *Journal of Language and Social Psychology* 27 (4): 409–21. http://dx.doi.org/10.1177/0261927X08322483.

Laflen, Angela, and Brittany Fiorenza. 2012. "'Okay, My Rant is Over': The Language of Emotion in Computer-Mediated Communication." *Computers and Composition* 29 (4): 296–308. http://dx.doi.org/10.1016/j.compcom.2012.09.005.

McKee, Heidi. 2002. "'YOUR VIEWS SHOWED TRUE IGNORANCE!!!': (Mis)communication in an Online Interracial Discussion Forum." *Computers and Composition* 19 (4): 411–34. http://dx.doi.org/10.1016/S8755-4615(02)00143-3.

Micciche, Laura R. 2007. *Doing Emotion: Rhetoric, Writing, Teaching*. Portsmouth, NH: Boynton/Cook.

Moor, Peter, Arv Heuvelan, and Ria Verleur. 2010. "Flaming on YouTube." *Computers in Human Interaction* 26 (6): 1536–46.

Selber, Stuart. 2004. *Multiliteracies for a Digital Age*. Carbondale: Southern Illinois University Press.

Sun, Susan Yue Hua. 2011. "Online Language Teaching: The Pedagogical Challenges." *Knowledge Management and E-Learning: An International Journal* 3 (3): 428–47.

Wallace, Patricia. 1999. *The Psychology of the Internet*. Cambridge: Cambridge University Press; http://dx.doi.org/10.1017/CBO9780511581670.

8

THINKING OUTSIDE "THE BOX"
Going outside the CMS to Create Successful Online Team Projects

Katherine Ericsson

This is the first time I've used something like this for a team project and I'm left wondering why we don't emphasize this idea in other classes. I know this course is specifically for Multimedia Authoring, but the whole idea of a team site with tasklists, calendars, file storage and a blog has made the entire process so much easier. It's helped so much with communication and collaboration, and even when I was gone for a week it made it so much easier to get back into the process.

—Student in Multimedia Authoring course

INTRODUCTION

This chapter provides instructors with a case study illustrating how to use an online shared workspace to facilitate a successful team project.[1] The student comment above was taken from the first semester the use of a shared workspace was attempted. The comment grabbed my attention because I hadn't considered that most of my students had never been asked to create and use a shared workspace to collaborate on a team project. I had merely incorporated it into the team project because I could not conceive of a way to allow students to successfully collaborate on a complex project within the CMS (Course Management System). Essentially, I was forced out of the CMS. After facilitating the team project for two years and carefully considering the key elements that have made the use of the shared workspace successful, I am now able to detail how the key elements intersect to create a truly collaborative team project experience for students. The key elements are explored in the founding concepts section of this chapter. A detailed overview of the case study follows and the chapter concludes with a discussion of the case study results and an exploration of the main findings from the case study.

DOI: 10.7330/9781607324850.c008

The chapter's underlying argument is that instructors and course designers need to seek out ways to incorporate shared workspaces into their team projects because it allows students to have control over their learning experience and prepares them to utilize new technologies in order to be successful members of the workforce.

FOUNDING CONCEPTS

This section explores the key elements, or theoretical concepts, which underscore the rationale for using an online shared workspace. It begins by arguing for a shift in the model of interaction between students and instructors; continues by exploring the relationship between online shared workspaces and the knowledge economy society; and concludes by examining the importance of collaborative activities that allow students to share information in order to create new knowledge.

Instructor Control

To begin, an exploration of instructor control is in order. Historically, instructor control over students and the classroom environment was a given. The instructor was in charge of most (if not all) decisions regarding curriculum design, curriculum delivery, assessment, in-class dynamics, etc. A definite hierarchy of power existed, with the instructor clearly at the top, often literally when lecturing from a raised podium at the front of the classroom. According to this schema, all knowledge, all learning was thought to originate from the instructor. This concept is wonderfully illustrated in the following model of F2F (face-to-face) interaction.

This schema, while still dominant, has slowly been changing. Especially within the context of writing instruction, wherein since the 1960s to the 1970s there has been a steady push toward cooperative writing activities such as peer review workshops. The push toward student interaction within the writing classroom results in the model of cooperative interaction as illustrated below.

This model illustrates cooperative interaction between students, yet the instructor is still on top and in charge of everything. Interestingly, that hierarchy of control has been built into the most commonly used CMS. Even in a CMS the instructor serves as the primary dispenser of knowledge, a virtual "sage on the stage." Rhetoric and Composition scholar Darin Payne (2000) notes that "A primary tenet of collaborative learning, then—the reduction of the student-teacher hierarchy—is countered in the very design of Blackboard, which composes both

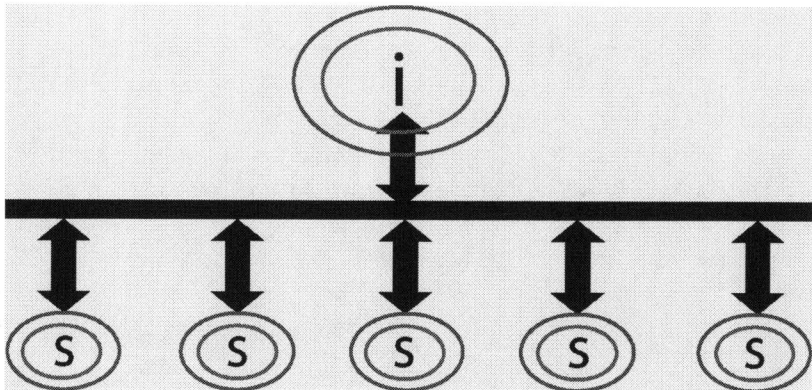

Figure 8.1. Model of F2F Interaction. Source: Brunk-Chavez and Miller 2007, sec. Digital Social Spaces.

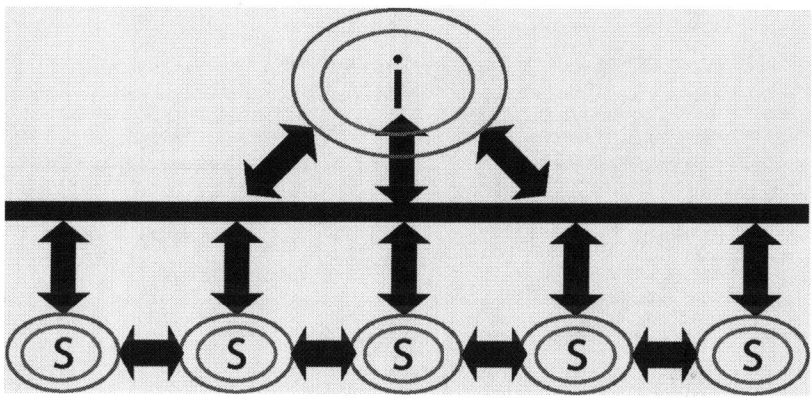

Figure 8.2. Model of Cooperative Interaction. Source: Brunk-Chavez and Miller 2007, sec. Digital Social Spaces.

teachers and students along traditionally sanctioned social lines" (sec. New Technologies as Facilitators of Cultural Reproduction).

Over the last two decades, writing instruction has taken the step out of the traditional F2F classroom setting to online and blended learning environments. In many ways, that step has afforded writing instructors a ready-made environment for cooperative interaction between students due the frequent use of discussion board activities in online learning environments. That step also resulted in a learning environment in which students must inherently produce more writing since almost all instructor-to-student and student-to-student communication is written. This chapter argues that the next step is toward the inclusion of a learning environment that does not place the instructor at the top: a learning environment where students are in control and the instructor acts as a facilitator. This step results in a collaborative model of interaction, which is illustrated in the figure below.

What is immediately evident when viewing this model is an uninterrupted circle; no longer is the instructor placed at the top. Not only is there no "top" or "power position," but the previous labels indicating "instructor" and "student" are removed from the schema. Before exploring the case study detailing how to incorporate this sort of a learning environment, it is important to consider why it is imperative that instructors relinquish some of their control over the students' learning experience and learning environment.

Relinquishing power is in keeping with writing instructions' historic embrace of student-centered learning, which aims to empower student writers. The inclusion of a learning environment where students are in control and the instructor acts as a facilitator empowers the students insofar as students have the creative buy in to author their own learning environment. The common vocabulary students use when referring to the CMS helps to demonstrate the significance of student-authored learning environments. As Rhetoric and Writing scholars Brunk-Chavez and Miller (2007) note, "[s]tudents end up using terms like 'visit' or 'access' in reference to the course webspace, and yet, don't have much in the way of buy in or contribution to the construction, development, or direction of that space. They essentially haven't 'moved in,' and are only 'visiting,' in a place/space that they can't really touch or modify, only look at" (sec. Digital Social Spaces).

The case study discussed later demonstrates having students create and use online shared workspaces entirely changes that dynamic as each team of students owns its workspace. They have created it; they can modify it; they can determine what tools to use in order to collaborate on their teamwork and how to use those tools to facilitate their collaboration. Having students create and use a shared online workspace is "teaching our students a way to be 'critically literate in a digital age'" (Selber 2004 quoted in Brunk-Chavez and Miller 2007, sec. Digital Social Spaces). Selber believes "that students are too often encouraged to learn how to use technology before they actually think about the implications of the technology." Authors Brunk-Chavez and Miller (2007) apply Selber's argument to instructors and note, "As instructors providing a gateway to a digital space for a course, we too would do well to apply our own analytical and critical skills to the technology we so often readily embrace and use" (sec. Digital Social Spaces).

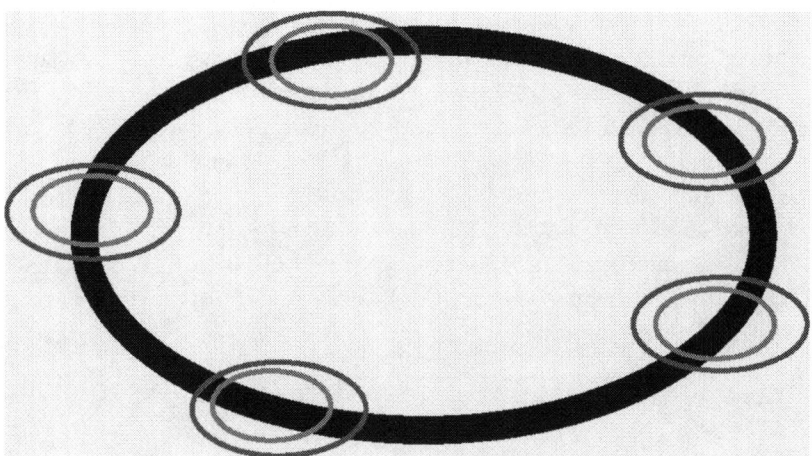

Figure 8.3. Model of collaborative interaction. Source: Brunk-Chavez and Miller 2007, sec. Digital Social Spaces.

Brunk-Chavez and Miller's article does an exceptional job of emphasizing the instructor's responsibility to critically analyze the technology used in the CMS. The article reveals that the onus is on the instructor (or course designer) to apply her critical skills and consider how she can give students creative buy in, can teach students to critically explore the implications of the technology they use, to circumvent the interface elements of CMS (or even a F2F classroom), which stymie creative efforts and reinforce the instructor's authoritarian position. While I agree with Brunk-Chavez and Miller's assertion that "instructors need to imagine and design a digital space wherein they can provide clear guidance and details for assignments and discussions, but also where they can also be open with their students about the shared experience of working collaboratively online," I do not entirely agree with their argument that "any CMS can be 'bent' to work for collaboration" (2007, sec. Digital Social Spaces). Rather than attempting to "bend" the CMS, I believe that successful and meaningful team collaboration should take place outside the CMS in a student-authored, online shared workspace because going outside the CMS allows for a break from the models of interaction that place the instructor as authoritarian.

While the later sections of this chapter explores ways in which instructors benefit from the use of online shared workspaces, one of the key ways instructors benefit is by having a dated and detailed "transcript" of the team's collaborative efforts. This "transcript" affords the instructor the ability to monitor and assess each student's work. In many regards, it also rewrites the instructor into a role more comparable to that of a workplace supervisor and/or project manager. While some educators might bristle at this new role, it better resembles the workplace reality students will face upon entering the workforce. Of course, this is not to say that the instructor neglects his or her duties as an educator. Rather, authors Oliveira, Tinoca, and Pereira (2011) argue for an "endorsement of collaborative learning contexts," wherein "the instructor should act mainly as a facilitator to the learning process, directing his participation towards the orientation of the community/group work in a productive direction" (1348).

Online Shared Workspaces and the Knowledge Economy Society

The 2013 EDUCAUSE Evolving Technologies Committee Report states that a CMS "provides an instructor with a set of tools and a framework that allows the relatively easy creation of online course content and the subsequent teaching and management of that course including various interactions with students taking the course" (1). As Payne notes, most university writing instructors use CMSs "partly because the university has a site license for it and partly because it is easy to use; teachers with little or no technological knowledge can host an entire course online with just a Web browser." CMSs are the easy go-to for most university instructors, but as previously mentioned it's important to consider how the CMS reconstructs the traditional power hierarchy of a F2F classroom. Payne (2000) asserts, "[r]egardless of what the teacher wants to do in this environment, he or she is authored to be an authoritarian" (sec. New Technologies as Facilitators of Cultural Reproduction).

To escape this authoritarian dynamic, it becomes vital that instructors envision ways to incorporate different learning environments into their teaching methods. An example of this is found in an online shared workspace. Some of the essential qualities of an online shared workspace (virtual workspace or team website) are as follows:

- located outside the CMS (or a F2F classroom)
- authored by students
- comprised of tools to assist students in their collaborative efforts
- accessed by the instructor via the invitation of the students

As previously noted, the problem with trying to "bend" a CMS to work toward collaboration (or having students collaborate within a F2F classroom) is that the instructor is placed in the authoritarian position.

By going outside of a traditional setting (whether it is a F2F classroom or a CMS) the instructor is no longer placed in that position. Instead, students are in control of their learning environment and learning process: they are the authors. They must determine *what* tools they will use in their online shared workspace as well as *how* they will use each tool. By providing only loose requirements for shared workspaces, instructors demonstrate their trust in the students' ability to author a learning environment that works for them. It empowers the students to actively and critically engage in their learning experience. This concept of student empowerment via virtual communities is supported in the research completed by scholars such as David McConnell (2006) and Isolina Oliveira. For instance Oliveira builds upon McConnell's work by noting that these types of online communities give students "ownership over the content and direction of their learning" by making students responsible for "managing their learning" experience (Oliveira, Tinoca, and Pereira 2011, 1348). The benefits of having only loose requirements for the shared workspace are also acknowledged in the article, "How Virtual Teams Use Their Virtual Workspace to Coordinate Knowledge." The authors of the article, Malhotra and Majchrzak (2012, sec. 7.1 Managerial Implications), explore the benefits of conceptualizing online workspace tools as "option sets" and allowing team members to select which tool to use and how to use each tool as opposed to specifying that a particular tool be used in a prescribed manner.

An online workspace hands over a significant amount of power to the students. The students are no longer "visiting" or "accessing" the instructor's domain (classroom or CMS); the students are deciding how to author their workspace and how to use their workspace. Within this setting, it is the instructor who must be invited to "visit" or "access" the students' domain. An online shared workspace also fosters the students' ability to be critically literate in a digital age. The value of that preparation becomes apparent within the context of knowledge economy theory. Knowledge economy theory explores the ways in which the global economy is transitioning from an "information society" toward a "knowledge society." Rather than having a focus on information or information sharing, the knowledge society is concerned with how knowledge is produced and coordinated among a group of individuals in a meaningful and transformative way. The call for educators to embrace pedagogical methods that respond to the economic factors that shape the workplace our students encounter has been addressed in previous scholarship. A good example of that call is found in the New London Group's (1996) work "A Pedagogy of Multiliteracies: Designing Social Futures." The article explores the complexities of developing pedagogies that respond to economic factors, while still advocating for teaching students to be critical and creative:

> In responding to the radical changes in working life that are currently underway, we need to tread a careful path that provides students the opportunity to develop skills for access to new forms of work through learning the new language of work. But at the same time, as teachers, our role is not simply to be technocrats. Our job is not to produce docile, compliant workers. Students need to develop the capacity to speak up, to negotiate, and to be able to engage critically with the conditions of their working lives. (sec. Changing Working Lives)

Within this examination of a pedagogy that prepares students to be critical participants within the knowledge economy, the authors discuss the concept of "productive diversity." By incorporating new media into our teaching methods, instructors are promoting collaborative working skills which can translate into the realm of work, wherein students can learn how to place their unique knowledge in dialogue with other students' knowledge (New London Group 1996, sec. Changing Working Lives). Not only does an online shared workspace challenge the notion of the instructor being the source of all knowledge and promote student confidence in authoring their own learning experience, it also demonstrates to the students the importance of coordinating their knowledge in a meaningful way to be active and productive members in the knowledge economy society.

Collaboration and Knowledge Sharing

In addition to exploring the difference in instructor control within the cooperative and collaborative models of interaction, Brunk-Chavez and Miller (2007) also explore the difference in student-to-student interaction. They note that while cooperative interaction typically involves "students divvy[ing] up the work [...] and then cobbl[ing] their results into a final presentation," collaborative interaction involves groups of students actively coordinating ideas and sharing knowledge in order to determine the best way to address a particular situation/task. Brunk-Chavez and Miller argue that collaborative learning empowers students because "unlike the cumulative talk that occurs in cooperative learning, collaborative learning encourages 'exploratory talk'" (2007, sec. Decentered, Digitized, but not Disconnected: Sharing our Shared Spaces). In exploratory talk "statements and suggestions are offered for joint consideration. These are then challenged and counter-challenged with justifications and alternative hypotheses" (Arvaja et al. 2000 quoted in Paulus 2005, 102). Exploratory talk is central to a successful collaboration; as author Oliveira, Tinoca, and Pereira (2011) emphasize "successful groups have a greater tendency to discuss its member's proposals and to link them with their prior conversations. On the other hand, less successful groups are more likely to reject or ignore its partner's contributions without weaving them with their prior conversations" (1349).

Although many students report that they dislike team projects, there is a clear need to provide students with the opportunity to develop collaborative working skills as it is a highly valued skill within the knowledge society. Indeed, as Learning Sciences and Technologies scholar Qiyun Wang (2010) notes, "[i]n the current knowledge society, work is becoming more knowledge-based, interdisciplinary and complicated. Collaborative learning is not a buzzword any more but becomes a necessity. It is hardly possible for an individual to complete sophisticated tasks without the support of others" (1270). Due to this reality, instructors must overcome both their own and their students' trepidations regarding team projects.

The main reasons students dislike team projects tend to relate to issues of creative control, scheduling, and assessment. Prior to the advent of new media, team projects placed a true burden on students as they were asked to negotiate schedules in order to find times that the group could physically meet and work together on the project. This burden is much lighter now that teams can use new technologies (e.g., Google Docs, Dropbox, Instant Messaging, Email, Facebook, etc.) to collaborate both synchronously and asynchronously. While present-day students use these technologies (to varying degrees), online students are exceedingly acclimated to technology-mediated learning. Having students use an online shared workspace allows students to retain some degree of control over scheduling as they can access the workspace when their schedule allows in order to asynchronously share ideas, questions and concerns, drafts, as well as check-in to see how other team members are progressing on tasks. The ability to jointly monitor and manage the project makes it so each team member has a fairly high degree of creative control over the project's development. Moreover, creative input or "exploratory talk" comprises one of the grading criteria for the case study team project described below.[2]

CASE STUDY
Context
This research was conducted during the 2012–2013 academic year in the online course titled *Multimedia Authoring: Exploring New Rhetorics*, which is a 300 level cross listed course.[3] The focus of the course is to help students explore both theoretical and practical considerations of multimedia authoring. The course is taught during a sixteen-week semester during the academic year and a twelve-week semester during the summer term. The team project takes place during the second half of the semester and lasts four weeks. Standard enrollment is thirty students per section.

Team Project Overview
The team project assigns teams to specific clients who are in need of organizational websites. The major deliverables for the project are a website proposal and website mockup. Each team's website proposal must persuade the client that the team understands the client's needs and is capable of creating a professional website for the client in a timely and affordable manner. Each team's website mockup must demonstrate to the client how the team has put ideas into practice so the client can see how the project is progressing.

Team Project Logistics
Each team consists of three to four students. Based on the student work produced earlier in the semester, the instructor identifies the more motivated and organized students in the course and assigns at least one of these students to each team in order to ensure that no team is entirely comprised of students who have procrastination tendencies. This process is fairly simple as the instructor can easily look back at the discussion board history to see who typically posts early and does a good job on his or her work. Teams are divided into students who wish to take on the role of the marketing and research professionals and students who wish to take on the role of the design and technology professionals for the project. The marketing and research professionals have primary responsibility for completing the website proposal. The design and technology professionals have primary responsibility for completing the website mockup.

The weekend before the team project begins the instructor emails each team, notifying students of team assignments and introducing each team to their respective client. The instructor uses the CMS email system to contact students. Each client is fictional and the instructor plays the role of the "client." Each activity for the team project consists of step-by-step instructions to help guide the students through the project. The first activity for the team project requires teams to begin communicating within the CMS to organize the team and begin work on the project. One of the requirements for the first activity is that each team submits a list of team assignments (which students are marketing and research professionals and which students are design and technology professionals) in a CMS discussion forum. Each student is required to post a reply to the list on the discussion in order to confirm that the team assignments posted are correct. This step is taken to ensure that there is no confusion regarding team assignments. Finally, students are asked to use that forum in the CMS in order to discuss and decide which design and technology professional will be in charge of creating the team website.

I selected Google Sites as the required platform for teams to use as their shared workspace (or team website) as it required students to author their own workspace, which would not be required if students used pre-packed project workspaces such as Teambox, Asana, Glasscubes, or Huddle. Also, Google Sites is free. If they would like to do so, students are allowed to use additional means of communication such as Google Hangout, Skype, or Camdip. Students are required to use Google Sites for their online shared workspace due to the variety of tools Google Sites affords, for example, Google Docs, Calendars, Task Lists, and other embeddable gadgets. It's also important to note that each student is graded individually for the activities that comprise the case study team project described in this chapter. In this way, the often-cited student complaint of having their grade be dependent on the work of others is avoided. Finally, it's important to note that in the case study described below, synchronous communication (e.g., conference calls or instant messaging) is not required as it acknowledges the additional burden synchronous communication requirements place on already busy students. However, in order to establish an active and organized team, it's imperative that instructors include specific due dates for the collaborative steps required to complete the project.

While clear deadlines are given for each step required for the Unit Three activities, there is more flexibility in the requirements for the shared online workspace (or team website) each team must create. The basic requirements ask that each team's website includes the following tools:

- team calendar with target dates
- announcement page such as a "Blog" or "Discussion Board" to communicate with team members
- the File Cabinet page to share files

Teams are asked to move all project-related communication to their team website as soon as it is constructed. All project-related communication must be posted on the team website. Teams are allowed to use other modes of communication (e.g., email, text, phone conferences), but a summary of that communication must be posted on the team website. This is due to the fact that all grading and assessment is based on the instructor's evaluation of the team website and the two project deliverables: the website proposal and the website mockup.

Once the each team's website is created, students are required to share the link to the team website in the CMS discussion board forum corresponding to team websites. Next, each student is required to review at least two other teams' websites, posting replies that explore the following questions: How are other teams setting up their shared workspace? What tools are they using to stay in touch? What tools are they using to set deadlines? What tools are they using to share documents and other project resources? Students are also encouraged to note any questions they may have, discuss challenges their team is having, and share strategies. The activity is an opportunity for students to share resources and see how other teams are using the team website to organize information and facilitate team interaction.

The remainder of Unit Three has teams collaborating on creating the two project deliverables (website proposal and website mockup) for the client. As noted before, the instructor monitors each team's website using the content contained on the website as well as each deliverable to assess individual grades for each student on each deliverable. Evidence of collaboration on each deliverable is heavily weighted in the grading rubric for both deliverables. The primary assessment is focused on collaboration; the quality of the deliverable is secondary. The final activity of Unit Three is a project evaluation wherein students evaluate the follow areas: Project Evaluation, Team Member Evaluation, and Self Evaluation.

Data Sources

In order to identify evidence of team dynamics and critically access the value of using team websites, course artifacts are analyzed in the next section. The three data sources analyzed are (1) student communication posted in the CMS during the first week of the team project; (2) student communication posted on three different team websites; and (3) comments received in the project evaluations. These three data sources best serve the purpose of this study as the first data source not only illustrates the importance of beginning the team project within the CMS, but also reveals student awareness of the value of using an online shared workspace to collaborate. The second data source provides insight as to how student use of the team website impacts team dynamics. Finally, an analysis of the project evaluations, the third data source, offers a chance to analyze student perceptions of the team project, with particular attention paid to comments relating to the collaborative interaction model and use of technology.

DISCUSSION OF RESULTS

Data Source One: Inside the CMS

The project begins inside the CMS when the instructor uses the CMS emailing system to email each team their client information. Students reply to that email to begin organizing themselves for the project. Next, teams respond to threads created by the instructor in a discussion board forum within the CMS titled "Project Introduction." This required step ensures that each team member confirms his or her role as either a marketing and research professional or design and technology professional. It also provides each team with a discussion area within the CMS to use for initial team communication. The use of the CMS email and the "Project Introduction" discussion board activity have resulted in successfully avoiding any issues relating to student confusion regarding team assignments. To date, I have not been contacted by students claiming to not know which team they are assigned to or which professional team (marketing and research professional or design and technology professional) they are assigned to.

The other required discussion activity within the CMS is the "Team Sites" activity where each team shares the link to their team website. This required step ensures that the instructor has access to each team's website and that teams are able to share tips and ideas for how to create and use their team websites. As illustrated in figure 8.4 below, this discussion activity promotes collaboration and knowledge sharing between teams as students are able to request support for constructing a shared workspace that facilitates team collaboration. Below, a transcript of this collaboration and knowledge sharing is seen in the student conversation regarding how to enable subscription features in order to monitor recent activity on a team website. In addition, the transcript illustrates students critically reflecting on the benefits of using shared workspaces for other purposes in their academic and personal lives.

POST TITLE: TEAM SITES; AUTHOR: MICHAEL 6/30/2012

After looking at all the team site forums, I wanted to make a specific comment on the concept of using team sites for collaboration on team projects. This is the first time I've used something like this for a team project and I'm left wondering why we don't emphasize this idea in other classes. I know this course is specifically for Multimedia Authoring, but the whole idea of a team site with tasklists, calendars, file storage and a blog has made the entire process so much easier. It's helped so much with communication and collaboration, and even when I was gone for a week it made it so much easier to get back into the process.

I don't know about the rest of you, but generally my classes are on campus here at WSU-Vancouver and we end up meeting a couple of times a week to work on team projects. Even in an on-ground course, a team site for collaborative projects is a great idea that I'll be taking with me for classes in the fall.

RE: HEAR! HEAR! AUTHOR: STEPHANIE 6/30/2012

This process is definitely easier for a team project than simply using a discussion board thread! Another plus for me is that the technology we are using seems fairly common in the business world but I hadn't ever been exposed to Google Docs or Sites, or Wix for that matter. Now that I am learning how to navigate within these tools I have additional marketable skills that will help me in the workplace. Fortunately for me I have a very patient team who are quick to help when I run into technical issues or can't figure something out!:-)

I can definitely see using these tools for other projects and classes. We have a family reunion in a year that I am heading up the planning for, and I've already decided that we will use a Google site with Docs, Photos, etc. so that all of us participating in the planning can easily communicate with each other.

~Stephanie

POST TITLE: TEAM 4—TEAM WEBSITE;
AUTHOR: JENNIFER 6/23/2012

Hi, everyone! Here's our website: [url to team website]

RE: TEAM 4—TEAM WEBSITE;
AUTHOR: JEFFREY 6/30/2012

This is pretty smooth looking. Myself, I want a big, neon, flashing calendar up front. But this looks great. The other thing is that I have yet to figure out a good way of communicating using these sites. I know I can sign up for RSS notifications or some crap, but I'm curious if anyone has found a better way of being notified within the site of new comments/content.

RE: HOW TO VIEW NEW COMMENTS/
CONTENT; AUTHOR: LIZ 6/25/2012

Jeff,

There are a couple of measures to you can take to be notified of new comments/content. First, our site has a page that lists all the most current posts, so everyone can see what's happened since they last logged in.

Second, you can subscribe to site updates so you will get "pinged" via email whenever something is added to your site. I have found this to be extraordinarily helpful. Just click on the "More" drop-down menu on the top right of your site (once you are logged in) and select "Subscribe to site changes." [. . .] You can also omit your own changes from the subscription, if you don't want to receive those. I actually like being notified of my own changes, though, because it allows me to double-check that my posts actually went through.

Have a great week!

Liz

Figure 8.4. Source: Transcript of Student Discussion within CMS "Team Sites" Discussion Forum. June 2012.

Students are asked to use the CMS email system to communicate with their client. In addition, the website proposal and website mockup are submitted in discussion board forums in the CMS. The project evaluations are submitted in a drop box in the CMS. In this way, all graded

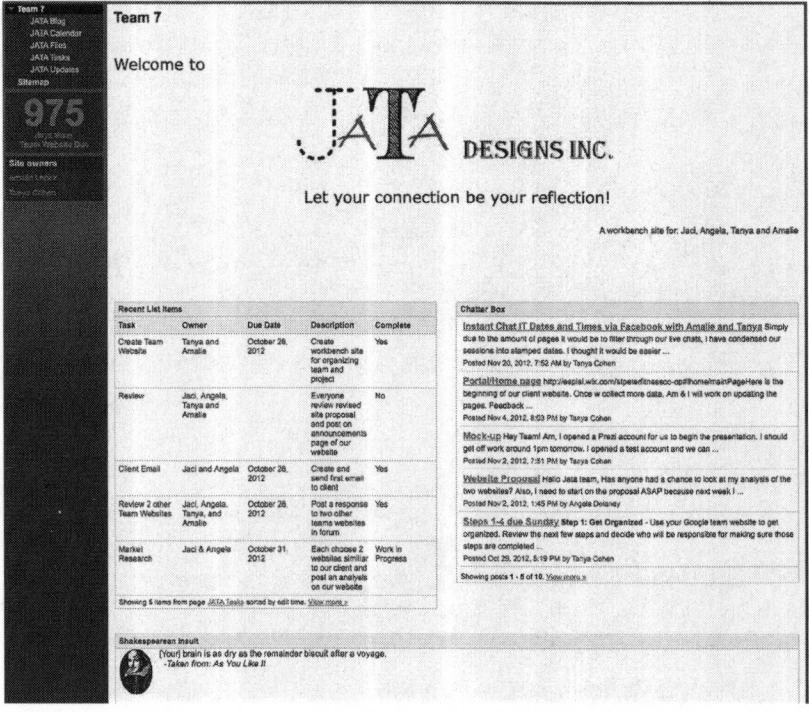

Figure 8.5. Source: Team Website: Example 1, JATA Designs Inc. October 2012.

deliverables are located in the CMS and student-instructor communication is located in the CMS. Keeping graded deliverables and student-
instructor communication inside the CMS allows the instructor to retain
records of those activities within the university endorsed CMS.

Data Source Two: Team Websites

Due to the loose requirements for the team websites, each team's website is unique. Below, figure 8.5 depicts one team's homepage.[4] Notice
that the team has a left navigation menu with collaborative tools (i.e.,
blog, calendar, files, tasks, updates, and count down clock). In addition to the left navigation menu items, immediately present on the
homepage is a list of items to track the completion of project tasks and
a "Chatter Box," which is a window display of the team's blog. Also,
important to note is the team name and logo JATA Designs Inc. and
team motto "Let your connection be your reflection!" The team name is
comprised of the first letter of each team member's name. The creation

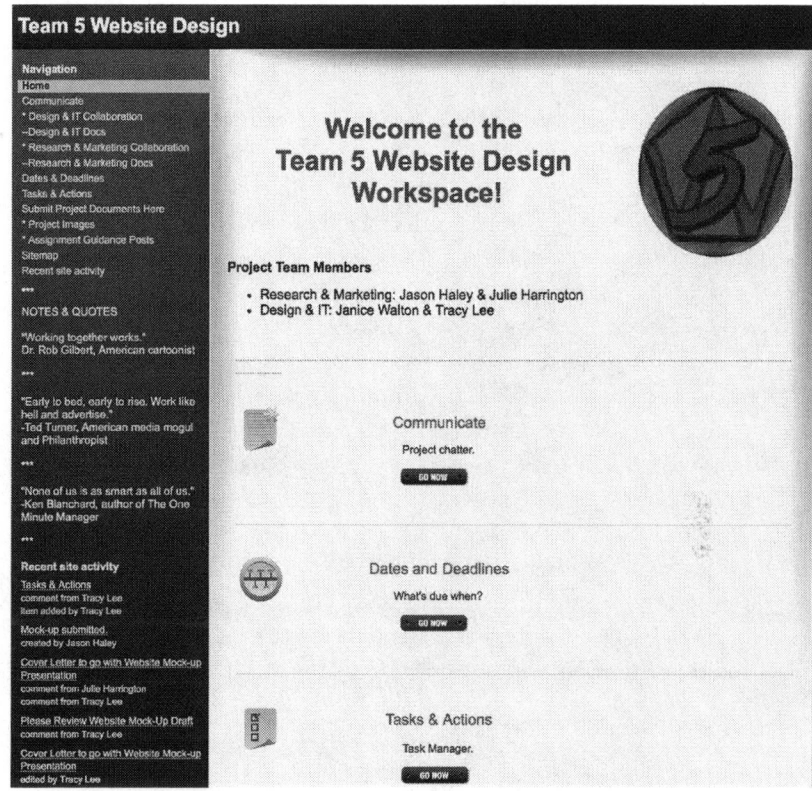

Figure 8.6. Source: Team Website: Example 2, Team 5 Website Design Workspace. October 2012.

of a team name and team logo demonstrates team bonding, effectively illustrates the claim that, "if done well, collaborative learning activities create a stronger connection between students learning together in a digital environment—in spite of their physical disconnection" (Brunk-Chavez and Miller 2007, sec. How Digitizing Decenters). Indeed, the two women working together as the design and technology professionals commented on the fact that working together was the highlight of the team project. As one of them stated in her project evaluation: *"Working with and brainstorming with my fellow design and technology professional has to have been the highlight of this project. [. . .] Even after this class is over we are going to remain great friends."*

Another example of a team website is included below in figure 8.6. Notice that this team's homepage has many of the collaborative tools used on the previous example, and it also includes a logo created by the team. A unique feature of this team's website is the team's use of quick links and sub-discussion boards. The sub-discussion boards are particularly interesting as it demonstrates the team's decision to provide separate discussion areas for the research and marketing collaboration and the design and technology collaboration. Therefore, these sub-discussion boards represent the team critically constructing a shared workspace that best facilitated their collaborative efforts. The sub-discussion boards help to filter the ideas, data and other content in a meaningful way, a way that allows the group to capitalize on the (shared knowledge) in order to solve problems and to learn from one another (Oliveira, Tinoca, and Pereira 2011, 1349). In this way, the team was able to filter content so only the most vital information was shared on the team's main discussion board, titled "Communicate: Project Chatter."

In order to illustrate the sort of "exploratory talk," which is central to effective collaboration, a transcript from a team discussion posted on a team website is included. In this discussion, Anna has presented some ideas for the team's consideration. Liz and Stephanie provide Anna with their feedback and build upon her ideas. The section of the discussion included below specifically illustrates the team providing constructive feedback that fosters successful team dynamics.

Data Source Three: Project Evaluations

As noted in the Founding Concepts section of this chapter, the positive benefits of collaborative learning environments are not automatic. However, to date the instructor has not had any instances where an entire team of students has failed to complete the team project activities.[5] Moreover, the instructor has received abundant positive feedback from students in their project evaluations discussing the use of the team websites. Many students note how the team website helped to circumvent issues encountered in previous team projects. For example, *"The shared workspace was a fantastic way to keep the project organized and on schedule. I wish I would have had this class earlier because it would have helped me with past team projects that did not got so well. I feel like those experiences could have been different if we would have had this shared workspace."* Another student's evaluation also mentioned problems with previous group projects and said, *"I was expecting this project would be no different and that myself and another team member would end up doing the majority of the work. That did not happen, and I was delightfully surprised to find that it is possible for an online course to have a team project where each team member contributes."*

LIZ 10:23 PM JUN 25, 2012

Kiva is an awesome organization! I love your funding ideas,[Anna]! [. . .]

STEPHANIE 9:44 AM JUN 26, 2012

Anna, I have to echo Liz's comment about how creative and innovative your funding ideas are! I think that is a major strength of our team that we should stress to the client. Many of the funding ideas don't even require that the client do anything other than the initial set-up and adding a link to his website, so it couldn't be easier for him to generate a lot of donations.

I was thinking that many of the funding ideas are so good that we only need to drive more viewers to our client's site in order to get them using the funding options. To that end, how can we steer more and more viewers to his site? I'll be thinking about this as well, but I wanted to throw it out there in this thread so that we could talk about it.

ANNA 3:06 PM JUN 26, 2012

Thanks team for your encouragement. I'm feeling over-whelmed at not being to navigate as quick as I would like! (I'm sure you have noticed my notes are all over the place!) It has taken me a Texas Mile to figure out the site! I think I'm up to speed. I'm now working on the comparison of the websites.

Figure 8.7. Source: Team Website: Example 3, Transcript of Team Website Discussion Thread. June 2012.

Another area often discussed in the project evaluations is the relationship between the team website and their team's level of collaboration. One student commented that, *"There were many benefits to completing this project, as a matter of fact, I wish this course had come earlier in my online college career, the collaboration methods used were new to me, but proved unbelievable beneficial to working as a team."* Another student emphasized that, *"the biggest benefit to this project was to get a chance to work more closely with classmates. In the virtual classroom it is much harder to build any sort of relationship with other students.* "This evaluation emphasized how enjoyable it was to see the deliverables come together knowing that each classmate had played a role in creating the deliverable.

Finally, many students discuss how using the shared workspace prepared them for the workforce. For instance one student said, *"By completing this project I felt we learned how to work as a team and work towards completing a single goal. In addition since this class was online we also had to learn how to complete this goal by communicating only through online databases. These skills are important in a world that is using technology more and more in the workplace.* "This sentiment can also be seen in this student's remark: *"I think that working with a team is a huge benefit in any class as it prepares you for future team work in your career.* "In the portion of the evaluation asking for student input on how to revise and improve the project one student noted, *"I do not suggest any revisions to this project because it is a lot like the "real world." In any job, you have to make allowances for and often wait for your coworkers to complete their tasks before the project can move forward. Even though it is frustrating, it is exactly like real life!"*

Admittedly, the feedback presented above paints a very positive picture of this particular team project. Obviously, some negative feedback was received. Most often that feedback is from students who simply do not enjoy working with other students. For example, *"Everyday situations arise where I get to try my communication skills. I don't need another new situation to hone them. I really don't benefit much from one more. They typically end up being an exercise in patience more than anything else. I realize not everyone has those opportunities so I can see their purpose."* The instructor also received requests to require synchronous communication as well as requests for more instructor feedback regarding the construction and use of the shared workspace: *"I would have appreciated instructor feedback on the shared site as we were collaborating, just to make sure we were on the right track."*

Instructor Facilitation

As previously noted, there have been no problems with students claiming to be unaware of team assignment or team responsibilities. Closely monitoring the initial activities for the project ensures that each team member is actively communicating with his/her team. If any student does not complete any steps of the initial team project activities, instructor intervention takes place in the form of an email to the student to ask the student to complete the missing work. Immediate instructor review of all team websites helps to identify whether any students are having trouble accessing or posting to the team website. If any students have not yet posted to the team website during the first week of the team project, instructor intervention takes place in the form of an email to the entire team to inquire whether all students are able to use the team website, identifying the team members who have not yet posted to the team website. To help keep teams on track, the instructor must post frequent reminders in the Announcements page of the CMS. These reminders consist of upcoming due dates, activity requirements, and examples of team websites and project deliverables.

Each team member is individually evaluated for each of the project deliverables. The evaluation is based on the instructor's careful review of each team website. This requires the instructor to review all content on the team website. As previously noted in the Case Study section of this chapter, evidence of collaboration on each deliverable is heavily weighted in the grading rubric for both deliverables. The main areas for evaluation are active collaborative efforts on the team's discussion area and file share area. Also noted in the Case Study section is the fact that the primary assessment is focused on collaboration; the quality of the deliverable is secondary. This assessment focus is based on the instructor's commitment to valuing the overall goals of the team project, which focus on skill development and collaboration.

The use of team websites provides the instructor with a transparent method for monitoring and evaluating participation. If there is no evidence of collaborative efforts that correlate to a portion of the grading rubric, the instructor notes this to the student. If the student claims to have collaborated, he or she must provide the instructor with evidence of collaborative efforts. It has been the instructor's experience that there is a strong link between the active use of the shared workspace and a group's successful collaboration. Less successful groups typically have fewer discussion posts and fewer files shared.

The importance of the instructor's facilitation at the beginning of the project is critical to ensuring that teams immediately begin using the team websites to collaborate on the project. However, instructor intervention within the team websites is minimal and only occurs during the evaluation of the two deliverables. This intervention does not take place within the team websites; the instructor never posts within a team's website. Instead, the instructor's intervention is conveyed via emails sent within the CMS and within each student's grading report for each project deliverable.

The previous exploration of constructive team dynamics on the team websites helps to illustrate that the team website itself is not typically the cause of team dynamic problems. Rather, the most common problems arise from the following:

- Total lack of student participation: student never completes any team project related activities.
- Minimal student participation: student participates minimally in team project activities and does not frequently visit or use the team website.
- Conflicting personalities between team members: student(s) with dominant personality tries to assert total control over project and/or student(s) with passive personality feels overlooked or has trouble asserting themselves into the collaborative process.

Instructor intervention in the form of email communication sent within the CMS can be used to address all of the issues noted above. It is possible to resolve the first two problems listed above via instructor intervention. However, it is difficult to solve the first problem as total lack of participation in the project is typically coupled with total lack of participation in the class. If a student does not respond to team or instructor intervention attempts, the instructor must encourage the team to continue working on the project without the input of the missing team member.

CONCLUSIONS

This chapter has argued that there is a need to seek out ways to incorporate shared workspaces into team projects in order to give students more control over their learning experience and prepare students to utilize new technologies in order to be successful members of the workforce. The purpose of analyzing this case study was to provide evidence that supports this chapter's argument by evaluating how the team websites foster a successful team dynamic in an a digital collaborative project and permit transparency in correspondence to mitigate miscommunication. In addition, an examination of the case study and data sources reveals strategies for improving future collaborative projects using a team website.

The first conclusion drawn is that it is possible to have students complete an entirely online team project and actually enjoy it. The second conclusion is that the use of team websites also allowed for transparency in the collaborative process. This transparency not only helps teams to negotiate miscommunications, but it also allows the instructor a dated-transcript of the team's collaborative efforts to use in evaluating each student's collaborative efforts. The final conclusion is that the instructor's attentive monitoring and timely guidance allows students to feel empowered and confident in their abilities to be effective virtual collaborators and multimedia authors.

FINAL THOUGHTS

It is the author's sincere hope that this chapter inspires other instructors to go outside the CMS or their F2F classroom and provide their students with the opportunity to take control over their learning environment and learning experience by using a shared workspace to collaborate on team projects. Furthermore, administrators reading this chapter should now be persuaded to allow and encourage their faculty to use technologies in addition to the ones licensed by their university. The quote opening for this chapter recognizes that the ease of using an online shared workspace within the context of this case study is unique as the course focuses on multimedia authoring. Integrating the use of a team website into a course that does not have that focus would most likely be more challenging and require the instructor to use video tutorials and other resources to guide students in the creation of the team website. If a team website were to be used within the context of a F2F classroom, instructors could potentially have teams create shared workspaces while in the classroom before moving the team activities on to the shared workspaces. The use of shared workspaces in team projects completed in F2F or hybrid courses would most likely have the same benefits as explored in this chapter. In addition, it is possible that the shared workspace would free up any in-class time that instructors may have had to dedicate to teams working together in the past.

By having students create and use shared workspaces outside of the CMS (or the traditional seated classroom), students can realize that not only do they understand the possible uses of various digital collaborative tools, they can apply that understanding by creating a shared workspace that allows them to collaborate asynchronously to complete a team project. That knowledge and skill set is extremely valuable in the knowledge economy society, wherein the innovative use of digital technology to share knowledge and accomplish tasks is increasingly required to be a productive member of the workforce. Future research to expand upon this chapter's findings is necessary in order to explore possible applications of new digital technologies for fostering collaborative learning experiences.

APPENDIX 8.A

DTC/ENGL 355 Lesson 3.2: Website Proposal		Student's Name
Your input for organizing your team website on the Announcements/"Blog" page	/26	
Your market research	/26	
Your work toward completing the proposal and/or the portal page	/26	
Your review of the proposal draft in your team website	/26	
Your input ensuring the revision and submission of the proposal	/26	
Final Score & Instructor Comments	/130	
Client Response		

APPENDIX 8.B

DTC/ENGL 355 Lesson 3.3: Website Mockup		Student's Name
Your brainstorming input on the Announcements/"Blog" page	/30	
Your collaboration toward completing the mockup	/30	
Your review of the mockup draft in your team website	/30	
Your input ensuring the revision and submission of the mockup	/30	
Final Score and Instructor Comments	/120	
Client Response		

Notes

1. The term "team" is used as opposed to "group" in this chapter as the term team connotes the idea of working together towards a goal. Also, the case study explored in the chapter involves teams.
2. See appendix 8.A and appendix 8.B for Team Project Grading Rubrics.
3. The course is housed in the WSU (Washington State University) English Department's Digital Technology and Culture degree program.
4. The legibility of figures 8.5 and 8.6 are not ideal. However, these figures are included to provide a general idea of what the team websites look like.
5. There have been cases where one team member fails to actively participate in the project, but never any cases where more than one team member or an entire team fails to successfully complete the team project.

References

Arvaja, M., P. Hakkinen, A. Etelapelto, and H. Rasku-Puttonen. 2000. "Collaborative Processes during Report Writing of a Science Learning Project: The Nature of Discourse as a Function of Ask Requirements." *European Journal of Psychology of Education* 15 (4): 455–66.

Brunk-Chavez, Beth, and Shawn J. Miller. 2007. "Decentered, Disconnected, and Digitized: The Importance of Shared Space." Kairos 11, no. 2.

EDUCAUSE Evolving Technologies Committee. 2013. "Course Management Systems (CMS)." *EDUCAUSE.edu*, October.

Malhotra, Arvind, and Ann Majchrzak. 2012. "How Virtual Teams Use Their Virtual Workspace to Coordinate Knowledge." *ACM Transactions on Management Information Systems* 3 (1): 1–14.

McConnell, D. 2006. "E-learning Groups and Communities." *British Journal of Educational Technology* 37 (6): 983–84.

New London Group. 1996. "A Pedagogy of Multiliteracies: Designing Social Futures." *Harvard Educational Review* 66 (1): 60–92.

Oliveira, Isolina, L. Tinoca, and A. Pereira. 2011. "Online Group Work Patterns: How to Promote a Successful Collaboration." *Computers & Education* 57 (1): 1348–57. http://dx.doi.org/10.1016/j.compedu.2011.01.017.

Paulus, T. 2005. "Collaboration or Cooperation? Analyzing Small Group Interactions in Educational Environments." In *Computer-Supported Collaborative Learning in Higher Education*, ed. T. Roberts, 100–124. Hershey, PA: The Idea Group. http://dx.doi.org/10.4018/978-1-59140-408-8.ch005.

Payne, Darin. 2000. "Collaborative Learning and Cultural Reproduction in Cyberspace: Publishing Students in Electronic Environments." *Journal of Electronic Publishing: JEP* 6 (1). http://dx.doi.org/10.3998/3336451.0006.109.

Selber, S. 2004. *Multiliteracies for a Digital Age*. Carbondale: Southern Illinois University Press.

Wang, Qiyun. 2010. "Using Online Shared Workspaces to Support Group Collaborative Learning." *Computers & Education* 55 (3): 1270–76. http://dx.doi.org/10.1016/j.compedu.2010.05.023.

9
COMMUNICATING WITH ADULT LEARNERS IN THE ONLINE WRITING LAB
A Call for Specialized Tutor Training for Adult Learners

Kimberley M. Holloway

INTRODUCTION

Using computers and the Internet to expand the space of the traditional writing center outside the physical walls of the center has become more common than it was a decade ago or even five years ago. Speculation on the causes of this phenomenon encompasses everything from the increased need of many students for remediation to administrators' concerns about the economy, which affects budgets and could lead to declining enrollments (Harris 2000a; Pemberton 2003). Whatever the reason, the fact is that the trend toward online writing centers or online writing labs (OWLs) is becoming the rule rather than the exception (Coogan 1999; Crump 2000; Harris, 2000b; Hobson 1998; Inman and Sewell 2000). At the same time that we have begun "wiring the writing center," as David Coogan says in his book on OWLS, *Electronic Writing Centers: Computing the Field of Composition,* we are also experiencing an influx of adult students who are taking classes in traditional and accelerated graduate and professional programs. These adult learners bring their own set of expectations and needs to higher education, and writing centers are no exception.

As a result of this move to expand to online venues, writing center directors have had to decide how to introduce OWLs to their writing centers in part as an effort to answer Cynthia Selfe's (1999) call to "turn our attention to technology and its general relationship to literacy education" (5). Writing center directors have also had to consider what many believe to be the negative aspects of the faceless, impersonal communication inherent in an OWL, worrying as Neil Postman (1992) does in *Technopoly: The Surrender of Culture to Technology* that in these new

DOI: 10.7330/9781607324850.c009

spaces, we will be in danger of "the deification of technology, which means that the culture seeks its authorization in technology, finds its satisfactions in technology, and takes its orders from technology" (71). Nevertheless, Purdue, which first introduced its OWL in 1994, "marked the beginning of an international movement to create web-accessible writing centers and WAC [Writing Across the Curriculum] programs" (Palmquist 2003, 403). In these early years of online writing centers, for we are certainly still in the initial stages of OWLs, we must find ways to effectively work with all students who use online services without losing the personal communication of the face-to-face (F2F) tutoring that is a strength of traditional writing centers. One way that we can address the concerns and needs of clients and tutors is to more deliberately train tutors to work with online clients of all kinds. Adult learners are one group of online clients who frequently use OWLs to obtain feedback on their papers, and their numbers in my own OWL are steadily rising. The traditional students who tutor in writing centers are sometimes not prepared to work with adult learners, who are usually older than the tutors and who bring to the session a strong focus, as well as anxiety, that traditional students often do not. As a result, tutors consult with their director more often about sessions with nontraditional students than those with traditional students, with whom they are usually more familiar. This situation suggests that we more deliberately train tutors to work with adult learners, to be aware of what they expect from a session, and to determine the best ways to work with them.

With this in mind, I performed a self-study of the OWL that I direct at King University, a Presbyterian, liberal arts university in northeast Tennessee. In this study, I compiled and analyzed the comments, questions, and requests that students who used our OWL included with their papers that tutors reviewed. The goal of this self-study was to help determine if specialized training is needed for undergraduate tutors to work with nontraditional students who use the OWL and what the focus might be if indeed tutors need this additional training.

NONTRADITIONAL STUDENTS ON CAMPUS

As Dickie Selfe (1995) points out in "Surfing the Tsunami: Electronic Environments in the Writing Center," beginning in the early 1990s the population of colleges and universities was changing; more students attended part time, more women were going to college, and "[o]lder students . . . [made up] an increasingly larger percentage of the student population" (316). He goes on to point out that these students usually have different kinds of responsibilities including jobs and families and "are often unable to commute to schools during the hours that many writing centers are available. As much as writing centers need to protect and develop their face-to-face interactive skills, they must also recognize that this very strength is a significant burden to a growing number of students" (316). Joanna Castner (2000) agrees, saying that "[t]he asynchronous nature of e-mail creates important advantages, especially for students who live off campus or who work most of their waking hours" (119). One way that writing center directors have addressed this "burden" has been to create an OWL to supplement their onground writing centers.

Colleges and universities, therefore, have been faced with determining the best ways to work with these students and address their needs, many of which are quite different from those of traditional students. Malcolm Knowles, Elwood Holton, and Richard Swanson, pioneers in the study of adult learning, posit that adult learners have specific characteristics and a different set of needs than do younger, traditional students. According to Knowles, Holton, and Swanson (2005), "[t]he six principles of andragogy are (1) the learner's need to know, (2) self-concept of the learner, (3) prior experience of the learner, (4) readiness to learn, (5) orientation to learning, and (6) motivation to learn" (3). While Knowles has revisited and revised his theories since they first appeared in the early 1970s, he still believes that teaching and working with this population of students must be approached differently from the way we teach more traditional students. Especially important in Knowles's principles are adult learners' motivation to learn and their more extensive life experiences. In my own writing center, tutors have sometimes felt unsure of how to work with adult learners who bring both focused motivation and life experience with them but also bring a high degree of anxiety about returning to school. These anxieties, in addition to a need for remediation, can make a tutoring session difficult. It is not surprising, then, that my tutors ask for assistance in these situations more than in any other.

Just as colleges and universities need to find ways to accommodate the needs of adult learners, writing centers and OWLs are also not immune to this need either. Tutors must be trained to work in F2F situations with different populations of students, and the same holds true for training students working in OWLs as well, maybe even more so. Because these students are, as Knowles has pointed out, ready and motivated to learn, while at the same time having less available time to visit campus writing centers, as Dickie Selfe (1995) has pointed out, OWLs have become their preferred, if not only, method of having papers reviewed. In my own OWL, for example, more Graduate and Professional Studies (GPS) students submit papers than do traditional students, with 180 GPS paper submissions in the three years of my study and only 118 submissions from traditional students during the same time frame. This fact led me to question whether there was a difference in the kinds of communication that GPS students had with my tutors as compared to the ways that they communicated with traditional students and to question whether, because of these students' attempts to dialogue with their tutors, my tutors needed more training. After all, because our campus was relatively small during the time of my study, though growing and thriving, most of my tutors knew or had classes with their clients who are traditional students. This was not, however, the case with the GPS students; these students are truly strangers to my tutors and bring with them a new set of anxieties and expectations that the tutors were not always prepared to address.

POTENTIAL COMMUNICATION PROBLEMS IN OWLS

The journey has not, however, been trouble-free for those writing center directors who have created online components for their writing centers, and many worry about the pedagogical value of OWLs. Ellen Mohr (1998), for example, worries about the potential for misunderstandings in OWL communications:

> I wonder how different the online messages are to the person-to-person dialogs taking place in 'real' centers. I think about how here on our JCCC [Johnson County Community College] listserv messages are consistently being misconstrued. A careless or thoughtless phrase, a sensitive reader, a general disregard for diversity and extent of audience can cause all sorts of problems such as hurt feelings, angry and hateful rebuttals, and new barriers to open communication. (161)

While Mohr's concerns are valid, specialized training for online tutors may help to solve this potential problem.

Michael Hammond (2000) used a communicative approach in his study of communication in online environments, and this approach has been useful in my own study. He writes that "[a] communicative approach is so called because it focuses on the exchange of information in order to cross an information gap" (258). When he analyzed certain communications posted by a particular student, he noted that the student was "trying to find a communicative voice" (259). In addition, in Diana Bell and Mike Hübler's study of virtual writing center communities, they write that they "classify computer technology as a social medium rather than a processing tool" (Bell and Hübler 2001, 57). Their study, which focused on developing ethos in email discourse, demonstrates that it is possible to dialogue in virtual areas such as OWLS. Students, especially adult nontraditional students using King University's OWL, are taking part in this kind of search for a communicative voice through the detail of their pre-review comments and their attempt to open a dialogue with their tutors. Thus, while communication may be difficult between student and tutor in an online environment, clearly many students in my OWL are finding ways to bridge the information gap. By examining the pre-review comments of adult learners using our OWL, I have come to believe that tutors would benefit from training that will help them to work specifically with this student population.

Not everyone believes, however, that OWLs foster communication between students and tutors. For instance, Castner questions the dialogic value of OWLs, saying that they go against the purpose of writing centers and concluding that asynchronous OWLs do not allow for dialogue. Chief among her reasons is that OWLs are not in line with the social constructivist thinking that most writing centers are based on because there is no collaborative dialogue involved in the communication, or, in a best case scenario, very little collaboration. However, some students, especially adult learners, seem to be finding ways to dialogue with their tutors. In the case of my OWL, in which we use Blackboard as the delivery system, adult learners use two primary ways to develop an ongoing conversation with tutors. First, they use the comment section of Blackboard to post questions and comments to tutors. These comments range from a simple mention of the topic of the paper or the class that it was written for to complete assignment directions with specific questions about both higher order concerns (HOCs) and lower order concerns (LOCs). A record of these comments and the answers to any questions are kept on file and appears on the FAQ page of the OWL. Second, some of these students resubmit papers one or more times, often with new questions, comments, or explanations.

Castner (2000) also points out that a potential problem in OWLs is that "[w]riting assignments can be hard to understand, and many factors complicate them further . . . Without dialogue between consultant and client, these complicating factors can keep the consultant from responding appropriately and/or keep clients from asking important questions" (125). This issue is, indeed, a potential problem that can hinder any real dialogue in an online tutoring session. My data suggests, however, that, though most undergraduates do not take steps to avoid this lack of dialogue, adult learners do attempt to communicate their instructors' requirements. In fact, 54.3 percent of the submissions from adult learners include either brief or detailed assignment requirements, while only 26.8 percent of the submissions from traditional students do. These adult learners are actively participating in the tutoring process by initiating communication with their tutors. As a result, tutors have a better idea how to respond to the students' assignments since they begin reading the work from a position of knowledge; they are able to focus more clearly on the potential problems in the paper and address those issues more effectively. When these tutors send comments back to the clients, the communication is more complete than if the tutor is commenting on the paper with no idea of the assignment requirements.

Another potential problem that Castner (2000) points out is that there is sometimes a disconnect between what the tutor knows and what the client does not know; terms such as "thesis," "organization," and "development" probably mean little to the client so that communication is hampered at the outset of an online session. She says that "clients struggle to articulate their writing-related questions" (126), therefore negating any chance for dialogic value in the online environment. While this is a legitimate concern for directors and tutors in OWLs, it does not seem to hold true in all cases. For example, nearly 42 percent of GPS students used words such as "thesis," and "development" in their pre-review requests that traditional students did. In addition, as Castner admits in this article, clients and tutors face this same issue in an F2F tutoring session just as online tutors do but states that only dialogue can help them overcome these potential misunderstandings. This idea raises the question of whether students are already working to overcome these difficulties through devices such as multiple submissions of the same paper or asking questions that the tutor then addresses in the reviewed paper. David A. Carlson and Eileen Apperson-Williams write that "Bohm (1996) reminded us that distance is an element of every discussion, even face to face" (Carlson and Apperson-Williams 2000, 7). In other words, there is a certain distance between the student/client and the tutor no matter the venue. The key seems to be the way in which that distance is closed. Tutor training designed to equip online tutors with techniques to overcome distance barriers in the online environment is one possible solution to this problem.

As for what this means for tutor training, Mark Shadle (2000) writes, "Overall, OWLs affect tutor training in complex and sometimes contradictory ways" (7). He points out that different OWL directors respond to this assertion in different ways: some say that the situation for OWLs is unique, and they approach tutor training as such; others say that they integrate onground theory and practice into their training for online tutors. Shadle then addresses the issues that ESL students have online, stating that there is "much to learn about online work with ESL students" (9) and their comfort levels in the online environment. I contend that the same might be said for nontraditional students: tutors must be trained to work with these students, who are often uncomfortable in cyberspace and who often do not speak the language of cyberspace. Many nontraditional students, who are digital immigrants rather than digital natives, are new to more than just higher education; many are uncomfortable using technology in general and are even more uncomfortable with the seemingly faceless online environment of computers, online classes, and OWLs. The less sure these students are of their skills in using computers and electronic communication, the more a possibility exists that they are also unsure of successfully communicating with a tutor online. Because of this possibility, writing center directors should consider steps they can take to address the needs of nontraditional students who use their OWLs. One such step is specialized training for all tutors.

While the mission of any writing center, online or onground, is to help students improve their writing skills, communication between the student and the tutor can mean the difference between a successful collaboration and an unsuccessful one. In fact, in OWLs, communication in writing begins before a tutor ever sees a student's paper. The ways that students compose messages to their tutors and the ways that the tutors respond to the messages can make a difference in the quality of the dialogue in an OWL. With this in mind, I began to study the kinds of messages that students posted with their papers when they used the OWL at King College (now King University as of July 2013) and discovered that these communications indicated more than just a mandate to study the ways students and tutors communicate. I determined that the most effective use of this data and my observations is to better train my tutors to work with a specific group of students: nontraditional, adult students. The resulting study led me to a paradigm shift in the way I approach tutor training for my OWL tutors.

BACKGROUND OF THE SELF-STUDY

When I became the director of King College's (now King University) writing center in 2003, I was tasked with making sure that all students were given the opportunity to work with tutors to improve their writing. While we had had a writing center for many years at King, this was the first time that a faculty member was given dedicated time to focus on and expand the writing center. When I began my job, I knew that one thing I would like to add was an online writing center. Between learning the ins and outs of my new responsibilities and teaching my classes, I considered this idea and how it could be implemented as soon as was feasible.

However, as I was considering adding this new dimension to our writing center, another issue was on my mind: the growing population of nontraditional adult students entering our graduate and professional programs. These students often lacked confidence in their writing skills because it had been years, decades for some, since they had completed writing assignments. In addition, many of these students attended class on one of our satellite campuses in the region and were not able to come to the main campus. Coupled with this new population of students eager to receive the help of writing tutors was that at the time our writing center was located only on the main campus in Bristol, Tennessee, and that all of the students I employed were undergraduates.[1] Because the only option we had in this time of growth was for the tutors to work on the main campus, I had to find another way to deliver our services to our nontraditional student population. An online writing center seemed to be the best option we had. In 2006, I decided that, with our growing population of GPS students, it was time to add an online component to our writing center. I felt ready to take the beginning steps in adapting our writing center to the influx of nontraditional students in both our traditional and GPS programs.

I decided to use our already-established Blackboard site as the home of the new online writing center. This decision was based on the premise that starting an online writing center was, at least at this stage, experimental and the fact that students were already familiar with Blackboard. This arrangement worked well for us, and we were able open the site for online tutoring. Since November of 2006, we have offered tutoring services for all students: traditional and nontraditional, online or onground. As I was sifting through the data from my writing center early in the 2009 Fall Semester, I began to notice a distinct trend in the comments students were making when they submitted their work to the OWL. In my initial data collection and analysis, I simply noticed that some students wrote longer, more detailed comments to the tutors than others did. Upon further analysis, however, I realized that the students who submitted the longest, most detailed comments were students in King's Quest program. The Quest program is for GPS students who need humanities credit in order to receive their degree from King. During this time, Quest is composed of four humanities-based classes: The Quest for Community, The Quest for Self, The Quest for Stewardship, and The Quest for Career and Vocation. These classes, taught by a variety of faculty in the College of Arts and Sciences, required students who were either part of the Register Nurse to Bachelor of Science in Nursing program or students in our Bachelor of Business Administration (BBA) program to write several long papers over the course of the semester. Because I teach classes in the Quest Program, I immediately recognized students' names, assignment topics, or professors' names and knew that many of these papers were from GPS students. Even a cursory look at the comments from these students showed me that nearly all of the students writing more detailed requests were GPS students. At this point, I knew that further research and data analysis would be necessary to understand the significance of my findings.

METHOD AND RESULTS OF THE SELF-STUDY

The data for my self-study were taken from OWL submissions between November 2006 and December 2009. During that time King's OWL received 307 paper submissions, with 189 of the submissions coming from students in the GPS and 118 submissions coming from students in the traditional undergraduate program. The fact that over 60 percent of the submissions we received were from GPS students during this time period was significant in several ways. First, I was surprised that only 38 percent of the submissions were from traditional students, who were required to take several writing intensive classes as part of the core curriculum and, for many, their major area of study. Second, during the first two years of this time period, more traditional students were enrolled at King than graduate students. That so many more graduate students were submitting to the OWL made me wonder what I should make of the situation. Based on this information, it would seem that a best practice for writing center directors would be to train undergraduate tutors in the best way to dialogue with nontraditional students, who are usually older than the tutors and who have different goals for and expectations of their education. I started by compiling data from my Blackboard records and dividing them into two main charts: GPS students and traditional students. I also included the students' comments, which are recorded on the Blackboard submission page, to the tutors. I then made a note of the kinds of pre-review comments that each student posted with his or her submission. These comments fit into five main divisions: specific requests, general requests, submissions that included both general and specific requests, other comments, and no comments. As I analyzed and charted the data, I found that some of what I saw fit my expectations; for example, based on my experiences with my onground writing center, I thought that more women than men would submit assignments and found this to be true: 76.6 percent of the submissions were from women, 14.3 percent were from men, and 9.1 percent were unreported. However, much of what I learned was not expected. In addition, knowing that OWLs are controversial, I wanted to see if the service we were providing our clients was what they needed. The data I had gathered led me to the conclusion that I should focus more on OWL tutor training for adult learners.

Specific Pre-Review Requests from GPS and Traditional Students by Type of Question

The data concerning the specific pre-review comments presented me with me my first surprise. While the GPS students did request help with grammar and formatting a significant number of times, the data I analyzed shows that traditional students were actually more interested in these issues than the graduates, with 82.7 percent of traditional students asking for help in these areas and 58.1 percent of the GPS asking for the same kinds of help. The fact that significantly more than 50 percent of all submissions requested help in grammar and formatting reinforced the kinds of training that I was already doing with my tutors. I was also surprised to find that a much higher percentage of GPS students requested specific writing guidance, including thesis statements, organization, and development, than traditional students. In fact, nearly 42 percent of the GPS students requested these higher order concerns (HOCs), while only 17.4 percent of the traditional students requested this kind of help. That GPS students were more concerned with HOCs issues bolstered my belief that I must train my tutors more deliberately to specifically address these problems for GPS students and for any traditional students requesting this kind of advice.

General Pre-Review Requests from GPS and Traditional Students by Specific Questions

GPS students also made more general pre-review requests/comments such as giving assignment directions, specifying which class or program the paper was written for, asking for a "review" or "proofreading," and other miscellaneous comments. Comments asking for a "review" or

Table 9.1. Specific Pre-Review Requests from GPS and Traditional Students by Type of Question

Comment	GPS		Traditional	
Format (APA, MLA, memo, etc.)	28	(45.2%)	14	(60.9%)
Grammar	8	(12.9%)	5	(21.7%)
General Writing	26	(41.9%)	4	(17.4%)
Total submissions with these requests	62		23	

"proofreading" indicate that the student either did not understand the services provided (proofreading requests) or had no specific questions or problems in mind (review requests). GPS students, for instance, were more likely to include assignment directions with their papers; over 35 percent of GPS students provided the tutor with assignment directions, while only 22 percent of traditional students included the directions.

One statistic showed that traditional students were much more likely to tell the tutor which class, professor, or program the paper was written for. My data shows that 40 percent of traditional students felt that this information was necessary, while only 6.6 percent of GPS students included this information. In this case, the traditional students seemed to be communicating with their tutors using the shorthand of giving them this class information, assuming that the tutor would understand what was necessary; very few GPS students made this assumption. Instead, they preferred to give tutors specific assignment details and writing requests.

The gap between the percentage of GPS students and traditional students posting miscellaneous questions and comments was not as significant as for those submitting general requests and comments. With 18 percent of GPS students and 12 percent of traditional students including this information, it is clear that some students in both groups believed that they needed some kind of dialogue with the tutor. These comments include explaining the kinds of revisions they made on a draft, asking for advice on specific problems they had encountered, asking questions about the review/submission process, and reporting problems with the system.

Both General and Specific Pre-Review Requests

Some students used the comments feature of Blackboard more extensively, giving the tutor as much information as possible to work with. By posting both general requests/comments and asking specific questions

Table 9.2. General Pre-Review Requests from GPS and Traditional Students by Specific Questions

Comment	GPS		Traditional	
Greets tutors	23	(10.7%)	1	(1.2%)
Expresses appreciation and/or thanks	122	(56.5%)	51	(60.0%)
Uses "please"	15	(6.9%)	5	(5.9%)
Complimentary close	9	(4.2%)	0	(0.0%)
Signs	63	(29.2%)	10	(11.8%)
Other comments	21	(9.7%)	27	(31.8%)
Total submissions with these elements	216		85	

about their writing, their grammar, or their formatting, these students actively initiated a dialogue in which they are attempting to provide the tutor with the best possible information to use while reviewing the paper. Considerably more GPS students took this step, 15.3 percent as compared to 4.2 percent of traditional students, demonstrating that training my tutors to read these requests and comments carefully so that they can respond in the best way is a revision that I should make in my online tutor training sessions.

Like Castner (2000), I wondered if we would be able to provide adequate tutoring to students, especially adult students, who used our OWL. In considering this question, Castner writes, "When clients ask me to edit their papers through email, I always wonder if they have other questions, but cannot articulate them" (126). I found that nearly 9 percent of GPS students and nearly 10 percent of traditional students ask for editing or revising as well posting other questions. Since just over 15 percent of the GPS students make other kinds of requests in addition to the general "reviewing" or "revising" questions that either add to or clarify what they need, I believe that GPS students are making efforts to communicate with their tutors by including as much information as possible. Including both specific and general requests seems to be one way that they are accomplishing this goal.

No Pre-Review Notes

On the other hand, some students did not take advantage of their ability to give the tutor any information about the paper that would be reviewed. Traditional students were much more likely to simply submit their papers with no requests or comments than were GPS students. Adult learners, then, seem to be more interested in communicating with the tutors who will be reading and reviewing their papers and in providing them with as much information as possible to complete the review. Knowles points to the fact that adult learners take charge of their educational experience in ways such as this is not surprising. This is one indication that tutors working with the GPS students in my OWL need more specialized training to work with adult learners who submit papers to our OWL. Training the tutors to continue the dialogue that adult learners begin, then, is a key consideration in the way that I should train my OWL tutors.

Miscellaneous Requests and Comments Made by GPS and Traditional Students

Even more interesting are the statistics showing the percentage of GPS students who included other kinds of comments and requests with their submissions, 216 GPS submissions as compared to only 85 submissions from traditional students. I was especially interested in the comments in which students expressed appreciation for the service and those including assignment directions. By including these comments and requests, students were taking the first steps in starting a dialogue with their tutors, in effect taking the lead in the tutor/client relationship. When coupled with including assignment directions or asking other questions, the student initiated the conversation and worked to establish a more personal tutoring relationship, more akin to what they would experience in an F2F session.

GPS students were more likely to try to establish a dialogue using these techniques than traditional students. However, traditional students expressed their appreciation or thanked the tutor for helping them in 60 percent of the submissions, and 56.5 percent of GPS students did the same, a statistically insignificant difference. However, as table 9.3 shows, many more GPS students than traditional students signed their submissions, 29.2 percent as compared to 11.8 percent of traditional students, and they were much more likely to greet the tutor and thus establish a more personal relationship.

CONCLUSIONS

The growing number of adult students in addition to the new kinds of services, such as OWLs, that writing centers offer indicate that tutors must be knowledgeable about the needs of nontraditional learners, especially those who submit papers via the OWL. Daniel Wagner and Richard Venezky have pointed out that "[t]here is a major need to develop structures that enable administrators, teachers, and tutors to

Table 9.3. Miscellaneous Requests and Comments Made by GPS and Traditional Students

Comment	GPS		Traditional	
Greets tutors	23	(10.7%)	1	(1.2%)
Expresses appreciation and/or thanks	122	(56.5%)	51	(60.0%)
Uses "please"	15	(6.9%)	5	(5.9%)
Complimentary close	9	(4.2%)	0	(0.0%)
Signs	63	(29.2%)	10	(11.8%)
Other comments	21	(9.7%)	27	(31.8%)
Total submissions with these elements	216		85	

make professional staff training and development an ongoing process" (Wagner and Venezky 1999, 25), and writing center professionals who train online tutors should keep this call in mind. The data from my own OWL demonstrates that adult learners are significantly more interested in communicating with their tutors and take steps in many cases to initiate a dialogue with them. When students post notes with specific requests, include complete assignment directions, and resubmit assignments, they are interested in giving the tutors as much information as they believe is necessary for the tutor to help them to improve their writing. When students greet tutors, express their appreciation, and sign their comments, they are attempting to establish a friendly working relationship with them. While this study shows that both traditional and nontraditional students do all of these things, it also shows that nontraditional students are significantly more likely to attempt to communicate and dialogue with their tutors in these significant ways.

Even though writing center directors train tutors to work with students by addressing both HOCs and LOCs concerns and also provide additional training to help tutors work with specific populations of clients such as ESL students, they must also begin to provide specialized tutoring for adult, nontraditional students. The data and the student tutoring logs in which tutors expressed concern over their tutoring sessions with adult students gathered in this study, point to the need for all tutors, online and onground, to be better prepared to work with these highly motivated but often underprepared students.

In addition, Castner (2000), in her study of the students in two of her classes who were required to use the online writing center, asked them if they did or did not email further questions to their online tutors and found that 16 of 29 students (55 percent) felt that they needed further dialogue with the tutor. She writes that her "students' responses suggest that more than half of them may need extended dialogue" (121). Castner's experience explains what many writing center directors have noticed in their experience with the adult, nontraditional students who submit papers to an OWL. Students who submit papers multiple times are attempting to further their dialogue with the tutor, though this may be true partly because tutors are trained to place notes on students' papers telling the students to contact them if they have other questions.

Ann Hager Moser (2008) suggests in her doctoral dissertation, *Theories, Techniques, and the Impacts of Computer-Mediated Conferencing in a University Writing Center: Toward a Model for Training Programs,* that "[s]tudents should be encouraged to begin creating metaphors of online tutoring, connecting those to their developing ideas about pedagogy, and they should work on constructing philosophies for CM [computer mediated] conferencing" (128). The data in this study suggests that writing center directors begin incorporating these needed adjustments to online tutor training sessions. As directors take steps to train their online tutors, they should keep in mind that they must be aware of the specific needs and expectations of adult students. Taking the time to acquaint tutors with theories of adult learning, such as Knowles's principles of adult students, will help them to better understand their nontraditional clients and make their work with them easier and more satisfying for both the tutor and the client. Tutors need to know that adult learners are not just older than they are, but that they are also just as nervous about their assignments and grades as the traditional students that the tutors know well. Incorporating this kind of information into their training helps tutors to see that, because these students are focused and goal-oriented, knowledge about nontraditional students and their learning strategies can lead to better, more productive tutoring sessions.

Writing center directors also need to train their online tutors on the importance of continuing the dialogue that their online clients initiate. Tutors do this by inviting their clients to email them if they have any other questions or concerns. Because dialogue is a key ingredient in tutoring sessions, the same must be true of online tutoring sessions as well. Tutors must be trained to open the way for better communication with their clients. Training them to use questions and invitations to further discuss a paper has helped tutors to make a concerted effort to continue the conversation as long as it is necessary. Writing center directors can also work with tutors on improving their skills in further cultivating and maintaining a dialogue with their online clients. Guided practice with nontraditional students and other learning opportunities, such as reading and applying theory and taking part in active research projects with writing center directors, can also help tutors to see the value of a strong dialogue with these tutees.

However, training tutors to work with adult students requires more than a simple session or two in which tutors are introduced to the characteristics and needs of adult students; they also need to complete a series of practice sessions with nontraditional students who have volunteered to help with this exercise. A multi-part training session for tutors working with nontraditional students online and onground should begin with reading excerpts from well-known texts on andragogy. Knowles's *The Adult Learner: The Definitive Classic in Adult Education and Human Resource Development* is a key text for understanding adult learners, but other articles about working with adult learners can be added to this classic (Knowles, Holton, and Swanson 2005). In further sessions, tutors should work with volunteer nontraditional tutees in both F2F and online sessions. Tutors in my writing center find that, after they have read theories about adult learning, the training sessions with these nontraditional students are more productive because of this background knowledge, and the practice with these tutees reinforces this knowledge.

Finally, writing center directors need to challenge their online tutors to remember that they are first and foremost tutors. This means that they are the client's first reader and, therefore, are responsible to help their clients to step away from what they have written and look critically at their own work in order to become better writers. As David Coogan (1999) writes, "email 'tutoring' encourage[s] a creative fissure between the self who wrote the paper and the self who wrote the email messages, allowing the student and, in some cases, the tutor, to explore alternative subject-positions in writing" (99). With well-trained tutors, the online environment can supply a space for this kind of work to happen.

While this study was limited to a relatively new OWL, and many students had yet to use it, it has brought up new questions for consideration. For example, a useful study would be to analyze the same data in a comparison of F2F sessions and online sessions. Understanding the differences or similarities between these two kinds of tutoring would also help me to more effectively train tutors in both F2F and online situations. Conducting a more extensive linguistic study of the pre-review comments of adult learners and other communications between learner and tutor would also shed light on the best ways to train tutors to work with their nontraditional clients.

Online writing centers are still in the early stages of their history, and all writing center directors must continue to analyze and study their own centers. Even a relatively new OWL can give other writing center directors ideas about those potential problems and potential strengths that must be addressed in the ways they run their OWLS and the ways that they train their tutors. Technology, programs, and student populations are constantly changing, and writing center professionals must be ready to revisit and revise their current practices as they strive to provide students with the best service possible.

Note

1. At the time of the publication of this essay, I have added both two master's-prepared Assistant Writing Center Managers and Writing Fellows to help address this issue.

References

Bell, Diana C., and Mike T. Hübler. 2001. "The Virtual Writing Center: Developing Ethos through Mailing List Discourse." *Writing Center Journal* 21 (2): 57–78.

Bohm, D. 1996. *On Dialogue.* London: Routledge.

Carlson, David A., and Eileen Apperson-Williams. 2000. "The Anxieties of Distance: Online Tutors Reflect." In *Taking Flight with OWLS: Examining Electronic Writing Center Work,* ed. James A. Inman and Donna N. Sewell, 129–39. Mahwah, NJ: Lawrence Erlbaum Associates.

Castner, Joanna. 2000. "The Asynchronous, Online Writing Session: A Two-Way Stab in the Dark." In *Taking Flight with OWLS: Examining Electronic Writing Center Work,* ed. James A. Inman and Donna N. Sewell, 119–28. Mahwah, NJ: Lawrence Erlbaum Associates.

Coogan, David. 1999. *Electronic Writing Centers: Computing the Field of Composition.* Stamford, CT: Ablex Publishing.

Crump, Eric. 2000. "How Many Technoprovocateurs Does It Take to Create Interversity." In *Taking Flight with OWLS: Examining Electronic Writing Center Work,* ed. James A. Inman and Donna N. Sewell, 223–33. Mahwah, NJ: Lawrence Erlbaum Associates.

Hammond, Michael. 2000. "Communication Within On-Line Forums: The Opportunities, the Constraints and the Value of a Communicative Approach." *Computers & Education* 35 (4): 251–62. http://dx.doi.org/10.1016/S0360-1315(00)00037-3.

Harris, Muriel. 2000a. "Making up Tomorrow's Agenda and Shopping Lists Today: Preparing for Future Technologies in Writing Centers." In *Taking Flight with OWLS: Examining Electronic Writing Center Work,* ed. James A. Inman and Donna N. Sewell, 193–202. Mahwah, NJ: Lawrence Erlbaum Associates.

Harris, Muriel. 2000b. "Preparing to Sit at the Head Table: Maintaining Writing Center Viability in the Twenty-First Century." *Writing Center Journal* 20 (2): 13–22.

Hobson, Eric H. 1998. "Straddling the Virtual Fence." In *Wiring the Writing Center,* ed. Eric H. Hobson, ix–xxvi. Logan: Utah State University Press.

Inman, James A., and Donna N. Sewell. 2000. "The Hatching of Taking Flight with OWLS: Promise and Possibilities." In *Taking Flight with OWLS: Examining Electronic Writing Center Work,* ed. James A. Inman and Donna N. Sewell, xix–xxiii. Mahwah, NJ: Lawrence Erlbaum Associates.

Knowles, Malcolm S., Elwood F. Holton, III, and Richard A. Swanson. 2005. *The Adult Learner: The Definitive Classic in Adult Education and Human Resource Development.* 6th ed. San Diego: Elsevier.

Mohr, Ellen. 1998. "The Community College Mission and the Electronic Writing Center." In *Wiring the Writing Center*, ed. Eric H. Hobson, 151–62. Logan: Utah State University Press.

Moser, Ann H. 2008. "Theories, Techniques, and the Impacts of Computer-Mediated Conferencing in a University Writing Center: Toward a Model for Training Programs." PhD diss., Virginia Polytechnic Institute and State University. Accessed January 10, 2010, from Digital Library and Archives, ETDS@vt.

Palmquist, Mike. 2003. "A Brief History of Computer Support for Writing Centers and Writing-Across-the-Curriculum Programs." *Computers and Composition* 20 (4): 395–413. http://dx.doi.org/10.1016/j.compcom.2003.08.013.

Pemberton, Michael A. 2003. "Planning for Hypertexts in the Writing Center . . . or Not." *Writing Center Journal* 24 (1): 9–24.

Postman, Neil. 1992. *Technopoly: The Surrender of Culture to Technology.* New York: Vintage Books.

Selfe, Cynthia L. 1999. *Technology and Literacy in the Twenty-First Century: The Importance of Paying Attention.* Carbondale: Southern Illinois University Press.

Selfe, Dickie. 1995. "Surfing the Tsunami: Electronic Environments in the Writing Center." *Computers and Composition* 12 (3): 311–22. http://dx.doi.org/10.1016/S8755-4615(05)80070-2.

Shadle, Mark. 2000. "The Spotted OWL: Online Writing Labs as Sites of Diversity, Controversy, and Identity." In *Taking Flight with OWLS: Examining Electronic Writing Center Work*, ed. James A. Inman and Donna N. Sewell, 3–15. Mahwah, NJ: Lawrence Erlbaum Associates.

Wagner, Daniel A., and Richard L. Venezky. 1999. "Adult Literacy: The Next Generation." *Educational Researcher* 28 (1): 21–29. http://dx.doi.org/10.3102/0013189X028001021.

PART THREE

MOOCs

10
MOOC MANIA?
Bridging the Gap between the Rhetoric
and Reality of Online Learning

Kristine L. Blair

For *The New York Times*, 2012 was "The Year of the MOOC," or the Massive Open Online Course. Even as the MOOCs have been identified by *The Times* and other forums as the next big thing in teaching and learning, for many of us in rhetoric and composition, the emphasis on fully online learning among genuinely distance students is still the exception rather than the rule. Despite our focus on integrating digital composing tools into the writing process, and the need for current faculty and future faculty training to make this integration an effective one, distance learning is often relegated to a few special issues in disciplinary journals such as *Computers and Composition,* a limited number of edited collections or how to treatments, or a topic frequently addressed in more interdisciplinary venues. Thus, it is ironic that both the academy and the larger culture is discussing the pros and cons of MOOCs as "the next big thing" when most faculty, if they have actually taught online, are often forced to do so whether they want to or not. I address this gap between rhetoric and reality by examining larger rhetorics of online learning, including those of access, democracy, and convenience, to question the impact of those rhetorics on the development of online learning. Grounding these rhetorics in the ongoing national debate about MOOCs, I call for conversations among university administrators and writing faculty to ensure we're not integrating online learning technologies for their own sake, but rather because they provide a range of learning opportunities with institutional structures that support and reward faculty for their innovation and labor. In this way, quality online instruction results from ongoing critical dialogue among administrators, faculty and students, allowing

DOI: 10.7330/9781607324850.c010

online learning to become a form of curricular engagement that better serves our local and global communities.

In her introduction to the June 2013 *CCC* Symposium on MOOCs, editor Kathleen Blake Yancey appropriately acknowledges rhetoric and composition's thirty-plus years of "attending to the technologies associated with composing and the teaching of composing" (Yancey 2013, 688). These early discussions of technology in the writing classroom celebrated its utopic potential; computers would not only improve the quality of student writing through an emphasis on process as opposed to product but also empower students though their access to online forums that would better equalize participation than their face-to-face counterparts, leading to students' overall professional success in college and beyond. This technological promise is as strong today as ever, and not only for writing studies. As I write this sentence on a Tuesday evening in August 2013, a commercial for Southern New Hampshire University appears on the television screen, pledging through its 180 online programs to make higher education accessible and affordable for all. Similarly, University of California, Los Angeles's (UCLA) Online Extension marketing campaign asks: "What do you get when you combine one of the nation's most elite universities with a revolutionary online learning environment? You get Empowered" (UCLA 2013). UCLA's advertising includes both web and television segments featuring successful program completers, along with instantly recognizable celebrities such as Sally Field, Pierce Brosnan, Cuba Gooding, Jr., and the late James Gandolfini.

Given larger cultural rhetorics of technology that are aligned with metaphors of access, innovation, and progress, it is not surprising that similar metaphors would infuse academia, particularly the illusion of 24/7, anytime anywhere virtual "learning communities" (Palloff and Pratt 2007). Despite these overly positive depictions of technology's impact, then and now, our own field has shifted toward a more critical cultural perspective that challenges the assumption that individuals and classrooms are empowered by sheer virtue of technology itself, and recognizes that the same structures of inequity and intolerance can occur just as frequently online as off. While these dynamics have often been addressed along the axis of race, gender, and sexuality, there can be other structures of access and inequality in today's online educational settings. As a former department chair and someone who has taught fully online courses, I also recognize the importance of online delivery in meeting the professional and personal needs of placebound, nontraditional college-age students who often work full time, raise families, care for aging parents, and have to commute long distances for day-time or evening classes. Very often these dynamics are gendered. As Cheris Kramarae (2001) notes in *The Third Shift: Women Learning Online:* "Many women balance job, community, and heavy family responsibilities against their academic work. They often have more serious financial burdens. Traditionally they have grappled with these difficulties while also facing inflexible class schedules and academic policies, inadequate childcare, lack of appropriate housing, and lack of reliable transportation" (5). Even with the increase in online courses to meet such students' needs, we frequently presume computer access when there is often lack of reliable access for a range of online students. Some students may retrieve course content from a machine at work and find a firewall, or may only be able to access a computer from a local public library, in part because the equipment they own or don't own at home is not sufficiently equipped.

Equally important concerns have focused on the material and political conditions surrounding the promotion of online learning and the increased tuition dollars that may be driving the growth of programs, impacting the academic labor and intellectual property of faculty. While these academic labor issues span the disciplines, they are compounded in rhetoric and composition in part because of the time-intensive nature of responding to multiple drafts of student writing as well as the contingent status of the many adjunct and graduate student instructors teaching writing at both the community college and university level. Because of the changing technologies—from the pen to the typewriter to the computer and now to mobile and handheld devices—that have impacted contemporary writing instruction, it has been vital that rhetoric and composition faculty "pay attention" (Selfe 1999) to the rhetorics of access surrounding technology. For Selfe, this attention includes understanding "how technology is now inextricably linked to literacy and literacy education in this country . . . we must help colleagues, students, administrators, politicians, and other Americans gain some increasingly critical and productive perspective on technological literacy" (24). Part of the process also involves opportunities for experimentation with the latest technologies both inside and outside the writing classroom, leading to even further academic labor concerns as the technology itself advances more rapidly than either policy or pedagogy, often involving a planned obsolescence of tools that have us swapping out cellphones, laptops, and other devices for newer, faster, better models, whether we need them or not.

The same can be said of online teaching tools, however, as the rush to technologize in the name of progress is a full-time job for those marketing and communication specialists who use social media to recruit students. It is natural that as our field has evolved from early product-based, computer-assisted approaches to writing instruction to digital pedagogies that mediate literate activity and identity (Hawisher et al. 1996, 83, 149), we have witnessed the shift from local area networks to wide area networks, from Web 1.0 to Web 2.0, and from the floppy disk to the USB drive that stores gigabytes over megabytes. The most prominent shift has been to learning or course management systems, and over the last decade, we have also witnessed a war of sorts in which platforms such as WebCT or Blackboard fight for dominance, with Blackboard winning that battle, only to be challenged by smaller, less well-known armies of tools from Desire2Learn to Canvas. Certainly, the rise of the course management system is tied not only to the rise of technology-infused teaching and learning across the disciplines but also to the shift to more diverse student populations. These populations have challenged our traditional understanding of a residential, brick and mortar classroom in favor of those virtual classrooms that can accommodate more students in ways that foster degree completion and increase tuition dollars. Even as more and more classes go online, relying on the institutionally supported course management system, or even the use of Web 2.0 tools from blogs, to wikis, to Facebook and Twitter, many faculty are engaged in constant debate with administrators about the constraints of online education, often arguing from a presumption of loss that an online course and the students who enroll in it cannot compare to a course in real time. To counter this concern, faculty development units have often partnered with educational technology services to support faculty making that transition, ready or not. Into this context enters the MOOC.

Like many writing faculty, I have struggled to keep up with literacy technologies even as I juggle with competing roles as a department chair, a graduate educator, and a journal editor. As someone who has also conducted a number of campus and off campus professional development workshops for faculty new to online teaching, I am aware of that need for "ramp time," or the opportunity to experiment with various tools and even to take the plunge and enroll in an online course prior to actually teaching one. Fortunately, as many colleges dive into the online learning enterprise, they often provide online training courses for the faculty themselves, buying into the adage that online teachers should be online students. Nevertheless, MOOCs represent an entirely new and different technological, curricular, and financial enterprise, and until roughly a year ago, not something with which many academic administrators, or many rhetoric and composition specialists for that matter, were familiar. Nevertheless, it was embarrassing for me when an emeritus faculty member in my unit emailed the Vice President for Academic Technology and me to rave about his experience in a MOOC and to solicit our opinions. As a department administrator, what was English's position on MOOCs? But at the time, what did I actually know about MOOCs? Admittedly, not much more than the larger national conversation that touted the potential democratic advantages to such learning environments, conversations not all that different from those earlier rhetorics of technology surrounding the integration of computers into the writing curriculum. As we have learned more about MOOCs from both a teacher and a student perspective, a number of conversations have become more critical as well.

As Steven Krause (2013) reflects on his experience as a student in a MOOC, "Listening to World Music was content without teaching; it felt less like being in a lecture hall and more like watching a cooking show . . . But I don't want to conclude by leaving the impression that MOOCs are a fad doomed for failure . . . Coursera and other MOOC providers are in the experimental stages and are still trying to discover and invent effective pedagogies" (694). But how do these "effective pedagogies" manifest themselves in a MOOC environment, and how possible is it to sustain them in light of the thousands who may initially enroll and the minuscule percentage of those who actually complete? Krause has helped to foster national dialogue among rhetoric and composition specialists in his co-edited collection *Invasion of the MOOCs: The Promise and Perils of Open Online Courses* (Krause and Lowe 2014). My own experience in a Coursera MOOC from Duke University titled "Think Again: How To Reason and Argue" was similar to Krause's. I enrolled more to see what all the fuss was about and found myself in a course of over forty thousand. In the welcoming message from the Coursera "Course Staff," one specific tip was that "You will get more out of the course if you share the adventure, so we suggest that you encourage a few friends and family to take the course with you." Given the large numbers of participants, there is little evidence that having people you know to bond with would counter any potential feelings of isolation in being in a discussion forum of thousands from around the world. Nevertheless, the goal of the instructors was that 30 percent of the thousands enrolled complete the course, and if that quota were met, the primary instructor offered to shave his head. The other goal I suspect was that the 30 percent or more buy the book that was recommended for the course, which just happened to be written by the instructor himself. After four weeks of listening to short video lectures, completing exercises, and taking a first quiz, I became a negative retention statistic. Admittedly, I had not chosen a topic that was of genuine interest but was instead easily accessible. This, combined with teacher-centered delivery models and thousands of people attempting to converse in a discussion board, deterred me from engaging with the teacher and with fellow students. I had no motivation to continue.

But clearly others do. Perhaps what makes MOOCs so intriguing inside and outside the academy is their presumed ability to bridge the gap between the two. In their cross between content management system and social networking, MOOC platforms such as Coursera, Udacity, and EdEx adopt a crowdsourcing model to learning course content and assessing student work. While the typical MOOC is not credit bearing, course completers earn a certificate, that while not the same as a degree, nevertheless can carry credence in a larger culture of professional advancement that values "certification" and "benchmarking" in ways that are impacting the academy. For instance, in a recent Webinar I conducted in November 2012 for Cengage about online learning, at the end of the session, a number of faculty participants queried about their certificates of completion. As adjunct faculty or those employed in other college settings where skills in teaching online may soon be tied to job security, the exigency for proof and/or reward for their time and effort is understandable. Moreover, such a process is similar to the badging and leveling models common to many game-based environments, which some educational theorists claim have a motivation potential that is equally powerful to a letter grade. Gaming literacies scholar James Gee (2005) refers to this as "The Achievement Principle," or the idea that "for learners of all levels of skill there are . . . rewards from the beginning, customized to each learner's level, effort, and growing mastery and signaling the learner's ongoing achievements" (67).

Naturally, such certification processes carry extra cache if they represent the academic branding of institutions like Harvard, Stanford, or the University of Michigan. Hence, another reason for the MOOC's popularity is the presumed global democratic access to the greatest minds in the twenty-first century academy. A review of Coursera partners reveals an impressive range of top-tier institutions and curriculum from Virology at Columbia to Engineering Mechanics at Georgia Tech. As a recent Educause (2013) Executive Briefing "What Campus Leaders Need to Know about MOOCs," early forays into MOOCs have primarily included disciplines that rely more on quantitative as opposed to qualitative assessment, a model consistent with the large lecture classes of the brick and mortar classroom. Other elements that correspond with this model include the typical "talking head" video lecture as well as the small study group session, which, instead of being led by an instructional assistant, are led by the students themselves, and in a MOOC environment are optional. As a result, the typical MOOC is a remediation of familiar teacher-centered genres, and admittedly, in light of the thousands that enroll, the possibility that they could be more student-centered, or encourage reflective activity through writing, may be utopic at this point. For Krause, the fact that writing prompts were never reviewed by the instructor of his "Listening to World Music" course but by fellow students, and that they were not "graded," impacted his overall motivation to spend significant time on them.

Although MOOCs may be new, student motivation issues are not. As Cheryl Hoy and I reported in our experience teaching online sections of intermediate writing for adult learners (Blair and Hoy 2006), very often students register for the online classes with the same end in mind, successful course completion, but the means may be very different, with some students actively participating in the learning community structure the instructor has constructed and others preferring a more correspondence school approach where they may work ahead and communicate less frequently with other students. As we experienced, both types of students were equally successful, but clearly the common variable was a motivation to see completion of the course as another means to an end in terms of competencies developed and credentials garnered. And very often, the factor that helped those students in the middle of this binary was the ability to maintain consistent contact with the instructor, typically through individual email, representing a vital form of interpersonal communication typical of quality teaching and learning, and a facet of most writing courses, both online and off.

It is our collective value of this type of student-teacher interaction that has led to concerns about the pedagogical benefits of MOOCs across the curriculum. In 2012 it have been the year of the MOOCs, and perhaps 2013 still is because of the debate surrounding them, but the balance between institutions signing with MOOC providers like Coursera and those expressing a healthy and public skepticism is shifting. Part of this shift is likely due to the increasing opportunity for MOOC courses to become credit bearing. A notable example is San Jose State University, who has recently suspended its pilot partnership with the MOOC provider Udacity. In "The Unexpected Resistance to MOOCs," Rachelle DeJong (2013) reports that "Of 3,500 [San Jose State University] students taking the Udacity math courses, the 100 credit-seeking enrollees found the courses too rushed, too reliant on the Internet, and too impersonal." Related issues involve scalability, which lead to the cancelation of a Coursera MOOC titled "Fundamentals of Online Education" when the use of Google tools for course communication simply couldn't sustain the group participation of the forty thousand plus participants (Jaschik 2013b).

Similar concerns have manifested themselves among writing studies specialists as well. Just as Yancey has devoted pages in *CCC* to first-hand discussions of MOOC learning, and just as schools that include The Ohio State University and Duke University have received Gates Foundation funding to develop and deliver MOOC writing courses through Coursera, the emerging consensus is that the typical MOOC experience is less conducive to the delivery of effective writing instruction. As the recent SUNY (State University of New York) Council on Writing's (2013) "Resolution on Massive Open Online Courses and the Teaching of Writing" powerfully states:

> Interactive work with student writers is at the center of our pedagogy, as many decades of scholarship in our field confirms it should be. We believe that the impossibility of this sort of mentorship in MOOC settings is likely responsible for their very high student attrition rates and frequently superficial levels of participation. For these reasons, the SUNYCoW [SUNY Council on Writing] opposes the prospect that MOOCs—or any other form of massive-scale instruction—might be accepted for credit in writing.

The SUNY Resolution and i-petition responds, in part, to the recent Open SUNY partnership between the institution and Coursera, which, as *The Times* reported, is not only designed to increase new student enrollments to over one hundred thousand across the SUNY system but also to accelerate graduation rates to three years (Lewin 2013b).

Speaking of writing teachers' historical struggles to keep up with technological change, Gail Hawisher, Paul LeBlanc, Charles Moran, and Cynthia Selfe make the following observation: "they complain, and rightly so, about the cost of technology, about teachers' and students' limited access and about our professional situation . . . When teachers of writing do keep up, they find themselves sounding like technoevangelists, almost annually excited about the pedagogical potential of some radically new-to-us technological development" (Hawisher et al. 1996, 13). Seventeen years later, writing teachers still find themselves in such a double bind, encouraging experimentation and innovation, as Krause does in his conclusion to his *CCC* MOOC Symposium contribution, but working to foster critical awareness of the possibilities and constraints of technology on our curricular and pedagogical goals. While these are important conversations to have with each other in the pages of *CCCs*, or this particular collection, it is through our role as technological literacy specialists that we can also serve our local institutional contexts as they debate about how, when, and where to successfully align technological innovation with instructional excellence. Otherwise, MOOCs or any other "next big thing" become a failed experiment, as institutions such as San Jose State University are beginning to discover, for ignoring the input of both teachers and students.

In his 2010 book the *Marketplace of Ideas*, Louis Menand challenges the process of graduate degrees in certain areas of the humanities taking much longer to complete than degrees in more professional areas, such as law or business. Granted, one benefit of distance delivery is its potential to help students struggling to cycle through degree plans maintain normative time to completion at the undergraduate and graduate levels. However, Menand's larger point is that "academics need to look to the world to see what types of teaching and research need to be done, and how they might better train and organize themselves to do it" (Menand 2010, 158). This is, of course, easier said than done.

Part of that "training" process involves closer attention to how MOOCs align with localized learning outcomes as well as with national standards, including the Quality Matters criteria of Learning Objectives, Assessment and Measurement, Instructional Materials, Learner Interaction, Course Technology, Learner Support, and Accessibility (Rubric). A representative contract between Coursera and the University of Michigan, published by the Chronicle of Higher Education, reflects a substantial amount of quality control over the content, particularly accessibility. Nevertheless, online environments require models of instructional design that foreground collective planning, building, implementation, and evaluation. MOOC curricula in some contexts do meet Quality Matters standards, as the organization has already begun to evaluate MOOCs via its Continuing and Professional Education Rubric. This has led to endorsement for supplemental programs such as Cuyahoga Community College's Math MOOC and a broader partnership with the Gates Foundation to evaluate its recently funded MOOC projects, including the writing MOOCs to which Krause and the SUNY Council on Writing allude. As Deb Adair, Quality Matter's Managing Director and Chief Planning Officer said of the Gates partnership:

> We are gratified to be invited to participate in examining the quality and efficacy of MOOCs to learn whether they have potential to become more than just a vehicle for access to free content . . . Can they be designed to

facilitate student learning? This is a critical question for the field to answer in understanding the potential role of MOOCs.

Regardless of the conclusions that are made about that role, decisions about whether to adopt MOOCs have to be made in ways that respect the model of university shared governance, and not surprisingly, many collective bargaining contracts include articles on distance learning, including issues of workload, compensation, and intellectual property. My own philosophy as a longtime department chair, a former faculty senate chair, and a University-wide information technology committee chair, involves making a pact with the faculty to develop policies about online learning that address continuing curricular concerns, as well as incentives and reward structures; to advocate for faculty and students by fostering a collective in which all stakeholders have a perspective to be heard; and to ultimately make decisions within a culture of transparency. Admittedly, this is not always within an individual faculty or administrator's control. But for any administrator, listening is an important part of that process, as well as identifying the strengths, weaknesses, opportunities, and threats of any curricular initiative, including online learning. But if faculty, especially writing faculty, are not there to be part of the dialogue, our concerns may go unheard and unheeded. Historically, writing faculty have had important experience and expertise to share about integrating technology into the curriculum, given our consistent emphasis on technology's impact on literate practice.

While the concept of a "learning community" has become an academic buzz term that can help to brand a university, Rena Palloff and Keith Pratt describe it as a co-learning process that is facilitated and sustained "through the mutual negotiating of guidelines regarding how the group will participate together" (Palloff and Pratt 2007, 41). Although Palloff and Pratt are referring to the online classroom itself, such a learning community model must apply to decisions about online learning in general, and MOOCs in particular. Based on the larger discourse on MOOCs and the continuing shift from the brick and mortar classroom to the digital classroom in colleges and universities from California to New Hampshire and back again, the debate needs to move from the pages of our journals and from the academic and corporate boardrooms to localized spaces where a larger host of stakeholders are invited to the proverbial table. Only then will the learning community concept so prevalent in academic culture shift from rhetoric to reality by enabling a more genuine conversation and partnership among administrators, faculty, and students and by fostering a broader understanding of what it means to be "empowered" online.

Even as I recommend the involvement of rhetoric and composition specialists in this conversation, however, our field has always been inter-disciplinary in scope. Thus we can and should also look to those already modeling alternatives to the traditional MOOC. This includes the recent development of a DOCC, or distributed open collaborative course in "Feminism and Technology" facilitated by feminist educators from a broad range of participating universities, from the New School to Penn State to the University of London. Speaking of the DOCC, co-developer Anne Balsamo contends that "A DOCC is different from an MOOC in that it doesn't deliver a centralized syllabus to the participants. Rather it organizes around a central topic . . . It recognizes that, based on deep feminist pedagogical commitments, expertise is distributed throughout all the participants in a learning activity" (Balsamo quoted in Jaschik 2013a). The leadership some writing programs are demonstrating at the national level with regard to MOOC development, coupled with the local leadership roles we have long played in student-centered learning in both face-to-face and virtual spaces, opens up significant opportuni-ties for rhetoric and composition specialists to participate in the dia-logue and experiment with the role such learning environments play within our own curriculum. Indeed, as the Ohio State University MOOC instruction team asserts, "it's still premature to make definitive claims about how (or how effectively) MOOCs will transform the teaching of writing. We can, however, take advantage of the opportunity afforded by the MOOC platform to take a sober look at what we've been doing in our classrooms" (Halasek et al. 2014, 165).

Ten years ago, Elizabeth Monske and I (2003) argued that it is impor-tant to question who benefits from the integration of online learning into the curriculum (Blair and Monske 2003). While the rhetorics of distance learning in the academy were still in their nascent stages, their tune was and is a familiar one with little change as we now survey the landscape of higher education in the twenty-first century. The terrain of online learning shifts each day; at my first drafting of this chapter, an August 2013 report from *The Times* (Lewin 2013a) reported that the Georgia Institute of Technology "plans to offer a MOOC-based online master's degree in computer science" through Udacity, but at a much lower cost ($6,660) than the face-to-face version of the degree. The emphasis on revenue stream either by increased tuition or by decreased costs has made online learning a standard option for many institutions from the community college to the Ivy League. Whether MOOCs are part of the distance equation, however, is a question neither administra-tors nor faculty can address at this moment in time. Just as Monske and

I questioned who benefitted then, in what ways do the University and the MOOC provider benefit in terms of both economic and cultural capital now? While at least one administrator quoted in *The Times* article acknowledges the fiscal benefit of online, "professional" (typically code for fee-paying) graduate programs, we must ask, in a rhetorical context that has been referred to as "MOOC Mania," whether there are other significant benefits to consider in future planning:

- To what extent are MOOCs the twenty-first century model of continuing education, providing access to a range of nontraditional populations and settings that bridge the gap between the academy and the community, where current and future audiences may include high school students, older adults, and global markets and corporate e-training?
- With which students, disciplines, and courses are MOOCs most effective? Which stakeholders should be involved in making that determination?
- In what context is a "certificate signed by the instructor" as valuable as a degree in hand?
- In what ways do faculty benefit (or not) from the distribution of online course content?
- In what ways do students benefit academically and professionally? In what ways can institutions evaluate the contribution of MOOCs to student success?

These are questions that can and should be collectively explored by a broader range of educational stakeholders than senior administrators in enrollment management or distance learning but by those most directly impacted by shifts in delivery models: teachers, students, and the local writing program and department administrators often called upon to represent them. We must all be part of that process, for inevitably, our historical role as curricular and technological innovators allows us to simultaneously be the voice of change and the voice of reason, as our institutions get caught up in MOOC mania, ready or not.

References

Blair, Kristine, and Cheryl Hoy. 2006. "Paying Attention to Adult Learners Online: The Pedagogy and Politics of Community." *Computers and Composition* 23 (1): 32–48. http://dx.doi.org/10.1016/j.compcom.2005.12.006.

Blair, Kristine, and Elizabeth Monske. 2003. "*Cui Bono?* Revisiting the Promises and Perils of Online Learning." *Computers and Composition* 20 (4): 441–53. http://dx.doi.org/10.1016/j.compcom.2003.08.016.

DeJong, Rachelle. 2013. "The Unexpected Resistance to MOOCs." *Minding the Campus: Reforming Our Universities*, August 7. http://www.mindingthecampus.org/2013/08/the_unexpected_resistance_to_m/.

Educause. 2013. "What Campus Leaders Need to Know About MOOCs."

Gee, James. 2005. *What Video Games Have to Teach Us About Learning and Literacy*. New York: Palgrave Macmillan.

Halasek, Kay, and Ben McCorkle, Cynthia L. Selfe, Scott Lloyd DeWitt, Susan Delagrange, Jennifer Michaels, and Kaitlin Clinnin. 2014. "A MOOC with a View: How MOOCs Encourage Us to Reexamine Pedagogical Doxa." In *Invasion of the MOOCS: The Promises and Perils of Open Online Courses*, ed. Steven D. Krause, and Charles Lowe, 156–66. Anderson, SC: Parlor Press.

Hawisher, Gail, Paul LeBlanc, Charles Moran, and Cynthia Selfe. 1996. *Computers and the Teaching of Writing in American Higher Education, 1979–1994: A History*. Stanford, CT: Ablex.

Jaschik, Scott. 2013a. "Feminist Anti-MOOC." *Inside Higher Education*, August 19.

Jaschik, Scott. 2013b. "MOOC Mess." *Inside Higher Education*, February 4.

Kramarae, Cheris. 2001. *The Third Shift: Women Learning Online*. Washington, DC: American Association of University Women.

Krause, Steven D. 2013. "MOOC Response about 'Listening to World Music' Symposium on Massive Open Online Courses." *College Composition and Communication* 64:688–703.

Krause, Steven D., and Charles Lowe. 2014. *Invasion of the MOOCS: The Promises and Perils of Open Online Courses*. Anderson, SC: Parlor Press.

Lewin, Tamar. 2013a. "Master's Degree is New Frontier of Study." *The New York Times*, August 17.

Lewin, Tamar. 2013b. "Universities Team with Online Course Provider." *The New York Times*, May 30.

Menand, Louis. 2010. *The Marketplace of Ideas: Reform and Resistance in the American University*. New York: W.W. Norton.

Palloff, Rena, and Keith Pratt. 2007. *Building Online Learning Communities: Effective Strategies for the Virtual Classroom*. San Francisco: Jossey Bass.

Selfe, Cynthia. 1999. *Technology and Literacy in the Twenty-First Century: The Importance of Paying Attention*. Carbondale, IL: SIUP.

SUNY Council on Writing. 2013. "Resolution on Massive Open Online Courses and the Teaching of Writing."

UCLA. 2013. "Empowered UCLA Extension: Certificate Programs for Adults."

Yancey, Kathleen Blake. 2013. "Editor's Note: Symposium on Massive Open Online Courses." *College Composition and Communication* 64:688–703.

11
WRITING AT SCALE
Composition MOOCs and Digital Writing Communities

Chris Friend, Sean Michael Morris, and Jesse Stommel

"Digital writing is political. It democratizes the act of writing in the sense that it both allows open participation in the creation of cultural content and redefines public writing as work that anyone—not just professional writers or academics—can do. From blogs to mashups to Twitter, to the greatest extent ever, we have the tools and the opportunity to write our own story, rather than suffering someone else to write it for us."
—Tanya Sasser, "Digital Writing as Handicraft"

INTRODUCTION

In 2006, as part of his job as the chair of a new online English program at the Community Colleges of Colorado Online (CCCO), Sean was tasked with designing first-year composition (FYC) courses within the WebCT learning management system (LMS). LMSs were closed systems, "walled gardens," in which learning was meant to take place through written or video lectures, discussion fora, and assignments (usually completed individually—group work is not easy inside most LMS frameworks). In other words, the design of the online classroom prohibited any but the least innovative writing pedagogies. And over time, some of those pedagogical tools, like the online discussion board, became as much a staple of online education as the lecture had been in the traditional classroom. While CCCO and other college systems around the country felt that offering distance education online was itself an innovation, the implementation of pedagogically limited LMSs kept online courses from interacting with their own medium: the web. This also meant that students—whose lives were increasingly being influenced by and represented on the Internet—were asked to leave behind their online lives at the very moment when they might most benefit from embodying them.

The conundrum Sean faced was that online courses simply do not operate the same as on-ground courses: the audience is not the same,

DOI: 10.7330/9781607324850.c011

the level of interaction and spontaneity in discussion cannot be replicated, and, most important, writing on the web (to which we also refer as "digital writing") is different from writing on paper. Despite the efforts made by word processing programs to mimic the page on a screen, writing online is more permeable, more malleable, more spreadable than analog writing with a pen, pencil, typewriter, and paper—indeed, even different from writing inside a contained word processing system.

When we write for the web, we do not write for print. This seems axiomatic, rational, and easy to accept. However, the case of online writing *instruction* is not so easily deduced, or reduced. The implications for writing on the web, specifically as opposed to writing for print, are various and sometimes surprising. And if we embrace the notion that the medium does not just dictate the message but also the method, we discover the multitude of ways in which digital writing and digital composition differ from, challenge, and undo more traditional writing. In this chapter, we argue that digital writing is unique and hasn't been adequately theorized, and that we must embrace the novelty of web-based writing in our composition pedagogies.

To some extent, massive open online courses (MOOCs) have attempted to respond to this novelty, integrating unique forms of peer review, reflection, and grading, and encouraging the use of blogging and social networks as part of their exploration of digital writing. Although massive in scale and experimental in nature, MOOCs have remained largely linear, reflecting online learning as it's been developed over the last decade—courses within LMSs that attempt to reconstruct classroom learning online.

A quick note about MOOCs here. MOOCs represent a fundamental shift in the scale, economic model, political economy, and pedagogy of the college classroom. As a one-size-fits-all reaction to the changing landscape of learning, though, the MOOC is a massive failure of imagination; however, as a model that might inspire new kinds of learning that can happen in all sorts of containers, the MOOC is a likeable beast. In November 2012, we chose to create a massive *digital* writing course precisely because successful MOOCs can force instructors to take a more student-driven (distinct from "student-centered") approach to learning, fostering emergent thinking in both student learning and course design. Siva Vaidhyanathan (2012) writes in "What's the Matter with MOOCs?,"

> Real education happens only by failing, changing, challenging, and adjusting. All of those gerunds apply to teachers as well as students. No person is an "educator," because education is not something one person

does to another. Education is an imprecise process, a dance, and a collaborative experience.

We sought to create a MOOC specifically designed to get at the "imprecise process" of digital writing. We called it Digital Writing Month (DigiWriMo), a slightly madcap, loosely designed MOOC, which not only sought to embrace novelty and reimagine writing in digital environments, but also worked to transform the process of online learning. It was not meant to be a linear, organized learning process, but rather one that was distributed across the web—nodally, rhizomatically, rampantly.

In this chapter, we situate our philosophy behind DigiWriMo within the context of composition pedagogy and its response (or resistance to) changes in writing technologies. After a brief review of the dynamic writing field, we discuss how we developed the course and balanced expectations with openness. Finally, we explore questions raised during and because of our experiences with DigiWriMo, highlighting the ways in which a flexible, month-long MOOC teaches us about working with digital texts in all our classes.

TOWARD A NEW THEORY OF WRITING

Composition pedagogy largely transitioned away from the process movement in the 1990s, shortly before digital composition became the standard for writing, and web-based publication took hold. With the field's attention fixed on important issues of genre, transfer, and multimodality, we may be inadvertently missing what Kathleen Blake Yancey, in her 2004 keynote address at The Conference on College Composition and Communication (CCCC), referred to as "a moment" (Yancey 2004, 297). She recognized a turning point in composition education, one created by a growing rift between student experience and student instruction. Many of the conventions taught in a composition classroom occur naturally, and without explicit instruction, on the web. When many of our students can adeptly navigate a political issue across online news reports, televised talk show interviews, up-to-the-moment Twitter reactions, and even meme images circulated on Facebook, our efforts to have students use a single genre in response to any rhetorical situation seems artificially separated from reality. Yancey asserts that today, we understand communication to involve multiple interrelated genres, "circulating across and around rhetorical situations both inside and outside school" (308). Writing instruction from the twentieth century does not adequately prepare students for the writing processes of the twenty-first. Yancey rightly asserts that the content of modern composition courses requires "a new vocabulary, a new set of practices, and a new set of out-comes" (308). We believe the rhetoric and composition field has yet to compensate for that new set of practices in its pedagogies. Until we develop a theory of digital writing practices, composition courses will occupy an untenable divide between theory-based content derived from print and practical application in digital spaces.

Early online composition courses leaned toward the content, rather than the application, side of this divide. Despite Yancey's call for a new set of outcomes for composition, early experiments in open online composition courses, including those that Sean designed for his online English program, as well as the first composition MOOCs, rarely focused on open online composition practices—practices Yancey called "the *content* of composition" (308; emphasis in original). While the writing process has changed over the past few decades, becom-ing more and more networked (while also being more individuated), those same decades have not seen an equal upheaval in composition pedagogical practices. The first group of composition MOOCs fea-tured remarkably familiar course content: Duke University empha-sized foundational skills like summary, analysis, argumentation, and support; the Ohio State University emphasized rhetorical thinking, rhetorical arguing, and rhetorical researching; while Georgia Tech emphasized critical thinking, rhetoric, and process (Tham 2013, 9). Similarly, the FYC courses at CCCO were yet based in the paradigm of the five-paragraph essay, and traditional conventions of process such as brainstorming, outlining, writing, editing, and rewriting. Rather than using the web to teach about writing on the web, this kind of course merely transfers writing for print into an online environment. Even though the courses took place on the web, they still emphasized a writing process firmly rooted in the traditions of print. They did not venture far from standard compositional practices, despite being con-ducted within a medium in which writers are reinventing writing.

How we write changed with the advent of the word processor. *Where* we write changed with the advent of the web. *Why* we write changed with the advent of blogging and again with the advent of social media. The writ-ing process no longer stops with "getting published." Not only has that goal been rendered commonplace with the countless platforms for blog-ging, microblogging, and status-updating, but online publication begins the responsive process built into Web 2.0 technologies. Once writing has been published to the web, it becomes available for re-use and re-mix, commentary and community. Kenneth Goldsmith (2011) writes of the joy inherent in writing through re-use, which "delivers emotion obliquely and unpredictably, with sentiments expressed as a result of the writing process rather than by authorial intention." Teaching writing in the age of re-use, therefore, asks that we move our focus from authorial intention onto a writing process that we may not yet entirely understand.

Digital writing—writing that anticipates re-use, re-mixing, remediation—alters how we think about words, their purposes, and their functions in a world of readers, writers, consumers, and producers. Digital writing allows our society to shape, or at least examine, that world through the lens of written discourse. In *Remix: Making Art and Commerce Thrive in the Hybrid Economy,* Lawrence Lessig (2008) asserts the value of a public that thinks through writing:

> Blogs are valuable because they give millions the opportunity to express their ideas in writing. And with a practice of writing comes a certain important integrity. A culture filled with bloggers thinks differently about politics or public affairs, if only because more have been forced through the discipline of showing in writing why A leads to B. (92)

Today's students learn the critical thinking involved in effective writing through social engagement. They see their writing coexist with others'; and analytic tools that count page hits, "likes," retweets, and re-blogs show the amount of influence and distribution garnered by a piece of writing. Success can be measured in terms of interaction with a quantifiable audience: how many times did a text get read, shared, or responded to? In effect, our students must become sensitive to what Jim Ridolfo has dubbed "rhetorical velocity." Rather than merely writers of simple static texts, students must "anticipate and strategize future third-party remixing of their compositions as part of a larger and complex rhetorical strategy that plays out across physical and digital spaces" (Ridolfo and DeVoss 2009).

By writing digitally, students get instant and as-it-happens feedback directly from their intended audience, rather than feedback from an individual teacher delayed by a week or more. Web-based writing brings with it new feedback mechanisms that have not been formally integrated into composition pedagogies. Feedback from the online audience eclipses instructor feedback—and even instructor grading—as more relevant, more immediate, and more meaningful. With web-based writing, because the audience can use and respond to student texts, students gain both a real, interactive audience as well as real-time feedback on their writing's effectiveness.

But the benefits of near-instantaneous feedback come with a challenge. Now there is no value to our writing except as it is made useful. What we write online gains purpose from what readers *do* with what we say—not just how our writing is interpreted, but how it is rebuilt, refabricated, repurposed—and we must write accordingly. And we must learn to teach writing accordingly by helping students develop tools for writing in ways that allow for and encourage networked ideals of re-use. With digital writing, every text begins at meaninglessness until it finds harbor and use elsewhere, becoming meaningful only by association. Writing for the web considers the inherent value—indeed, the intention—of virality in the medium. Today, "going viral" acts as a lure to motivate online writers to produce more, publicize better, or be wittier. Indeed, if writers create digital content while ignorant of the need for distributable texts online, they miss an essential point of writing digitally: web-based texts belong to the web once they are published.

Institutions of learning did not invent digital writing; rather, it has evolved on its own as a response to social media and online personal networks. It has been further facilitated by creative design and technology (such as Google Docs, GitHub, Markdown, and other web-aware writing tools) frequently used by non-academics, and in many cases, people who call themselves "coders," not writers. Quite simply, the tools we use for writing change the ways we write and share our work. Even as discussions of "intellectual property" proliferate and fear of student plagiarism runs rampant, the notion of singular authorship is losing traction. Phenomena like fan fiction have re-opened the way to writing that is borrowing, writing that is repurposing, writing that is "uncreative" but deeply original. These innovations have occurred largely outside the purview of the composition or writing classroom, and have taught those students—usually before they come through the door—an entirely different set of writing rules and processes than those they'll learn in class.

The disconnect between technological innovation and changes in writing instruction have not gone unnoticed. Yancey (2004) observes that "the members of the writing public have learned . . . to write, to think together, to organize, and to act . . . largely without *our* instruction" (301). Today's students choose from among myriad tools to construct their diverse texts, and their composing practices may be quite different from traditional academic composition instruction. The meaning of *composition* has expanded, and the writing process has changed, from the influence of online technologies. Our instruction should change to reflect the new composing possibilities. We cannot avoid teaching writing technologies any more than students can avoid using them.

In "Teaching in a Culture of Writing and Technology," Chris M. Anson (1999) writes, "our key roles—as those who create opportunities and contexts for students to write and who provide expert, principled response to that writing—must change in the present communications and information revolution" (275). We must teach new writing technologies to help students make sense of their processes in the modern environment. And we must be prepared to let them teach us (and each other) new skills, new tools, and new literacies that draw from or build on those technologies. The CCCC issued its Position Statement for Online Writing, suggesting that "an online writing course should focus on writing and not on technology orientation or teaching students how to use learning and other technologies" (Conference 2013). This position risks decontextualizing writing by suggesting that writing and the tools of writing can be treated separately. Admittedly, the Position Statement argues that "students [should] focus on learning composition and not on learning technological platforms or software," placing the emphasis on writing while acknowledging that the technological is involved. But teachers need to avoid creating classrooms that are disconnected from the digital. It is a mistake to think students will not try to employ digital tools to write, and equally erroneous to believe that the digital—housed in the pockets of every student—can disappear when learners walk from the hallway to their seat in class. When we teach students to write, we teach them a process inherently infused with technology. Digital writing relies on technologies that cannot be separated from their creative processes, and therefore, teaching composition without the technologies involved equates to teaching half a subject.

To be clear, digital writing, as invented by those who do it, is as much a process informed by the voices of the writers (working communally, collaboratively, or convergently) as it is by the design of the technology within which that writing takes place. Christina Haas (1996) warns that ignoring the influence of technology on our writing process "discourages any examination of how technology shapes discourse and how it, in turn, is shaped by discourse" (22). Effective composition instruction helps students see how language works within a discourse; we must therefore include an examination of writing technology not just in our pedagogies but also in our course content. Because writing and technology are inseparable, efforts to teach one without the other are not merely reckless but frankly impossible. When students learned to use word processors to write their texts, they had to learn how to use cut/copy/paste features; otherwise, they wrote as they would with a typewriter . . . and therefore missed the point. Likewise, skills appropriate for print-minded texts bear no resemblance to those used to write in pixels. Certainly, there are comparisons that could be made between the changes of the digital age and those of the industrial age, but conflating these moments obfuscates the very distinctive effect each new tool has on our writing products and processes.

As its associated technologies have become more complex, the act of writing has transformed. One might say that today, more than ever, technology is technique. The machine determines the method, if you will, and if we wish to help our students improve the method, the machine must also be investigated, even (or especially) as those machines change. To pretend otherwise risks obsolescence. We need a pedagogical approach to composition that accommodates, examines, and uses the affordances of web-based writing.

DREAMING UP DIGITAL WRITING MONTH

Digital Writing Month, a one-month MOOC exploring digital writing and literacy, began with a phone call. Brainstorming ways to bring attention to his newly birthed English and Digital Humanities program, Jesse called Sean and said, "I want to do something like NaNoWriMo [National Novel Writing Month]." Run by the San Francisco non-profit Office of Letters and Light, NaNoWriMo is a kind of hybrid proto-MOOC. The event is held over the thirty days of November, during which writers each produce a fifty thousand–word novel. As the website for the event says, the event is "a fun, seat-of-your-pants approach to novel writing . . . Valuing enthusiasm and perseverance over painstaking craft, NaNoWriMo is . . . for everyone who has thought fleetingly about writing a novel but has been scared away by the time and effort involved." Jesse wanted something that would encourage people to play, create, compose, write, and craft—something that would get the attention of young bloggers, of middle-aged Internet novices, of educators and technologists.

Digital Writing Month set two goals for participants in its inaugural year. The first: finish the month with fifty thousand digital words. The second: figure out what digital writing is—how it's made, and what it consists of. We described the event as "a (somewhat) insane month-long writing challenge, a wild ride through the world of digital writing, wherein those daring enough to participate will wield keyboard and cursor to create 50,000 words of digital writing in the thirty short days of November." Our approach to the event was to break open the boundaries of writing, beyond the concerns of genre and form, and to enlist people into an experiment designed to discover what digital writing is through the enacting of the same. We didn't look for participants to write novels, essays, short stories, or poems, but made all of these—along with Facebook updates, tweets, blog posts, text messages, webcomics, and more—valid applications of digital writing. We envisioned a project that had only a marginal understanding of itself, one which, through the active participation and content-generation of its writers, would discover what it was trying to accomplish. We believed that digital writing was still an entirely new pedagogical (if not creative) field, and we knew the only way to uncover digital writing was to do digital writing, en masse.

We made a choice to house the course on the open Internet, resisting the urge to build a course within an LMS, and instead working to create a community of writers using a Wordpress blog, a Twitter hashtag, and a Disqus forum. We encouraged writers to come up with creative ways to manage their word count, and to share their methods with the digital writing community. We also did not limit the expression of "writing" in new forms: video, animation, comic strips, images made from words, and more. Because our proposal was that digital writing is something yet undiscovered, we could hardly frame the course around composition and writing in a printed context. Web-based writing confuses the distinction between what is writing and what is composition because these things don't live separately on the web.

Before long, a conversation opened up about the nature and meaning of "digital words." With a requirement to reach fifty thousand words, participants began to ask, "What is a digital word?" "What counts as writing?" Some proposed that reblogging, retweeting, sharing, or even "liking" already made digital words could count because those words move into a new context and were new words. Tanya Sasser (2012) wrote in "Defining Digital Writing,"

> For some, the challenge of Digital Writing Month is not so much the word count as it is figuring out what exactly digital writing is (and is not). Do emails count? What about retweets? What about images and videos? How do you "count" those? What about all of the words we delete during the process of drafting and revising? Do those count even though they're no longer "there"? . . . Which digital "words" don't count? . . . Where do ideas end and authorship begin?

In other words, the word count goal was not necessarily literal. In fact, several participants realized that they would reach the fifty thousand–word goal quickly, and without effort, if they included all the words they cast into the Internet through their various social networks, blogs, e-mails, and more. The word "count" became a lens through which to consider the nature of digital writing, the constancy of it, and the idea of authorship. In addition, the flexibility with which participants handled

word count allowed those who normally balk at writing, or say they simply "aren't writers," to see that writing was not only commonplace in
their lives, but always and everywhere a potentially creative act.

Sean posted "The Specter of the Author" during the second week of
the course, responding to participants' thoughts about the new nature
of authorship. There, he says,

> Write what you know, and the world will write upon it. The world will tweet
> it, "like" it, share it, parse it, abbreviate it, duplicate it, splice it, excerpt
> it. And each new iteration and variation on your text becomes less your
> text and more the text of the world. Your testament, which you so care-
> fully crafted and which your mother said was so you, becomes ever more
> recrafted as it is dispersed; and, ever more applied to others, it begins
> to resemble that text their mothers would recognize as so them. But of
> course that text is only them as long as it hovers in suspense, unredistrib-
> uted, unrepurposed, unshared, unauthored.

Or, as Barthes (1975) much more succinctly (but without the
Internet) said: "The true locus of writing is reading" (147). The participants of DigiWriMo soon discovered that their work gained new value
after it was redone by others; and each of them was able to make famous
their compatriots by redoing their work. It became clear that collaboration and communal writing, then, is not simply the product of a cooperative effort, an essay or story written by many hands, but writing sub-
jected to the act of sharing, and thus rewritten and rewritten.

A FLURRY OF CURSORS

The work of real-stakes writing depends on collaboration, a complex
transaction that demands more than just the simple transfer of words and
ideas from a writer to a page and then to a reader. In the most productive collaborations, our ideas live coterminous on the page with the ideas
of our sources and our peers. In the days leading up to DigiWriMo, we
worked more to build a strong community of participants than we did to
assemble content for them to consume. Digital Writing Month began with
a midnight launch, gathering participants from all around the world into
a grand experiment, one that invited discovery and play. Twitter participants counted down to the start, a mob excitedly refreshing the course
website as the countdown reached zero. From the outset, participants in
the event were asked to "conspire, collaborate, co-author, cooperate, col-
lude, and even compete" to reach their fifty thousand–word goal.

In DigiWriMo, we worked together, co-composing with a large group
of learners, investigating the ways that collaborative writing can be used

to support learner-centered composition pedagogy. What we encountered in our experiments was a series of brilliant, chaotic but also coordinated, efforts as group members dynamically delegated the various tasks that go into the creation of an essay, story, or poem. We organized the writing of collective poems with hundreds of participants, where each author could only contribute a single word. We coordinated an effort that had approximately one hundred people co-author a forty-two thousand–word novel in a single day. The goal of these experiments was less about product and more about process—about learning to navigate mass collaboration within a digital environment. Collaborative writing, whether between a group of three or hundreds, is a dance that depends on careful orchestration, flexibility, a meta-level consideration of process, and a commitment to play.

The novel in a day experiment ran from midnight to midnight on November 3, 2012. Fifty-five authors signed their names to the final document, which remains openly accessible on the web. (We offered access to the event and document without requiring sign-in, so the number of additional anonymous participants is difficult to estimate.) The task itself was proclaimed with a simple setup: "1 Day. 1 Novel. 50,000 words. A Throng of Authors." The guidelines, co-authored by participants inside a Google Doc on the previous day, included: writing is synchronous, not sequential; writers should defer to text already in the document, rather than wildly deleting; writers shouldn't worry about how or where their words "fit"; and writers should pick a section of the novel and revel in the "flurry of cursors." The group decided that the novel would be a series of interconnecting vignettes, featuring an appearance (in some cases a mere cameo) by the DigiWriMo mascot, Digi the Duck. Some writers expressed trepidation at the start, and many participants chose to compose in a calmer environment outside the Google Doc, cutting and pasting a vignette wholesale into the novel. As we all got more and more comfortable with each other, though, the collaborations became increasingly intimate, with dozens of cursors flitting across the document.

One of the participants, Elizabeth Switaj (2012), writes in her blog post about the experience, "The closer the collaboration, the more likely you are to create something greater than you could have made independently." Switaj writes about the initial hesitation many contributors felt to collaborate at the sentence level. What we observed was an increased intermingling of cursors as the day proceeded and community formed around the task. We also noticed that vignettes composed outside the document were less likely to inspire continued work from other participants once added to the novel. The most successful vignettes were the ones where authors deliberately created gaps and prompts for other writers inside their paragraphs and even inside their sentences. Many vignettes offered subtle second-order commentary on the experiment itself, which demonstrated a consideration of digital writing and how collaborative work happens on the web.

Some examples from three vignettes follow, each reflecting in some way on the nature of digital writing. The first vignette reads almost like a set of instructions for writers working inside the document, asking contributors to skip gleefully from one vignette to another—to not let cursors get stuck.

> One doesn't often consider how cobblestones might feel under the feet of a duck, but walking through the square was more difficult than Digi imagined it would be. Bricks get hot, and there are no shoes for webbed feet. One simply must walk quickly, skipping from puddle to puddle, as ducks do. And he did. He did it very well indeed.

Even this early in the co-authored document, writers were consciously and subtly working with one another to encourage collaboration. As well, by suggesting that writers and character skip "from puddle to puddle, as ducks do," the authors of this small bit urge those who will follow toward experimentation and play.

The counting of words is central to NaNoWriMo. In DigiWriMo, the discussions were less about reporting counted words and more about asking how, why, and what we count. Within digital writing, counting words is a red herring, leading to a slew of quandaries like how to count images, code, co-authored words, etc. The following excerpt is from the third vignette, which was co-composed by at least six authors who seem to be addressing this problem of counting words:

> 56. 60. 64. 70. Counting the cobblestones like small square letters in a giant heap of words. Words that burn holes in pockets. Words that ask for sentences. And paragraphs. And small ducks to help arrange them into stories. And poems. And novels. "Novels like this one," said the boy, looking down at the lines written across the cobblestones below his feet. 74. That's the number he liked best.

We embarked on a challenge to write fifty thousand words in a month, but nearly wrote that number in a single day. In composing his post for DigiWriMo, "On the Horrors and Pleasures of Counting Words," Jesse counted the words from every e-mail and tweet he composed in October: 32,366 words sent by e-mail and 10,134 words sent by tweet. In November, Chris counted the 1,168 words he tweeted on election night alone, not to mention the 8,043 words he wrote on a single day in his responses to student writing. In the wake of the sort of trans-formations at work in the technological age, it seems sensible to turn the sheer magnitude of digital writing to our advantage. Our pedagogies must embrace the various alternate modes of communication in which students (and we) are proving so prolific.

Finally, this excerpt from the fourth vignette illustrates the under-standing we came to during the course that the goal of Digital Writing Month was not to make words but to connect people:

> She stopped, still staring out at the square. "People . . . they're like places. You can't tell things from the surface. Events happen, and pass, and some-times don't leave a mark. Even when they do, sometimes you have to know where, and how, and why to look." She sighed.

This ounce of narrative, sheltered as it was by itself, seemed to reflect on the entire cooperative writing experience. Here, the character stops in the square to look around at who walks by, what takes place. And underneath the small soliloquy, we can hear the author reflecting on the process of communicating via networks, collaborative writing spaces, and the Internet: "sometimes, you have to know where, and how, and why to look."

What was most meaningful about the novel in a day experiment is the way that it encouraged participants, from the start, to inhabit each other's sentences—to put their words more fully into conversation with the words of others. One of the final activities of the month had partici-pants writing Twitter Essays of exactly 140 characters to define writing digitally. Janine DeBaise (@writingasjoe) tweeted, "My fingers tap the keys. I pause to consider. Who on earth is listening? Could be anyone, anywhere. I keep typing #digiwrimo #twitteressay."

THE PLEASURES OF DIGITAL TEXTS

Beyond the concerns of composition instruction, beyond even the concerns of the educational endeavor, something is happening to lan-guage and writing in the digital age. The texture of it, its species, is changing. Writing online might be considered what Roland Barthes (1975) calls "writing aloud." As he writes in *The Pleasure of the Text*: "*Writing aloud* is not expressive . . . it is carried not by dramatic inflec-tions, subtle stresses, sympathetic accents, but by the *grain* of the voice, which is an erotic mixture of timbre and language, and can there-fore also be, along with diction, the substance of an art" (66–67). For Barthes, words and language have a material quality. However, he takes this a step further when he describes "writing aloud," vocalizations that bring character and not content to words, shifting value almost entirely from the signified to the signifier, from what words represent to what they can be made to do.

Roland Barthes writes further about the interactivity of written texts: "What I enjoy in a narrative is not directly its content or even its structure, but rather the abrasions I impose upon the fine surface" (12). His use of the word "abrasions" suggests that there is something almost violent about the way we interact with a written text. He also suggests that reading is something we "impose" upon a text and not something a text imposes upon us. Digital writing tears at the text's cohesive fabric, punctures its skin, rips its pages and paragraphs, dissects its innards. This is what digital writing asks of us, as well.

Digital Writing Month may have closed at the end of that November, but it hardly reached a conclusion. Instead, the community of digital writers, including teachers, students, administrators, technologists, were left to reformulate what they thought about writing, digital writing, and the nature of authorship in the digital age. Through our continued work with those writers, and our further meditations on digital writing, we feel confident offering the following tenets:

1. Digital writing is *networked*. The digital text is connected, as are its readers and writers. Everything on the Internet is metonymic. In digital space, everything is *next to* everything else: people, ideas, high-culture, low-culture, art, trash, literary texts, plagiarized texts, etc. What the web lacks in depth, it makes up for by having a good deal more surface. Digital writing harnesses this broad surface by emphasizing links, networks, and communal context. Digital writing brings the text into more direct conversation with its sources, dismantling hierarchies of critical thought. The work of the reader and the work of the writer are coterminous on the page.

2. Digital writing is *collaborative*. Conventional notions of authorship are contested in digital space. Many digital texts are coauthored, unattributed, or blended on the page so that it becomes impossible to distinguish one author from another. Loss Pequeño Glazier writes in *Digital Poetics: The Making of E-Poetries*, "We do not want to be distracted by the 'image versus text,' or other essentially analog debates" (Glazier 2008, 178). In digital space, image and text have a simultaneity, a dependence, an inseparability. Digital writing invites its reader (once a mere satellite) into a more intimate, more provocative dance. Even when the work is not produced by multiple authors/artists, it becomes collaborative when it's given generously to its readers.

3. Digital writing is *defiant*. Digital space is always already new, creating and recreating itself even as we look at it (and live within it). Digital writing is neither contained nor obedient. It defies its own virtuality by being textured and lively, three-dimensional and populous. It speaks to us from a (usually) flat screen with the potential to engage us in a tangible and visceral way.

Digital writing is as much about how we express an idea as it is about where the idea's expressed, and why. This is composition of a different order. It is composition that does not always begin with words, but with the choice of mode, container, and network. Because the array of fora for expression are as many as sites on the Internet, the choice of word does not need to come first; instead, the choice of medium precedes the writing. And the knowledge that all vocalizations will be re-vocalized, rewritten, and distributed by others (in an analogue to the oral tradition) influences as much the choice of what to say as the choice of where to say it.

The LMS has as its thesis the limitation of modes of learning. It is not as transformable a space as an on-ground classroom. However, ingenuity and intention, a critical look at how online spaces can be made more permeable, and a desire to experiment and play, can open even limited course containers to innovative and creative pedagogy. What must be advocated is an acknowledgment that, while the Internet has not necessarily changed the way people learn, it does present new modes of invention—modes that offer brilliant, unexplored territory for writing, reading, and learning.

References

Anson, Chris M. 1999. "Distant Voices: Teaching and Writing in a Culture of Technology." *College English* 61 (3): 261–80. http://dx.doi.org/10.2307/379069.
Barthes, Roland. 1975. *The Pleasure of the Text.* New York: Hill and Wang.
Conference on College Composition and Communication Committee for Best Practices in Online Writing Instruction. 2013. "A Position Statement of Principles and Example Effective Practices for Online Writing Instruction (OWI)." March. http://www.ncte.org/cccc/resources/positions/owiprinciples/.
Glazier, Loss Pequeño. 2008. *Digital Poetics: The Making of E-Poetries.* Tuscaloosa: University of Alabama Press.
Goldsmith, Kenneth. 2011. "It's Not Plagiarism: In the Digital Age, It's 'Repurposing.'" *Chronicle of Higher Education*, September 11. http://chronicle.com/article/Uncreative-Writing/128908/.
Haas, Christina. 1996. *Writing Technology: Studies on the Materiality of Literacy.* New York: Routledge.
Lessig, Lawrence. 2008. *Remix: Making Art and Commerce Thrive in the Hybrid Economy.* New York: Penguin Press. http://dx.doi.org/10.5040/9781849662505.
Ridolfo, J., and D. N. DeVoss. 2009. "Composing for Recomposition: Rhetorical Velocity and Delivery." *Kairos: A Journal of Rhetoric, Technology, and Pedagogy* 13, no. 2.

Sasser, Tanya. 2012. "Defining Digital Writing." *Remixing College English*, November 3. http://remixingcollegeenglish.wordpress.com/2012/11/03/defining-digital-writing/.
Switaj, Elizabeth. 2012. "What I Learned from #DigiWriMo's Novel Experiment." November 4. http://www.elizabethkateswitaj.net/2012/11/learned-digiwrimo-novel-experiment/.
Tham, Jason. 2013. "Before Twilight: A Survey of Composition MOOCs." Presented at *Computers & Writing 2013*. http://www.slideshare.net/JasonCKTham/preparing-for-the-moocacolypse.
Vaidhyanathan, Siva. 2012. "What's the Matter with MOOCs?" *Chronicle of Higher Education*, July 6. http://chronicle.com/blogs/innovations/whats-the-matter-with-moocs/33289.
Yancey, K. 2004. "Made Not Only in Words: Composition in a New Key." *College Composition and Communication* 56 (2): 297–328. http://dx.doi.org/10.2307/4140651.

SOME TEXT OF THIS PAPER IS ADAPTED DIRECTLY FROM:

Morris, Sean Michael. 2012. "Digital Writing Uprising: Third Order Thinking in the Digital Humanities." *Hybrid Pedagogy*, October 8. http://www.hybridpedagogy.com/Journal/files/Digital_Writing_Uprising.html.
Stommel, Jesse. 2010. "Scholarship and Digital Space." *Pity Poor Flesh*, March 3. http://pitypoorflesh.wordpress.com/2010/03/03/scholarship-and-digital-space/.

ABOUT THE AUTHORS

DANIEL RUEFMAN is the director of first-year composition at the University of Wisconsin–Stout. His research interests include digital writing pedagogy, multimodal composition, and poetics.

ABIGAIL G. SCHEG holds a PhD in composition from Indiana University of Pennsylvania. She is currently a course mentor for general education composition at Western Governors University. She has also worked as a dissertation chair for numerous institutions. Scheg is the author or editor of several texts including: *Reforming Teacher Education with Online Pedagogy Development, Implementation and Critical Assessment of the Flipped Classroom Experience, Critical Examinations of Distance Education Transformation across Disciplines,* and *Bullying in Popular Culture: Essays on Film, Television, and Novels.* She also serves as a reviewer for several journals and publications in the areas of composition, creative writing, educational technology, and distance education.

KRISTINE L. BLAIR is professor of English at Bowling Green State University, where she teaches courses in digital rhetoric and scholarly publication in the Rhetoric and Writing Doctoral Program. In addition to her publications in the areas of gender and technology, online learning, electronic portfolios, and teacher training, Dr. Blair currently serves as editor of both the international print journal *Computers and Composition* and its separate companion journal *Computers and Composition Online.* She is a recipient of the CCCC Technology Innovator Award and the Computers and Composition Charles Moran Award for Distinguished Contributions to the Field.

JESSIE C. BORGMAN began teaching face-to-face in 2006 and has taught online since 2009. She works for four schools: two for-profit, a community college, and a four-year university. She has presented at several conferences including CCCCs, C&W, and TYCA. She is an expert panelist for the CCCC Committee for Effective Practices in Online Writing Instruction. She has also published in the *OWI Open Resource* and designed/authored a Pearson *Mercury Reader* for her online English Composition courses. She is the co-creator of The OWI Community (owicommunity.org), a website dedicated to online writing instruction. Her research interests include online writing instruction, course design, genre studies, two-year colleges, and writing program administration.

MARY-LYNN CHAMBERS has her PhD in technical and professional communication from East Carolina University. She has taught English in Virginia and North Carolina at community colleges and universities. Her instructional focus is composition and literature, with a research focus in online education at HBCU schools. She enjoys interacting with her students and inspiring them to write better, think more critically, and love literature. This professor views the classroom as an opportunity to make a difference.

KATHERINE ERICSSON is an online writing instructor for Washington State University and Eastern Oregon University. Her research and teaching interests include technical/professional writing, digital rhetoric, identity politics, and online education. She has been teaching entirely online for over six years. Prior to teaching, Katherine worked in the publishing industry and also worked online for Smarthinking and John Hopkins University's Center for Talented Youth.

CHRIS FRIEND is assistant professor of English in the Department of Language Studies and the Arts at Saint Leo University. He is also the managing editor of *Hybrid Pedagogy* and the producer of *HybridPod*, a podcast exploring conversations of critical digital pedagogy, listening for ways to empower students and champion learning. Chris holds a PhD in texts and technology from the University of Central Florida. His research works to define hybridity and collaboration in education, with particular attention to their influence in first-year composition courses. He tweets at @chris_friend, and his personal website is at chrisfriend.us.

TAMARA GIRARDI is an assistant professor of English in Harrisburg Area Community College's Virtual Learning program. She holds a PhD in English from Indiana University of Pennsylvania and has taught online classes since 2007. She conducts research on online pedagogy, online learning environments, Twitter and Facebook as learning tools, young adult literature, and creative writing studies. She also writes young adult fiction.

HEIDI SKURAT HARRIS is an assistant professor of rhetoric and writing at the University of Arkansas at Little Rock, where she teaches in and oversees the graduate certificate in online writing instruction, as well as teaching technical writing, rhetoric, and nonfiction online. She has published in *Disrupting Pedagogies in the Knowledge Society* and the *WAC Journal* and coedited a special issue of *Across the Disciplines*. She is a member of the CCCC Committee for Effective Practices in Online Writing Instruction and has presented at CCCCs, NCTE, the Conference of Distance Learning Administrators, and the United States Distance Learning Association.

KIMBERLEY M. HOLLOWAY is associate professor and chair of technical and professional communication at King University in Bristol, Tennessee. She has taught composition, literature, and technical communication classes and served as the director of the writing center and the director of the Academic Center for Excellence at King since 1998. She is currently a PhD candidate at Indiana University of Pennsylvania and is finishing her dissertation on the identity formation of adult nontraditional students in their work with writing center tutors.

ANGELA LAFLEN earned her PhD from Purdue University and is currently an associate professor of English and co-director of women's studies at Marist College. She teaches in the areas of digital writing, technical communication, and literature and gender. She has presented her work at meetings of the Modern Language Association and the Conference on College Composition and Communication, and her work has appeared in *Computers and Composition*, *Modern Language Studies*, and *Kansas English*, among others. Her published work focuses on online pedagogy, visual rhetoric, and gender issues. She is author of *Confronting Visuality in Multi-Ethnic Women's Literature* (Palgrave Macmillan, 2014).

LENI MARSHALL, PhD, teaches English and age studies at the University of Wisconsin–Stout. Her research focuses on age studies in North American minority and majority literatures and cultures. Advisory editor for *Age, Culture, Humanities*, she also has served at the leadership level for the AGHE, ENAS, GSA, NANAS, NWSA, and MLA. With Valerie Lipscomb, she edited *Staging Age: The Performance of Age in Theatre, Dance, and Film* (2010). Her most recent book, part of the SUNY Press's Feminist Theory and Criticism series, is *Age Becomes Us: Bodies and Gender in Time* (2015).

SEAN MICHAEL MORRIS is co-director of both *Hybrid Pedagogy*—a digital journal of learning, teaching, and technology—and Digital Pedagogy Lab. He is also senior editor for research and education at Instructure. Sean is interested in the practice of critical digital pedagogy as a social movement, while also strongly identifying with the post-digital. He learns, teaches, and theorizes from a contemplative perspective. He can be found on Twitter as @slamteacher, and his personal website is at seanmichaelmorris.com.

DANIELLE NIELSEN is an assistant professor of English at Murray State University, where she teaches composition, professional and technical writing, and British literature courses. Her current research interests include assessing accessibility and student success in composition and technical writing courses. She has previously published articles in *Nineteenth-Century Gender Studies*, *The Latchkey: A Journal of New Woman Studies*, *ELT: English Literature in Transition*, and the *CEA Forum* and has articles forthcoming in *Computers and Composition* and the *Journal of Technical Writing and Communication*.

DANI NIER-WEBER lives in the Catskills and works in the SUNY system as an assistant professor of English at Sullivan County Community College. She has a BA in elementary education from Smith, an MA in English from Butler, and a PhD in English, concentration rhetoric and composition, from Ball State. She has taught a variety of classes, from composition and women's literature to technical and creative writing, and previously served as writing center director at three universities. She taught English as a second language in Germany for thirteen years, where her two sons were born, and has taught numerous writing workshops in a medium-security correctional facility.

JESSE STOMMEL is assistant professor of digital humanities in the Department of Liberal Arts and Applied Studies at University of Wisconsin–Madison. He is also founder and director of *Hybrid Pedagogy*, a digital journal of learning, teaching, and technology. Jesse is an advocate for lifelong learning and the public digital humanities. He teaches courses about digital pedagogy, digital storytelling, horror film, and Shakespeare. He experiments relentlessly with learning interfaces, both digital and analog, and works in his research and teaching to emphasize new forms of collaboration. He can be found on Twitter @Jessifer.

INDEX